HANDBOOK OF QUALITATIVE RESEARCH METHODS ON HUMAN RESOURCE MANAGEMENT

HANDBOOKS OF RESEARCH METHODS IN MANAGEMENT

Series Editor: Mark N.K. Saunders, *University of Birmingham, UK*

This major series will provide the starting point for new PhD students in business and management and related social science disciplines. Each *Handbook* will give definitive overviews of research methods appropriate for particular subjects within management. The series aims to produce prestigious high-quality works of lasting significance, shedding light on quantitative, qualitative and mixed research methods. Each *Handbook* consists of original contributions by leading authorities, selected by an editor who is a recognized international leader in the field. International in scope, these *Handbooks* will be an invaluable guide to students embarking on a research degree and to researchers moving into a new subject area.

Titles in the series include:

Handbook of Research Methods on Intuition
Edited by Marta Sinclair

Handbook of Research Methods on Human Resource Development
Edited by Mark N.K. Saunders and Paul Tosey

Handbook of Research Methods on Trust
Second Edition
Edited by Fergus Lyon, Guido Möllering and Mark N.K. Saunders

Handbook of Qualitative Research Methods on Human Resource Management
Innovative Techniques
Edited by Keith Townsend, Rebecca Loudoun and David Lewin

Handbook of Qualitative Research Methods on Human Resource Management

Innovative Techniques

Edited by

Keith Townsend

Associate Professor of Employment Relations, Griffith Business School, Griffith University, Australia

Rebecca Loudoun

Senior Lecturer, Griffith Business School, Griffith University, Australia

David Lewin

Neil H. Jacoby Professor Emeritus of Management, UCLA Anderson School of Management, USA

HANDBOOKS OF RESEARCH METHODS IN MANAGEMENT

Edward Elgar
PUBLISHING

Cheltenham, UK • Northampton, MA, USA

Published by
Edward Elgar Publishing Limited
The Lypiatts
15 Lansdown Road
Cheltenham
Glos GL50 2JA
UK

Edward Elgar Publishing, Inc.
William Pratt House
9 Dewey Court
Northampton
Massachusetts 01060
USA

A catalogue record for this book
is available from the British Library

Library of Congress Control Number: 2016935792

This book is available electronically in the **Elgar**online
Business subject collection
DOI 10.4337/9781784711184

ISBN 978 1 78471 117 7 (cased)
ISBN 978 1 78471 118 4 (eBook)

Typeset by Servis Filmsetting Ltd, Stockport Cheshire
Printed and bound by CPI Group (UK) Ltd, Croydon, CR0 4YY

Contents

PART III   INNOVATIONS IN DATA COLLECTION METHODS

PART IV   INNOVATIVE DATA ANALYSIS

Figures

Tables and boxes

TABLES

BOXES

Editors

Keith Townsend is Associate Professor of Employment Relations at Griffith University, Australia. His research spans a wide range of areas including a focus on line managers (including frontline managers), employee involvement and participation in decision-making, industrial relations and human resource management, working time and work–life balance, and employee misbehaviour and resistance. These broad themes are brought together with an overarching approach to better understanding the complexities of managing people within the modern workplace. His research has been published in journals including *Human Resource Management Journal, Work, Employment and Society* and *Human Resource Management* (US). He has also published in the area of qualitative research methods including the book *Method in the Madness: Research Stories You Won't Read in Textbooks*. Keith is active in the practitioner community, having spent seven years on the Industrial Relations Society of Queensland executive and three years on the Australian Labour and Employment Relations Association National Council.

Rebecca Loudoun is Senior Lecturer at Griffith University, Australia and a member of the Griffith Centre for Work, Organisation and Wellbeing. She has been employed in the university sector for more than two decades where she consults, researches and teaches in the area of human resource management, employment relations and work health and safety management. Over the last 15 years Rebecca has successfully completed research projects and consultancies for several international and Australian-based agencies on the impact of state-wide workplace changes on workers. Through these projects Rebecca gained considerable experience in undertaking in-depth qualitative and quantitative research with workplace health and safety officials and representatives. She is equally competent with the theory and application of qualitative and quantitative research methods, and has completed formal postgraduate studies in how to develop questionnaires, audit and interview schedules; published using data derived from quantitative, qualitative and mixed method studies.

David Lewin is Neil H. Jacoby Professor Emeritus of Management at UCLA Anderson School of Management, USA. He is the author of many published works on such topics as human resource strategy, human resource management practices and business performance, workplace and organisational dispute resolution, and compensation and reward systems, including executive compensation and public sector pay practices. Professor Lewin serves on the editorial boards of *Industrial and Labor Relations Review*, *Industrial Relations*, *California Management Review* and *Journal of Change Management*, is a Fellow and Director of the National Academy of Human Resources, serves as a Managing Director and Head of the Labor and Employment Practice for the Berkeley Research Group (BRG) and is a member of The Conference Board's Evidence-Based Human Resources Advisory Panel. David consults widely on human resource management issues with business, government and voluntary organisations in the United States and abroad. He also serves as an expert witness in employment litigation. His current expert retentions involve issues of no-poaching, the reasonableness of executive compensation, gender discrimination, retaliatory termination, employee and managerial misclassification and independent contractor versus employee status.

Contributors

Peter Ackers, Professor of Employment Relations, Department of HRM, Faculty of Business and Law, De Montfort University, Leicester, UK.

Sara Branch, Research Fellow, Griffith Criminology Institute, Griffith University, Australia.

Roslyn Cameron, Research Fellow in Human Resource Management, Curtin Business School, Curtin University, Australia.

Catherine Cassell, Deputy Dean and Professor of Organisational Psychology, Leeds University Business School, Leeds University, UK.

Gail Clarkson, Lecturer in Organisational Behaviour, Leeds University Business School, University of Leeds, UK.

Julie Cogin, Professor and Director, Australian Graduate School of Management at UNSW and Deputy Dean, UNSW Australia Business School, University of New South Wales, Australia.

Jacqueline Ewart, Associate Professor, School of Humanities, Languages and Social Science, Griffith University, Australia.

Matthew T. Hardin, Consultant, Teacher and Chemical Engineer, Leeds, UK.

Michael Humphreys, Professor of Organisation Studies, Durham University Business School, Durham University, UK.

Richard Johnstone, Professor and Director of Research, School of Law, Queensland University of Technology, Australia.

Mark Learmonth, Professor of Organisation Studies and Deputy Dean (Research), Durham University Business School, Durham University, UK.

David Lewin, Neil H. Jacoby Professor Emeritus of Management, UCLA Anderson School of Management, USA.

Rebecca Loudoun, Senior Lecturer, Department of Employment Relations and Human Resources, Griffith Business School, Griffith University, Australia.

Fatima Malik, Lecturer in Employability and Enterprise, University of Bradford School of Management, University of Bradford, UK.

Almuth McDowall, Course Director for the MSc Human Resource Development and Consultancy, Birkbeck, University of London, UK.

Ju Li Ng, Research Fellow in Management, UNSW Australia Business School, University of New South Wales, Australia.

Werner Nienhüser, Professor of Work, Human Resource Management and Organisational Studies, University of Duisburg-Essen, Germany.

Laura S. Radcliffe, Lecturer in Organisational Behaviour, Management School, University of Liverpool, UK.

Sheryl Ramsay, Senior Lecturer, Department of Employment Relations and Human Resources, Griffith Business School, Griffith University, Australia.

James Richards, Associate Professor of Human Resource Management, School of Management and Languages, Heriot-Watt University, UK.

Céline Rojon, Lecturer in Human Resource Management, University of Edinburgh Business School, University of Edinburgh, UK.

Sally Sambrook, Professor of Human Resource Development, Bangor Business School, Bangor University, UK.

Mark N.K. Saunders, Professor of Business Research Methods, Birmingham Business School, University of Birmingham, UK.

Keith Townsend, Associate Professor of Employment Relations, Department of Employment Relations and Human Resources, Griffith Business School, Griffith University, Australia.

Kerrie L. Unsworth, Professor and Chair in Organisational Behaviour, Leeds University Business School, Leeds University, UK.

Richard Winter, Senior Lecturer in Management, Research School of Management, Australian National University, Australia.

1 Qualitative research in HRM: innovation over stagnation

Keith Townsend, Rebecca Loudoun and David Lewin

Qualitative research methods are now common in social sciences and particularly research on relations at work such as industrial relations, industrial sociology and human resource management (HRM). However, to date semi-structured interviews and in-depth interviews seem to dominate publications, with occasional job observation and ethnographical studies appearing. This book explores the actual and potential contribution of qualitative research methods to progressing understanding in the broadly interpreted field of HRM and considers innovative methods to broaden inquiry further.

Miles, a seminal writer in these methods, noted in the 1970s that "qualitative data tend to overload the research badly at almost every point: the sheer range of phenomena to be observed, the recorded volume of notes; the time required for write up, coding, and analysis can all be overwhelming" (1979, p. 590). Significant technological developments have occurred since this time with, for example, digital recorders, ubiquitous desktop and notebook computers and hand-held devices (for example, personal mobile phones) that can be used for video and photographic recording now readily available. Additionally, transcription software (for example, Dragon Naturally Speaking) and analysis software (for example, NVivo) have been designed to support the qualitative researcher. This rapid development and technology and software has allowed the validity of qualitative techniques to flourish in recent decades providing new insights to data and also allowing researchers to experiment with qualitative data collection techniques that otherwise might have been impossible, or too costly.

The book is divided into four parts with respected international authors contributing from their various fields of expertise. Authors were asked to choose a form of qualitative data collection and/or analysis they were experienced in using, and to consider how it could be used in the broad field of HRM. The term "innovative" is used here to mean rarely used in the field of HRM. To explain this using an example, one could hardly call historical analysis innovative, however, we contend that given historical analysis is rare in the modern business school where HRM research is typically housed, using a historical approach to modern problems is innovative for the HRM researcher.

QUALITATIVE RESEARCH AND RESEARCH DESIGN

The first step in any research undertaking, whether primary or secondary research, is the determination of the design to be used.[1] In qualitative research, potential designs range from pure laboratory experiment and quasi-experiment to field-based survey, interview, observation and participant observation. More than one of these methods may be used in a particular study. Such multi-method research or triangulation is aimed at determining whether the findings from one method converge with or diverge from the findings from another method or methods. The more that the findings from multiple methods converge, the more confidence one has in those findings, and the converse is true as well.

Despite (or perhaps because of) its key importance to the qualitative research process, a particular research design may lead to a change in the original design. In essence, this is what occurred in the famous Hawthorne study. In that work, the researchers intended to measure the effects of lighting (or, as it was expressed and measured at the time, candle wattage) on worker productivity. To do so, a field-based quasi-experiment was created in which six employees of the Hawthorne plant were assigned to an enclosed space (that is, room) in the plant in which the workers continued their regular work of producing and assembling certain components of telephones and in which the researchers could control the amount of lighting. In the original research design for this study, the concept of a work group or team was nowhere to be found. Rather and based on the prior industrial engineering-based work of Taylor (1911), who focused on the effects of job design and redesign on worker productivity, the Hawthorne researchers focused on the effects of an external, environmental characteristic of work, namely, the amount of lighting (or candle wattage), on worker productivity. It was only after the accidental discovery during the Hawthorne study that lighting was not positively correlated with productivity that the researchers began to consider that something other than lighting might be affecting such productivity. To determine what that "something" was, the researchers decided to talk with – interview – the workers. After doing so, the researchers concluded that the strong "we-feeling" among those workers was key to explaining why their productivity was very high even under the condition of extremely poor lighting. The concept of we-feeling was subsequently relabelled "group norms" and quickly became central to organisational behaviour and HRM – and has remained so ever since.

By contrast, studies conducted by Roy illustrate how a qualitative research design may have considerable staying power (Roy, 1952, 1959). As with the Hawthorne researchers, Roy was also interested in the determinants of worker productivity. However, his preferred research design was that of participant observation. For this purpose, Roy became hired as a production worker in several different settings and systematically documented his experiences therein. This approach, which continued throughout his career as an industrial sociologist, enabled him to show how workers could obtain a certain amount of autonomy even under highly restrictive production requirements and how such autonomy could positively affect productivity (Roy, 1959). But he also showed how group norms could form and be maintained such that they restricted worker productivity (Roy, 1952).

Also notable about these particular studies is that while they are regarded as leading historical examples of qualitative research, they also illustrate that "data" for such research may be both quantitatively and qualitatively obtained and analysed. Hence, substantial quantitative data were obtained during the original Hawthorne studies, and those data have been extensively analysed by many subsequent researchers (for example, Levitt and List, 2011). By contrast, data of the type obtained by Roy and other participant-observation researchers are highly qualitative and are typically analysed ethnographically (for example, Burawoy, 2001).[2] In both instances, however, the choice of research design is key as is the lesson that no particular research design in immutable. A design can and should be changed based on unanticipated factors and findings.

As previously mentioned, the Hawthorne studies and Donald Roy's and Michael Burawoy's research are just a few of the many studies that have used qualitative data to give us new insights and understandings in the field of HRM. What is the state of HRM studies at the moment though? Saunders and Townsend (forthcoming) have examined the changes in empirical, qualitative research articles in ten top ranked journals. As we can see in Table 1.1, Saunders and Townsend found that there was, with some variation between journals, a 10 per cent reduction in the publication of interview-based, qualitative research articles in 2013 compared with the same journals a decade earlier in 2003. Does this mean that qualitative research is no longer fashionable in business schools? Experienced researchers like John Godard (2014) caution against the "psychologisation" of business schools and the focus on quantitative research that comes with that shift. We suggest that similar to these classic studies of the industrial sociology era – a body of literature many of today's HRM

Table 1.1   Published interview-based articles, comparison 2003 and 2013, ten top ranking journals

Field	Journal name	2003	2013	% change	Total interview articles
		Interview as %	Interview as %		
General Management	*Journal of Management Studies*	55.74	32.43	−23.31	46
	British Journal of Management	62.50	39.47	−22.03	25
	Asia Pacific Journal of Management	40.00	17.78	−22.22	16
HRM/ Employment Relations	*Industrial Relations*[a]	11.54	9.38	−2.16	6
	Human Resource Management	47.05	23.68	−23.37	17
	Work, Employment and Society	55.17	62.79	+7.62	43
	Human Resource Management Journal	50.00	47.83	−2.27[b]	20
Organisation Studies	*Human Relations*	57.89	47.17	−10.72	47
	Group and Organisation Management[a]	6.25	4.55	−1.70	2
	Organisation	72.73	66.67	−6.06	22
Total		45.89	35.17	−10.62	244

Notes:
[a]   As there was a small number of relevant interview-based articles in IR (6 of 58) and GOM (2 of 42 empirical articles) the authors included another journal from these categories (*Human Resource Management* and *Organisation*, respectively) into the analysis.
[b]   Rounding effect.

Source: Adapted from Saunders and Townsend (forthcoming).

researchers "grew up" on – qualitative research can be both innovative and timeless when designed well.

It is commonly accepted that the design of a research project should relate specifically to the research questions for which the researcher seeks answers. Not all questions lend themselves to qualitative inquiry, and often there is an under-reporting of qualitative data in quantitative research reporting (Saunders and Townsend, forthcoming). In Chapter 2, Roslyn Cameron examines a sample of mixed method studies published in the HRM journals to determine the role of qualitative methods in mixed methods study designs. The analysis has a specific focus on the role of qualitative methods in terms of key dimensions that characterise mixed methods studies: purpose; priority of methods; implementation (sequential or concurrent); and design. The author finds that this approach to HRM research offers opportunities to add perspectives to phenomenon and complex research problems. Mixed methods are also shown to assist in levering off strengths of one data collection approach and countering the weaknesses of the other(s).

Rebecca Loudoun and Keith Townsend suggest in Chapter 3 that quantitative approaches to research tend to lend themselves to longitudinal studies far easier than qualitative studies but they argue that this does not mean qualitative research cannot be longitudinal. It is usually easier to see that one number is higher or lower than the other in a quantitative analysis and hence make interpretations of how the matter at hand has changed over time. It can be more difficult though to interpret swathes of interview transcripts and infer meaning about experiences of change. The chapter reports on two time periods of a qualitative, longitudinal study where the researchers experimented in the quantifying of qualitative data – specifically, the use of keywords – in an attempt to find a baseline for measuring differences in employee experiences at a multi-site organisation. In addition, the chapter demonstrates how this approach to data collection and analysis provides a nuance of data that is not available with survey data collected.

In the final chapter in Part I, Chapter 4, Sally Sambrook considers the use of autoethnography design in research projects showing that when researching highly personal aspects of HRM, such as employee engagement, autoethnography provides a novel and more nuanced understanding of HRM phenomena.

INNOVATIONS IN DATA SOURCES

Following the design stage, the next step in the research process is to determine the source of the data. Part II of the book considers the many sources available to the researcher beyond the traditional interviews with workplace actors. In Chapter 5, Richard Johnstone suggests that in order to engage with the regulatory framework surrounding HRM, researchers may need to examine labour law rules and principles. The chapter provides an introduction to doctrinal (sometimes called "analytical") legal research, and discusses other approaches to researching law that draws on qualitative social science research methods. Using the law is hardly innovative, but it is rare within the realm of HRM.

Sheryl Ramsay, Sara Branch and Jacqueline Ewart focus their chapter

(Chapter 6) on the important, innovative contribution that news media research can make to the field of HRM. Through an exploratory study into workplace bullying, the researchers analyse the public representations of HRM issues through the use of news media. The authors point out that news media can allow the researcher to consider aspects of public perception of HRM issues like workplace bullying, for example.

Throughout the early days of the democratisation of the internet, James Richards used "workplace blogs" for some innovative research. His chapter (Chapter 7) looks at conducting research with employee bloggers – employees often suspicious of outsiders and not an easily recruited source of workplace information. Conventional gatekeepers, such as HR managers, will often take a dim view of employees talking to researchers about taboo topics, like workplace misbehaviour and discontent. Richards provides an insider take on four key methodological challenges and dilemmas faced when conducting a qualitative study of employee blogging practices.

Many researchers will have been exposed to the HR manager who seems to hold the view that their organisation is organised around a wonderfully innovative model of people management that will leave all employees engaged and excited about work, while enhancing performance and productivity levels. In reality, this is rarely the case. To avoid what could be referred to as "analysis amnesia" it is occasionally important to consider the entire body of work on a research topic rather than simply focusing on research advances and seminal studies. Indeed, when it comes to many topics in both research and practice, there is more than a century of research throughout the industrialised era alone. In Chapter 8, renowned industrial relations historian Peter Ackers takes a modern journey throughout historical research arguing a historical view to modern analysis is an important innovation from which HRM researchers could well benefit.

Similarly, in Chapter 9 Kerrie Unsworth and Matthew Hardin draw on ideas that are very old, philosophical methods to illuminate to HRM researchers that there are many ways to look at the problems of the modern workplace. The authors argue that by using philosophical methods and thinking about HRM and work in different ways new insights may be possible that elude researchers using other inductive or deductive techniques.

INNOVATIVE DATA COLLECTION

The third part of this book hosts six chapters on innovative data collection techniques. It begins with Chapter 10 and a contribution from Keith

Townsend, who adopted a method from the "solution-focused therapy" field, where people would traditionally be visiting a psychologist and be asked (with a preamble) if a miracle occurred and their life was perfect, what would be different? Townsend's team asked this question of employees in a workplace as an experiment in data collection. They were very interested to understand if a traditional "problem-focused" interview style would collect the same, or comparable, data to a "solution-focused" approach.

With the advent of the ubiquitous hand-held phone/camera, the general public seems to be visually documenting almost every moment of their lives, more so than in any other era in time. Why should we not adopt this innovation as a research method? In Chapter 11, Catherine Cassell, Fatima Malik and Laura Radcliffe explore the use of photo-elicitation methods in a study of how people manage their daily work–life balance and conflict. In doing so, the chapter outlines some important methodological issues for those who seek to use these methods and concludes that photo-elicitation techniques have much to offer HR researchers.

In another chapter that draws on the qualitative research element of a mixed methods project, Céline Rojon, Mark Saunders and Almuth McDowall outline in Chapter 12 how the repertory grid technique can be used as the first stage within a sequential mixed methods research design. After explaining the method, its usage in HRM and related fields, an example of individual workplace performance research illustrates its utility for informing survey design.

In a similar vein to Chapter 3, Werner Nienhüser in Chapter 13 explores the basic concept behind the free verbal associations (FVA) method that the spontaneous associations a person makes in connection with an object (such as "work" or "tax") reflects his or her attitude towards that object. The chapter explains FVA using the example of a telephone survey of 3203 individuals about their attitudes towards employee participation in decision-making, an ongoing research matter in the HRM field.

Laura Radcliffe (Chapter 14) explores another data collection technique that is not new per se, but is innovative in the field of HRM research. The chapter explores the use of diary studies to highlight the importance of capturing, and understanding, complex daily practices and experiences. The author found this approach to have the ability to look at issues in a new light, uncovering important new insights and helping to understand the daily dynamics of complex issues and experiences.

The final chapter (Chapter 15) in Part III, presented by Mark Learmonth and Michael Humphreys, explores the idea of "autoethnographic vignettes" – theoretically informed stories (vignettes) drawn from our own lives (auto) about our observations of working life (ethnography).

The authors explore the value and potential impact of practitioner knowledge within academic writing, especially writing concerned with the lived experience of working lives. The chapter notes some pitfalls to avoid as well as some ideas for those who are interested in constructing their own vignettes. In an important link to the practitioner community, the authors suggest this approach can improve the working relationships between practising managers and academics, potentially providing insights into topical and perhaps difficult organisational issues.

INNOVATIVE DATA ANALYSIS

Conversations about data analysis with a scholar who performed empirical qualitative research throughout the early stages of modern HRM in the 1980s would differ in many ways from the use of computer technology used in analysis in the second decade of the twenty-first century. In Part IV, the chapter by Julie Cogin and Ju Li Ng (Chapter 16) outlines how computer-supported software can be used in qualitative HRM research. Even though a number of different computer packages have been available for many years, they remain relatively underutilised by HR scholars. Despite the numerous advantages, the use of computer-assisted qualitative data analysis software (CAQDAS) has not been without controversy, and the authors explore some of the "myths" and "truths" of CAQDAS with recommendations for effective use in HRM research.

Gail Clarkson presents cognitive mapping procedures in Chapter 17 as a way to structure and simplify thoughts and beliefs, to make sense of them and communicate information about them. Cognitive mapping, Clarkson argues, might usefully be employed in the context of cross-cultural HRM research and the use of mapping methods is considered in the context of one research study. This approach is found to hold great potential in the context of large-scale studies. The author recommends casual cognitive mapping for researchers looking to elicit and compare anything other than a small number of cause maps on a longitudinal or cross-sectional basis.

The final contribution, from Richard Winter (Chapter 18), illustrates another element of mapping, specifically how to derive behavioural role descriptions from the perspectives of job-holders. Code mapping of interview data and the use of role maps reveal the personal meanings managers attribute to their work roles and social interactions – proactive behaviours often missing from traditional approaches to job analysis. This is an excellent but underutilised means of analysis for various aspects of HRM research.

The authors of the chapters and the editors of this volume are passionate qualitative researchers who all see a great deal of value in the way qualitative research can illuminate the field of work. We hope that this book serves as both a guide and inspiration to current and future qualitative researchers.

NOTES

1. Primary research is research in which new data and documents are created and analysed. Secondary research is research in which existing data and documents are analysed. In primary research but not in secondary research, the researcher determines the research design to be used. To illustrate using an example discussed further below, the original Hawthorne study was designed by Mayo, Roethlisberger and Dickson (see Mayo, 1933; Roethlisberger and Dickson, 1939). It was not designed by other researchers, such as Franke and Kaul (1978), who subsequently reanalysed data from the Hawthorne study.
2. A classic field-based study that employed an observation-based research design and also featured combined elements of quantitative and qualitative analysis is Coch and French (1948).

REFERENCES

Burawoy, M. (2001), "Manufacturing the global", *Ethnography*, **2** (2), 147–59.

Coch, L. and French Jr, J.R. (1948), "Overcoming resistance to change", *Human Relations*, **4** (1), 512–32.

Franke, R.H. and Kaul, J.D. (1978), "The Hawthorne experiments: first statistical interpretation", *American Sociological Review*, **43** (5), 623–43.

Godard, J. (2014), "The psychologization of employment relations?", *Human Resource Management Journal*, **24** (1), 1–18.

Levitt, S.D. and List, J.A. (2011), "Was there really a Hawthorne effect at the Hawthorne plant? An analysis of the original illumination experiments", *American Economic Journal: Applied Economics*, **3** (1), 224–38.

Mayo, E. (1933), *The Human Problems of an Industrial Civilization*, New York: Macmillan Company.

Miles, M. (1979), "Qualitative data as an attractive nuisance: the problem of analysis", *Administrative Science Quarterly*, **24**, 590–601.

Roethlisberger, F.J. and Dickson, W.J. (1939), *Management and the Worker*, Cambridge, MA: Harvard University Press.

Roy, D. (1952), "Quota restriction and goldbricking in a machine shop", *American Journal of Sociology*, **57** (5), 427–42.

Roy, D. (1959), "Banana time: job satisfaction and informal interaction", *Human Organization*, **18** (4), 158–68.

Saunders, M.N.K. and Townsend, K. (forthcoming), "How many participants are sufficient? An analysis of research articles using qualitative interviews in highly regarded organization and workplace journals", *British Journal of Management*, doi: 10.1111/1467-8551.12182.

Taylor, F.W. (1911), *The Principles of Scientific Management*, New York: Harper Brothers.

PART I

DESIGNING
QUALITATIVE PROJECTS

2 The role of qualitative methods in mixed methods designs
Roslyn Cameron

INTRODUCTION

Mixed methods research is growing in popularity across many business and management disciplines. It is now often referred to as the third methodological movement and has an ever-expanding base of research texts and a strong body of foundational literature, seminal authors and methodologists. Although mixed methods research designs vary in complexity across a continuum of simple to highly complex, many of these studies can be described as being very innovative and at times also multidisciplinary. Mixed methods prevalence rate studies across many business and management disciplines not only demonstrate the rates at which mixed methods is being published in top ranking discipline-based journals but also rate the number of quantitative and qualitative studies being published. Grimmer and Hanson (2009) undertook a study of the *International Journal of Human Resource Management*, analysing 828 articles published between 1998 and 2007. They found 49.4 per cent of articles were quantitative, 23.6 per cent of the published articles were conceptual or theory based, 16.3 per cent were qualitative and 10.7 per cent used a mixture of both qualitative and quantitative (Grimmer and Hanson, 2009). The role of qualitative methods in mixed methods study design is the focus of this chapter that analyses a sample of mixed methods studies published in human resource management (HRM) journals. The analysis has a specific focus on the role of qualitative methods in terms of key dimensions that characterise mixed methods studies: purpose; priority of methods; implementation (sequential or concurrent); and design.

Mixed methods research (MMR) has emerged as a legitimate methodology growing in popularity and acceptance across a broad range of disciplines. There are a growing number of texts and journals publishing mixed methods and seminal authors and mixed methodologists. The contentious issues that have been identified in the MMR community include paradigmatic or conceptual stances in MMR, the language or nomenclature of MMR, practical issues in applying MMR and the interface between the conceptual, the methodological and the methods

(Tashakkori and Teddlie, 2010, p. 12). This chapter first provides an overview of MMR prevalence rate studies across business and management disciplines before looking at these and related studies from within the HRM discipline. This is followed by an exploration of the role of qualitative methods in mixed methods studies: purpose; priority of methods; implementation (sequential or concurrent); and design. The chapter concludes with some personal reflections of using MMR designs on large national workforce development projects and a concluding discussion on when to use MMR.

MIXED METHODS PREVALENCE RATES STUDIES

Mixed methods prevalence rates studies have been described by Alise and Teddlie (2010, p. 103) as a "new line of research [that] has emerged in mixed methods (MM) over the past 5 years: one that examines the prevalence rates of methodological approaches within the social/behavioural sciences. In this line of research, investigators determine the proportion of qualitative (QUAL), quantitative (QUAN), and MM research studies that occur within journals in the social/behavioural sciences over a specified time period". Molina-Azorin and Cameron (2015) summarised these prevalence rate studies across several business and management disciplines (international business, marketing, management, HRM, strategy, organisational behaviour, career development, vocational education and training, entrepreneurship, information system and project management) (Table 2.1).

As can be seen from Table 2.1, Grimmer and Hanson (2009) undertook a study of the *International Journal of Human Resource Management*, analysing 828 articles published between 1998 and 2007. They found 49.4 per cent of articles were quantitative, 23.6 per cent of the published articles were conceptual or theory based, 16.3 per cent were qualitative and 10.7 per cent were a mixture of both qualitative and quantitative. In terms of the empirical articles and those not coded as conceptual or theory based, 64.61 per cent were quantitative, 21.33 per cent were qualitative and 14.06 per cent were mixed qualitative/quantitative (Grimmer and Hanson, 2009, p. 6).

Grimmer and Hanson (2009) further analysed the qualitative and mixed methods papers to explore what types of qualitative methods were used and whether authors supplied justification for the use of qualitative methods. They found 15 per cent of these articles explicitly justified the use of the qualitative methods and the "predominant justification centred on the ability of qualitative data to offer more insight and a deeper

Table 2.1 Prevalence studies in business disciplines

Studies	Prevalence rates of empirical works			Disciplines/number of journals	Period	Search strategy	Total number of articles reviewed
	QUAN	QUAL	MIXED				
Hurmerinta-Peltomaki and Nummela (2006)	68%	15%	17%	International business/4 journals	4 years (2000–03)	Manual (all articles reviewed)	484 articles (394 empirical)
Hanson and Grimmer (2007)	75%	11%	14%	Marketing/3 journals	10 years (1993–2002)	Manual	1195 articles (736 empirical)
Molina-Azorin (2008)	78% (80% strategy, 78% operations, 76% entrepreneurship)	10% (5% strategy, 12% operations, 16% entrepreneurship)	12% (15% strategy, 10 % operations, 8% entrepreneurship)	3 subfields in management (strategy, operations management, entrepreneurship)/4 journals	5 years (2003–07)	Manual	916 articles (732 empirical)
Grimmer and Hanson (2009)	65%	21%	14%	Human resource management/1 journal	10 years (1998–2007)	Manual	828 articles (633 empirical)
Molina-Azorin and Cameron (2010)	83% (82% strategy, 87% organisational behaviour)	5% (4% strategy, 6% organisational behaviour)	12% (14% strategy, 7% organisational behaviour)	2 subdisciplines within management (strategy and organisational behaviour)/2 journals	7 years (2003–09)	Manual	871 articles (717 empirical)
Cameron (2010a)	9%	69%	22%	Vocational education and training/1 journal	6 years (2003–08)	Manual	152 articles (106 empirical)
Cameron (2010b)	51%	43%	6%	Career development/1 journal	6 years (2004–09)	Manual	99 articles (63 empirical)
Cameron (2011)	46%	40%	14%	Management/conference papers	1 year (2007)	Manual	281 papers (197 empirical)

Table 2.1 (continued)

Studies	Prevalence rates of empirical works			Disciplines/number of journals	Period	Search strategy	Total number of articles reviewed
	QUAN	QUAL	MIXED				
Miller and Cameron (2011)	32%	28%	40%	Business administration/ Doctor of Business Administration research projects	12 years (1996–2007)	Manual	186 research projects
Molina-Azorin (2011)	72% (78% strategy, 67% entrepreneurial)	14% (5% strategy, 23% entrepreneurial)	14% (17% strategy, 10% entrepreneurial)	2 subdisciplines within management (strategy and entrepreneurship)/4 journals	10 years (1997–2006) strategic 8 years (2000–07) entrepreneurial	Manual	1330 articles (1072 empirical)
Harrison and Reilly (2011)	–	–	2%	Marketing/9 journals	7 years (2003–09)	Electronic and manual	2596 articles
Molina-Azorin (2012)	77%	8%	15%	Strategic management/1 journal	27 years (1980–2006)	Manual	1431 articles (1086 empirical)
Molina-Azorin et al. (2012)	68%	21%	11%	Entrepreneurship/5 journals	10 years (2000–09)	Manual	955 articles (742 empirical)
Sankaran et al. (2012)	–	–	1.48%	Project management/3 journals	7 years (2004–10)	Electronic and manual	1755 articles (214 articles identified in search)
Venkatesh et al. (2013)	–	–	3%	Information systems/6 journals	7 years (2001–07)	Manual	–

Source: Molina-Azorin and Cameron (2015, pp. 471–2).

Table 2.2   Usage of research methods in qualitative and mixed research

Research method	Number of articles reporting usage (percentage)
Case study	153 (18.5%)
Interview – semi-structured	144 (17.4%)
Secondary data	86 (10.4%)
Questionnaire	58 (7.0%)
Interview – structured	31 (3.7%)
Interview – in-depth	30 (3.6%)
Observation	18 (2.2%)
Focus group	10 (1.2%)
Interview – unstructured	5 (0.6%)
Internet/email	0 (0.0%)

Source: Grimmer and Hanson (2009, p. 19).

understanding of the phenomena under investigation than purely quantitative data. Qualitative data was said to be able to answer questions of "how" and "why" versus "what", that is, to address the underlying causes of observed phenomena, to provide more richness of information, to enhance validity, and to allow for more effective sense-making" (Grimmer and Hanson, 2009, pp. 7–8). Table 2.2 summarises the qualitative methods used and the frequency of their use in qualitative and mixed methods articles in ascending order.

This study is now dated and extending the study from 2008 to 2015 may show a trend towards more mixed methods articles being published as acceptance levels and the popularity of the methodology increases.

Gallardo-Gallardo et al. (2015) undertook a bibliometric and content analysis of the literature related to talent management between 2001 and May 2014, which resulted in a total of 273 journal articles being identified. These were coded and the remaining 139 articles were subjected to further analysis. These 139 articles were then summarised in terms of being either theoretical or empirical with empirical articles being coded as either qualitative, quantitative or mixed as summarised in Table 2.3.

It appears from the talent management literature analysed in this study that conceptual (38.8 per cent) and qualitative (33.1 per cent) approaches are those most published followed by quantitative (20.1 per cent) and the least published being mixed methods (7.9 per cent). However, if this analysis is undertaken on the empirical (qualitative, quantitative and mixed methods) articles the percentages for quantitative (54.1 per cent) approaches is over half of these articles followed by qualitative (32.9 per cent) at one third. The percentage of mixed methods articles (13 per cent)

Table 2.3   Summary of talent management literature, 2001–14

Paper type	Method	Total	Percentage (%)	Percentage empirical (%)
Theoretical	Conceptual	54	38.8	
Empirical	Qualitative	46	33.1	54.1
	Quantitative	28	20.1	32.9
	Mixed	11	7.9	13
	Total	139	100	100

Source: Adapted from Gallardo-Gallardo et al. (2015, p. 269).

is comparable with the Grimmer and Hanson (2009) study (14 per cent). However, the use of qualitative approaches is much higher (32.9 per cent) than the Grimmer and Hanson (2009) study (21 per cent).

ROLE OF QUALITATIVE METHODS IN MIXED METHODS STUDIES: PURPOSE, PRIORITY OF METHODS, IMPLEMENTATION (SEQUENTIAL OR CONCURRENT) AND DESIGN

Those analysing the utility and publishing of mixed methods studies in prevalence rate studies have identified several issues. First, that many authors claim to be using mixed methods studies when they are doing this only superficially (Cameron, 2011; Cameron et al., 2015). Others identified that some are utilising mixed methods but don't draw from the mixed methodology foundational concepts, seminal authors, research designs, notation system or nomenclature (Fetters and Freshwater, 2015). As a result, these studies have often used different systems in analysing the dimensions of the published mixed methods studies they have identified in their respective prevalence studies. Cameron (2014, p. 8) summarised these dimensions by looking at the analytical frameworks used over 15 prevalence rates studies in the fields of business and management and found:

> In terms of the analytical frameworks used to further analyse the identified MM studies, several dimensions/aspects of the papers were examined. These included the purpose or rationale for using MM (n = 8), the use of a MM research design (n = 6), matrix for determining implementation and priority (n = 4), matrix for determining data collection and data analysis (n = 4), levels of value add (n = 2), main/primary data collection method (n = 2), data col-

lection methods used (n = 2), data priority, methods and analysis (n = 2) and, sequence and priority of data collection (n = 2).

As was done in 8 of the 15 studies in the Cameron (2014) study, research-ers looked at whether authors of mixed methods studies explicitly stated the rationale or purpose for using mixed methods. The priority of the data and its sequence were also sources of analysis. Bainbridge and Lee (2013) undertook a study of the use of mixed methods in a particular area of HRM research related to the study of the relationship between HRM and performance as first undertaken by Boselie et al. (2005) within a date range of 1994 to 2003. They did this via a review of articles published in top tier management journals and field-specific HRM journals between 2000 and 2011. They drew upon the five mixed methods purposes first proposed by Greene et al. (1989) (summarised in Table 2.4 that also pro-vides examples).

Not only is the purpose for utilising mixed methods important but also the priority given to each method as symbolised in the now much accepted mixed methods notation system first developed by Morse (1991) and further expanded by Morse and Neihaus (2009) and Cameron (2012). In this notation system quantitative research is represented by "QUAN/ quan" and qualitative research by "QUAL/qual" in the overall study. Upper case is used when the method has priority and lower case when it is less dominant. In some cases the research can have equal status. Implementation is another important dimension of MMR designs and this is categorised by whether the data collection was undertaken sequen-tially (represented by "→") or simultaneously (represented by "+"). The priority and implementation dimensions are at the heart of the visual depictions that represent MMR designs. Table 2.5 summarises the result of the Bainbridge and Lee (2013) analysis in terms of purpose, priority of methods used and the implementation of the data collection.

In terms of the innovations employed in MMR I would like to cite a recent paper by Alony et al. (2014) in which the researchers applied a MMR tool used in marital research and applied this to the HRM topic of employee turnover. They found a general consensus amongst scholars to the various factors that lead to voluntary turnover but note the lack of their ability to predict such turnover. These studies tend to rely on self-reporting answers and so the prediction models have very limited ben-efits to organisations. Alony et al. (2014) therefore turned to the marital research literature on marital separation and more specifically voluntary marital separation. They found that "Much like voluntary turnover, marital voluntary separation was initially studied using self-reported

Table 2.4   Purposes for using mixed methods

Purpose	Description	Example
Triangulation	Seek convergent or corroborative results by collecting multiple data on same phenomenon.	An example of this may be the use of both quantitative and qualitative data on the organisational climate of a large organisation using multiple methods: organisational climate survey; focus groups with organisational teams; in-depth interviews with frontline managers. All data collection methods are focused on the same aspects of the organisational climate. However, the data are collected from different samples or subsamples in this case.
Complementarity	Explore interconnected and/ or distinct aspects of a phenomenon by building on strengths and weaknesses of each data collection method.	An example of this may be the exploration of outsourcing HR functions in organisations. A broad online survey of organisations from a specified sample population would seek to collect data on the use of outsourcing HR functions across the sample. The results of this may then be combined with semi-structured interviews whereby chief executive officers are asked to explain and clarify the decision-making processes behind outsourcing or not outsourcing the HR function.
Exploratory/ initiation	Examine similarities, contradictions and new perspectives.	The results from a survey may be contradictory to the results from some qualitative data collection, which then is further explored within the line of inquiry.
Expansion	Add breadth and scope to a project.	"A researcher might survey HR managers about their implementation plan for a new set of HRM practices before making field observations of the process by which the practices were implemented" (Bainbridge and Lee, 2013).

Table 2.4   (continued)

Purpose	Description	Example
Development	Use methods in ways to complement one another.	A researcher(s) may undertake interviews to inform the development of a survey instrument that contains measures or concepts developed from the analysis and results of the qualitative component of the study (interviews/focus groups).

Source: Adapted from Greene et al. (1989) and Bainbridge and Lee (2013).

surveys. However, it was only when an interactional perspective was employed that predictive empirical results emerged" (Alony et al., 2014, p. 190). A MMR-based tool that converts qualitative interview data into quantitative measures proved to have an accuracy of over 90 per cent in predicting voluntary marital separation. The researchers went on to apply a customised model of the tool to investigate voluntary staff turnover. The relationship diagnostic tool relies on qualitative data (the interview) and in an employment setting this needs to be done when the interviewer is external and independent of the employer and the employee must be guaranteed confidentiality.

In concluding, the researchers found there was "a preference for MMR that is complementarity oriented, has a greater weight placed on the quantitative component, that is sequentially implemented and that follows a QUAN → qual design" (Bainbridge and Lee, 2013, p. 2). Clearly, there is room to move for HRM researchers to be more adventurous in the choice of MMR designs and for choosing to have the qualitative components of the MMR design as dominant. Only two studies in Table 2.5 have a QUAL dominant study (Budhwar et al., 2006; Townsend et al., 2011). However, 6 of the 16 studies have equal status.

PERSONAL REFLECTIONS OF USING MIXED METHODS IN HRM RESEARCH

I now draw upon personal experiences utilising MMR designs in large-scale multidisciplinary workforce development research for the Australian rail industry. Both involved mixed methods approaches. Figure 2.1 summarises the research design for the skilled migration research project. The

Table 2.5 Characteristics of mixed methods studies examining the HRM–performance relationship: purpose, priority, implementation and design

Author	Journal	Purpose	Priority	Implementation	Design
Budhwar (2000)	*BJOM*	Expansion	Equal status	Sequential	QUAN + QUAL
Truss (2001)	*JMS*	Expansion	Equal status	Simultaneous	QUAN + QUAL
Bartel (2004)	*ILRR*	Development	Different status – quantitative dominant	Sequential	qual → QUAN
Hatch and Dyer (2004)	*SMJ*	Complementarity	Different status – quantitative dominant	Sequential	QUAN → qual
Browning (2006)	*IJHRM*	Triangulation	Different status – quantitative dominant	Sequential	qual → QUAN
Budhwar et al. (2006)	*JLR*	Exploratory	Different status – quantitative dominant	Simultaneous	QUAL + quan
Clarke (2006)	*IJHRM*	Triangulation	Different status – quantitative dominant	Sequential	QUAN → qual
Khilji and Wang (2006)	*IJHRM*	Development/ Complementarity	Equal status	Sequential	Sequential QUAL → QUAN
Shipton et al. (2006)	*HRMJ*	Complementarity	Equal status	Simultaneous	QUAN + QUAL
Tessema and Soeters (2006)	*IJHRM*	Complementarity	Different status – quantitative dominant	Simultaneous	QUAN + qual
Tsai (2006)	*IJHRM*	Expansion	Equal status	Simultaneous	QUAN + QUAL

Nikandrou and Papalexandris (2007)	*HRMJ*	Complementarity	Different status – quantitative dominant	Sequential	QUAN → qual
Rao (2007)	*IJHRM*	Complementarity	Different status – quantitative dominant	Simultaneous	QUAN + qual
Othman (2009)	*CCM*	Triangulation	Equal status	Sequential	Sequential QUAL → QUAN
Innocenti, Pilati, and Pelusco (2011)	*IJHRM*	Complementarity	Different status – quantitative dominant	Sequential	QUAN → qual
Townsend et al. (2011)	*PR*	Triangulation	Different status – qualitative dominant	Simultaneous	QUAL + quan

Note: Academy of Management Journal (*AMJ*), Administrative Science Quarterly (*ASQ*), British Journal of Industrial Relations (*BJIR*), British Journal of Management (*BJOM*), Cross Cultural Management (*CCM*), Human Relations (*HR*), Human Resource Management (*HRM*), Human Resource Management (*HRMJ*), Industrial & Labor Relations Review (*ILRR*), International Journal of Human Resource Management (*IJHRM*), Journal of Applied Psychology (*JAP*), Journal of International Business Studies (*JIBS*), Journal of Labor Research (*JLR*), Journal of Management Studies (*JMS*), Personnel Psychology (*PPsych*), Personnel Review (*PR*), Strategic Management Journal (*SMJ*).

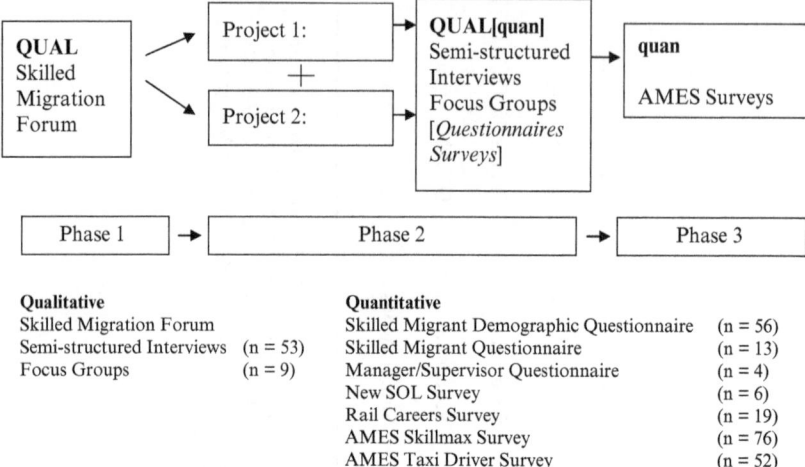

Source: Adapted from Cameron et al. (2011, p. 20).

Figure 2.1   Sequential exploratory research design: three phases of data collection

research design was exploratory and used a variety of qualitative and quantitative methods across three main sequential research phases. The results from the first phase of the research determined the focus and direction of the latter phases, allowing the research process to be emergent. In addition, the context in which the research occurred was volatile as government policies changed. For the researchers there was a strong sense of dealing with a "moving target". Phase 1 involved a Skilled Migration Forum with key stakeholders. The information derived from the forum informed further qualitative and quantitative data gathering relating to attracting and retaining onshore skilled migrants and the recruitment of offshore skilled migrants – both issues identified by the industry at the forum. These data were gathered in phase 2 and a third phase involved data collected from participants in a government service dedicated to assisting onshore skilled migrants gain employment in Australia within their respective professions.

The three phases of data collection allowed a range of perspectives and data from key stakeholders across the Australian rail industry, which was a requirement of the project as it was national but it was difficult to get large numbers of surveys in phase 2. These quantitative instruments were complementary to the main qualitative data collection. The third phase of quantitative data collection was undertaken externally from the

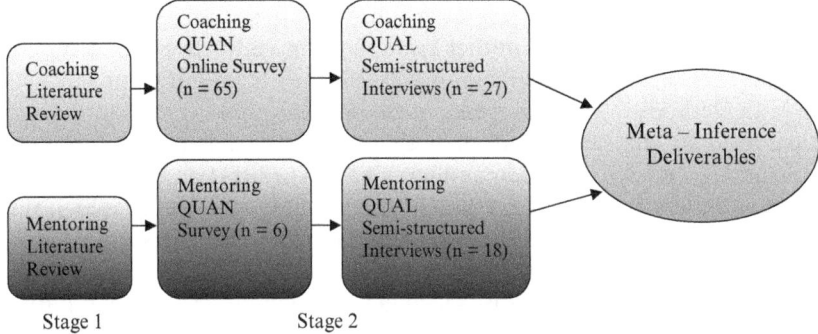

Figure 2.2   Concurrent mixed model research design

Australian rail industry and again allowed the research team to gather larger amounts of quantitative data.

The second workforce development research project for the Australian rail industry also used a MMR design. Figure 2.2 summarises the MMR design for the skills recognition project. This project explored the use and application of mentoring and coaching, two related but distinct HRD practices gaining popularity across the world. The research team was spread across two universities with one group looking specifically at mentoring and the other at coaching. A concurrent mixed model research design was employed as this design best suited the two strands (mentoring and coaching) of the research project and allowed for different combinations, sequencing and weightings of data collection in each parallel strand. This allowed the research team to focus on each area in depth and to bring the findings together to produce deliverables that reflected the differing nature, theoretical foundations and practices of the two (mentoring and coaching) whilst also twinning these practices for greater customisation for the industry.

This research design suited the structure of the project with its two distinct focal areas: mentoring and coaching. The research team had a diversity of research skills that were maximised by using the research design chosen.

WHEN TO USE MIXED METHODS

There are several issues that will ultimately determine whether a mixed methods approach is the most suitable or appropriate. The first key issue will be the paradigmatic stance of the researchers involved. Second, the research problem and the research questions posed will determine the approach to be utilised. Another issue that may influence the methodological choices researchers make is whether they have sufficient skill sets in both methods to be employed and whether they have the resources and time to undertake the mixed methods study that tends to be more time consuming and resource demanding. Cameron (2011) asserted the need for researchers embarking on MMR approaches to be methodologically trilingual, which takes Tashakkori and Teddlie's (2003) assertion even further from their "methodologically bilingual" claim. Whereas methodological bilingualism means skilled in both qualitative and quantitative research methods, methodological trilingualism refers to:

> Not only do they need strong grounding in their chosen quantitative and qualitative methodologies and associated paradigms but they also need to be cognisant, knowledgeable and fluent in the theoretical foundations of mixed methods, the specific mixed methods methodological issues (research designs and typologies, mixed methods sampling, data priority, implementation and integration) and the quality frameworks that have been developed for mixed methods. (Cameron, 2011, p. 262)

In more complex research, several methods may be used and again the skill sets of the researcher(s) may determine the data collection methods chosen. In large research teams, there is likely to be a mix of these technical research skills and experiences that can mean it is more conducive to taking a mixed method approach.

MMR designs offer opportunities to add perspectives to phenomena and especially complex research problems. Kiessling and Harvey (2005) argued this point in relation to strategic global human resource management (SGHRM). They asserted that SGHRM researchers used predominantly quantitative methods alongside western theories and methods for undertaking research and that "these methods and theories frequently do not capture the 'fabric' of global phenomenon that include complex interactions of culture, institutions, societal norms and government regulations, among a few concerns. The mixed method approach is proposed to add the 'fabric' required, illustrating the depth and flexibility needed to explore the SGHRM issues" (Kiessling and Harvey, 2005, p. 22).

Mixed methods can also assist in levering off strengths of one data collection approach and to counter the weaknesses of the other(s).

Ultimately, the research problem and question(s) will be seen through the paradigmatic stance and worldview of the researcher, which in turn will determine the research approach undertaken. The dictatorship of the research question, methodological logic and congruence are all key drivers in the methodological decisions researchers make. These methodological choices, no matter what approach is taken, must be rigorously defended.

REFERENCES

Alise, M. and Teddlie, C. (2010), "A continuation of the paradigm wars? Prevalence rates of methodological approaches across the social/behavioural sciences", *Journal of Mixed Methods Research*, **4**, 103–26.

Alony, I., Hasan, H. and Sense, A. (2014), "Mixed methods to the rescue: addressing the problem of employee turnover using marital research", *International Journal of Multiple Research Approaches*, **8** (2), 190–200.

Bainbridge, H. and Lee, I. (2013), "An analysis and review of mixed methods research designs utilised in the study of the relationship between HRM and performance", Paper presented at ANZAM Conference 2013, Hobart, Australia, December.

Bartel, A.P. (2004), "Human resource management and organizational performance: evidence from retail banking", *Industrial and Labor Relations Review*, **57**, 181–203.

Boselie, P., Dietz, G. and Boon, C. (2005), "Commonalities and contradictions in HRM and performance research", *Human Resource Management Journal*, **15**, 67–94.

Browning, V. (2006), "The relationship between HRM practices and service behaviour in South African service organizations", *International Journal of Human Resource Management*, **17**, 1321–38.

Budhwar, P.S. (2000), "Strategic integration and development of human resource management in the UK manufacturing sector", *British Journal of Management*, **11**, 285–302.

Budhwar, P.S., Luthar, H.K. and Bhatnagar, J. (2006), "The dynamics of HRM systems in Indian BPO firms", *Journal of Labor Research*, **27**, 339–60.

Cameron, R. (2010a), "Mixed methods in VET research: usage and quality", *International Journal of Training Research*, **8**, 25–39.

Cameron, R. (2010b), "Is mixed methods used in Australian career development research?", *Australian Journal of Career Development*, **19**, 53–67.

Cameron, R. (2011), "Mixed methods in business and management: a call to the 'first generation'", *Journal of Management & Organization*, **17**, 245–67.

Cameron, R. (2012), "Applying the newly developed extended mixed methods research (MMR) notation system", Paper presented at the British Academy of Management 2012 Conference, Cardiff, Wales, 11–13 September.

Cameron, R. (2014), "What are mixed methods prevalence rate studies analysing?", Paper presented at the 13th ECRM 2014 Conference, London, June.

Cameron, R., Joyce, D., Kell, P. and Wallace, M. (2011), *Final Report Skilled Migration Project*, Brisbane, Australia: CRC for Rail Innovation.

Cameron, R., Sankaran, S. and Scales, G. (2015), "Mixed methods use in project management research", *Project Management Journal*, **46** (2), 90–104.

Clarke, N. (2006), "Why HR policies fail to support workplace learning: the complexities of policy implementation in healthcare", *International Journal of Human Resource Management*, **17**, 190–206.

Fetters, M. and Freshwater, D. (2015), "Publishing a methodological mixed methods research article", *Journal of Mixed Methods Research*, **9** (3), 203–13.

Gallardo-Gallardo, E., Nijs, S., Dries, N. and Gallo, P. (2015), "Towards an understanding of talent management as a phenomenon-driven field using bibliometric and content analysis", *Human Resource Management Review*, **25** (3), 264–79.

Greene, J.C., Caracelli, V.J. and Graham, W.F. (1989), "Toward a conceptual framework for mixed method evaluation designs", *Educational Evaluation and Policy Analysis*, **11**, 255–74.

Grimmer, M. and Hanson, D. (2009), "Qualitative and quantitative research published in the *International Journal of Human Resource Management*, 1998–2007", Paper presented at the annual meeting of the Australian and New Zealand Academy of Management (ANZAM), Melbourne, Australia.

Hanson, D. and Grimmer, M. (2007), "The mix of qualitative and quantitative research in major marketing journals, 1993–2002", *European Journal of Marketing*, **41**, 58–70.

Harrison, R.L. and Reilly, T.M. (2011), "Mixed methods designs in marketing research", *Qualitative Market Research: An International Journal*, **14** (1), 7–26.

Hatch, N.W. and Dyer, J.H. (2004), "Human capital and learning as a source of sustainable competitive advantage", *Strategic Management Journal*, **25**, 1155–78.

Hurmerinta-Peltomaki, L. and Nummela, N. (2006), "Mixed methods in international business research: a value-added perspective", *Management International Review*, **46**, 439–54.

Innocenti, L., Pilati, M. and Pelusco, A.M. (2011), "Trust as moderator in the relationship between HRM practices and employee attitudes", *Human Resource Management Journal*, **21**, 303–17.

Khilji, S.E. and Wang, X. (2006), "'Intended' and 'implemented' HRM: the missing linchpin in strategic human resource management research", *International Journal of Human Resource Management*, **17**, 1171–89.

Kiessling, T. and Harvey, M. (2005), "Strategic global human resource management research in the twenty-first century: an endorsement of the mixed-method research methodology", *International Journal of Human Resource Management*, **16**, 22–45.

Miller, P. and Cameron, R. (2011), "Mixed method research designs: a case study of their adoption in a doctor of business administration program", *International Journal of Multiple Research Approaches*, **5**, 387–402.

Molina-Azorin, J.F. (2008), "Mixed methods research in business management: a comparison of the use of mixed methods in three specific areas", Paper presented at the IV Mixed Methods Conference, Cambridge, UK.

Molina-Azorin, J.F. (2011), "The use and added value of mixed methods in management research", *Journal of Mixed Methods Research*, **5**, 7–24.

Molina-Azorin, J.F. (2012), "Mixed methods research in strategic management: impact and applications", *Organizational Research Methods*, **15**, 33–56.

Molina-Azorin, J.F. and Cameron, R. (2010), "The application of mixed methods in organisational research: a literature review", *Electronic Journal of Business Research Methods*, **8**, 95–105.

Molina-Azorin, J.F. and Cameron, R. (2015), "History and emergent practices of multimethod and mixed methods in business research", in S. Hesse-Biber and R.B. Johnson (eds), *The Oxford Handbook of Multimethod and Mixed Methods Research Inquiry*, New York: Oxford University Press, pp. 466–85.

Molina-Azorin, J.F., López-Gamero, M.D., Pereira-Moliner, J. and Pertusa-Ortega, E. (2012), "Mixed methods studies in entrepreneurship research: applications and contributions", *Entrepreneurship & Regional Development*, **24**, 425–56.

Morse, J. (1991), "Approaches to qualitative-quantitative methodological triangulation", *Nursing Research*, **40** (2), 120–23.

Morse, J. and Niehaus, L. (2009), *Mixed Method Design: Principles and Procedures*, Walnut Creek, CA: Left Coast Press.

Nikandrou, I. and Papalexandris, N. (2007), "The impact of M&A experience on strategic HRM practices and organisational effectiveness: evidence from Greek firms", *Human Resource Management Journal*, **17**, 155–77.

Othman, A.E.A. (2009), "Strategic integration of human resource management practices: perspectives of two major Japanese electrical and electronics companies in Malaysia", *Cross Cultural Management*, **16**, 197–214.

Rao, A.S. (2007), "Effectiveness of performance management systems: an empirical study in Indian companies", *International Journal of Human Resource Management*, **18**, 1812–40.

Sankaran, S., Cameron, R. and Scales, J. (2012), "The utility of mixed methods in project management research", in *12th EURAM Conference Proceedings, Social Innovation for*

Competitiveness. Organisational Performance and Human Excellence, Rotterdam, 6–8 June.

Shipton, H., West, M.A., Dawson, J., Birdi, K. and Patterson, M. (2006), "HRM as a predictor of innovation", *Human Resource Management Journal*, **16**, 3–27.

Tashakkori, A. and Teddlie, C. (eds) (2003), *Handbook of Mixed Methods in Social & Behavioral Research*, Thousand Oaks, CA: Sage.

Tashakkori, A. and Teddlie, C. (eds) (2010), *Handbook of Mixed Methods in Social & Behavioral Research*, 2nd edn, Thousand Oaks, CA: Sage.

Tessema, M.T. and Soeters, J.L. (2006), "Challenges and prospects of HRM in developing countries: testing the HRM–performance link in the Eritrean civil service", *International Journal of Human Resource Management*, **17**, 86–105.

Townsend, K., Lingard, H., Bradley, L. and Brown, K. (2011), "Working time alterations within the Australian construction industry", *Personnel Review*, **40** (1), 70–86.

Truss, C. (2001), "Complexities and controversies in linking HRM with organizational outcomes", *Journal of Management Studies*, **38**, 1121–49.

Tsai, C.-J. (2006), "High performance work systems and organizational performance: an empirical study of Taiwan's semiconductor design firms", *International Journal of Human Resource Management*, **17**, 1512–30.

Venkatesh, V., Brown, S. and Bala, H. (2013), "Bridging the qualitative-quantitative divide: guidelines for conducting mixed methods research in information systems", *MIS Quarterly*, **37**, 21–54.

3   Anchoring qualitative methods for longitudinal studies
Rebecca Loudoun and Keith Townsend

INTRODUCTION

This chapter details an innovative research methods approach to measuring change in experiences at work over multiple time periods and worksites. Using a recent research project in a large public sector organisation we describe a longitudinal study where baseline qualitative, interview data were "anchored" in such a way that subsequent changes in responses could be tracked over time at an individual and an aggregate level. While qualitative research is generally considered the superior option for exploring "how" rather than "how many" questions, and for understanding phenomena from the perspectives of those being studied (Pratt, 2009), deliberate strategies need to be used when trying to evaluate changes in people's experiences over time.

Significant technological developments have occurred, with digital recorders, ubiquitous desktop and notebook computers, transcription or voice recognition software, computer-aided qualitative data analysis software (for example, NVivo) all becoming readily available to support the qualitative researcher. Despite this, qualitative research does not lend itself naturally to easy comparison over different time periods.

In the current project the researchers were well aware prior to any data collection that considerable challenges to eliciting information would be present as the organisation was beset by low levels of both morale and trust in executive management. While we utilised an online survey of standardised measures in a range of areas, we also implemented a method of inquiry that has not, to the best of our knowledge, been considered in human resource management (HRM) research to date. The interview schedule involved "word association", a technique that has been used in psychology for a century and in market research for decades. This research method, while providing the authors with a means of placing a measurement on the T1 experience of employees, was not without its problems. Participant interpretations of the questions and instructions were varied and, furthermore, when it came time for the researchers to code the data, many responses proved complex and ambiguous.

The chapter explores this technique and the challenges and benefits it offers to researchers using a longitudinal research design. First, we examine the literature that influenced our approach in choosing this data collection method. This is followed by an explanation of the data collection approach adopted in the larger project. Finally, positive and problematic aspects of this data collection method are presented in the discussion. This chapter does not have research questions as such; rather, it tells a story of an experiment in data collection, how this method compares with more "mainstream" survey methods and provides some consideration for further use of this method.

LITERATURE REVIEW: QUALITATIVE RESEARCH TECHNIQUES

Although the contribution of qualitative research has been criticised in certain quarters, the value of this research over time is undeniable (Cassell and Symon, 2007). Qualitative research in the workplace or organisational realm is designed ultimately to link events and meanings during the construction of a social reality (Van Maanen, 1988, p. xxi). Achieving these aims, however, can be "extremely challenging" at times, with difficulties reported around phrasing questions in a way that their meaning is clear and interpreted the same by all interviewees (Gephart, 2004, p. 460). In addition, a "lack of widespread agreement" among interviewees means that it is very difficult to present the "correct" experience (Graves, 2002, p. 169). According to Alvesson, "it is easy to underestimate the problem of relying on responses to questions as valid sources of information" (2011, p. 1).

As another example, researchers must be cognisant of the reality that interviewees might have differing interpretations of the interviewer's or interviewers' research protocol. Again, Alvesson (2011), while in support of qualitative techniques, argues that the complexity and uncertainty of the research practice is such that meaning taken from interviews is contestable. Scheurich (1997, p. 71) offers the view that it is not just contestability of interpretation that needs to be considered but also that interviewees can actively control parts of the interview where "they may push against or resist (his) goals, intentions, questions and meanings". HRM scholars (particularly those with an industrial relations background) are typically resistant to the post-modernist view that there are no facts, only interpretations that depend on the meaning individuals ascribe to them. Nevertheless, survey questions and interview questions can be prescribed different meanings depending on the context. It is unreasonable to expect then that all interviewees will interpret questions the same way.

THE WORD ASSOCIATION TECHNIQUE

Psychologists have used word association tests for more than 100 years, with Galton (1880) and Jung (1904–07) being two well-known proponents of the technique. Word association is considered one type of "projective technique" where participants are given a stimulus and are asked for an immediate response (Lykke Nielsen and Ingwersen, 1999). The psychological perspective suggests that the response "projects" aspects of the participant's personality (Spiteri, 2004). The method is used to minimise ideation (Lindzey, 1959, p. 163) or capture an immediate, unfiltered response (Carter et al., 2013). The technique is used frequently in the area of consumer motivation or market research (Donaghue, 2000), particularly when consumers find it difficult to articulate their feelings, beliefs, attitudes and motivations about a product (Webb, 1992, pp. 125–6).

Kidder (in Webb, 1992, p.125) says projective techniques are useful for:

> encouraging in subjects a state of freedom and spontaneity of expression where there is reason to believe that subjects cannot easily evaluate or describe their motivations or feelings . . . or where topics on which subjects may hesitate to express their opinions . . .

In a related field, Carter et al. (2013) discuss the use of projective techniques in the human resources practitioner community, arguing that their use was quite common until the early 1990s when popularity waned owing to a general agreement that they were too time consuming. HRM researchers are often less interested in the personalities of research participants, instead focusing more on their experiences. Hence, it seemed possible that this approach could pay dividends when investigating matters in an organisation that was known to have problems with employee morale, trust and culture if a more time-efficient process could be found for coding the data.

DATA COLLECTION APPROACH

The research project for which these data were collected is an ongoing study designed to measure change in one division of an Australian public sector organisation with approximately 2000 employees. The research design incorporated a multi-method data collection approach with responses measured at three time points over a two-year period (that is, T1 at June 2013, T2 at June 2014 and T3 at June 2015). An online questionnaire was designed using published, validated scales measuring a range of organisational and individual level variables. The scales of interest for this study included training opportunities, satisfaction with supervisors and overall job satisfaction. These questions were supplemented with standard demographic questions and some organisational specific questions.

The qualitative and quantitative data collected for this project were designed to identify and measure changes in employee and line manager perceptions of the effectiveness of enterprise bargaining, managerial strategies and line manager training over the time period of the study. Prior to the commencement of the project, however, the researchers realised that adopting traditional approaches to collection and analysis of qualitative data was unlikely to allow tracking of individuals over time and detect any changes in perceptions over time.

TIME 1 DATA COLLECTION

Beyond the quantitative component of the project, six executive-level, head office managers were interviewed at T1 and 52 interviews with staff at all levels of the organisation were conducted across five of the 15 worksites. At each worksite a vertical and horizontal representation of the workforce were interviewed. All participants were randomly selected from the staff list and invited to participate in the interviews, except for the site manager of each of the five sites who were all interviewed.

This type of ongoing measurement is somewhat rare in qualitative HRM research, so the researchers drew from different disciplines such as marketing and psychology for ideas on data collection methods. We considered this a reasonable approach as, after all, one of the key components of HRM as a field of study is the capacity of researchers to draw from different disciplines for theory – why not methodology?

The interviews began with a period of rapport building where the interviewers would ask about the interviewees' background and share overlapping experiences. Following this an explanation of the remaining interview process was provided as follows:

> I am going to ask you a handful of questions over the next 30 minutes or so. For many of the questions I would simply like you to give the first three words that spring in to mind, kind of like a word association exercise. For example, if I was to say "sky" you might say "blue", "cloud" and "grey".

It was following this outline that the interviews would generally begin. Three examples of interview questions within the interview protocol are as follows:

1. When you think about your immediate line manager, what are the first three words that spring to mind?
2. When you think about your site manager, the senior-most person at this worksite, what are the first three words that spring to mind?
3. When you think about the relationship between the union and management in this organisation, what are the first three words that spring to mind?

After documenting responses, the researchers then asked the interviewee to expand on them by way of providing an example to illustrate why the word they chose describes or is associated with the event or person in question. The purpose of this follow-up was to gain a deeper understanding of the respondent's views on the matter and to ensure they had understood the meaning of the word correctly.

The next stage of data analysis involved the researchers discussing their findings between interviews, and then again at the end of the day for consistent and divergent themes. This process formed a loose version of convergent interviewing, a technique advocated by Dick (1998) and, more recently, Jepsen and Rodwell (2008). The rigour of qualitative interviews might be questioned, but Jepsen and Rodwell argue that convergent interviewing improves internal validity, external validity, reliability and objectivity – measures that are essential in research methods. Developing themes could then be further investigated at the next data collection point, in this case, within just a day or two.

At the completion of each set of interviews, the words provided by each interviewee were transferred to an Excel spreadsheet and given a colour allocation. Positive descriptive words were coded green, negative descriptors were coded red, neutral words were coded yellow and those words that did not seem to fit this initial allocation were coded grey. This approach was not originally designed to overcome problems with confidentiality or reporting but we quickly discovered benefits in these areas. These unanticipated benefits are considered in the following section. This section also outlines challenges and potential pitfalls with this data analysis identified throughout the first stage of the project as well as strategies considered to overcome them.

TIME 1 ANALYSIS: CHALLENGES AND BENEFITS

The main problems with the approach outlined related to the imagination and vocabulary of some of the people interviewed. The first of these problems was that some employees could not think of three words about the event, person or process in question. This didn't appear to be the result of a lack of knowledge of the topic, it was simply that they were lost in the many thoughts they had about it and how interrelated those thoughts were. To disentangle them and come up with three separate words was too difficult for some people. Attempts to walk around the topic until an appropriate descriptor was identified made some of the interviews overly long for the time allocated.

Another problem was the inability of some people to express their thoughts using an appropriate descriptor. For example, when asked about the relationship between the relevant union and management, the researchers expected the employees to use words that described "the relationship". One employee responded, "well, I reckon that staff representatives are too cosy with the union here, but I'm not sure of a word that you could use for that". From this description the word "cosy" stood out as the descriptor but in this instance (and many others) the researchers did not think the standout word provided an accurate representation of the interviewee's views. For example, if the researchers were to return to the dataset at T2 and see the word "cosy" that might conjure warm, positive thoughts, not the negative connotations that the employee was trying to convey. On some occasions when an employee would provide a monologue, the researcher was able to select a keyword and ask the participant if that was a fair representation of what they were thinking. But, as in the example of "cosy" above, this was not always the case. Hence, a short phrase was recorded.

It became clear early on that much care and attention on the part of the researcher was needed when taking notes in the interviews to ensure positive and negative connotations were interpreted correctly and the general meaning of words were not taken as a given. Interpretation of events and words is essential for the qualitative researcher. We do not measure volume as such, nor do we measure numerical associations, we interpret meaning. This can be problematic as was the case with one employee who was quick with his first word, "rabble". The interviewer's first thought was that this would be a negatively coded word. When pressed on what he meant by rabble, he went on to explain that in his view, the union was such a "rabble" and it was wonderful to see. He liked that his union appeared slightly disorganised, but excitable on issues. For this employee, "rabble" should not be coded red as a negative word, but green as something he liked. Additionally, on some occasions, the researcher chose a keyword from the statement and asked the participant if they felt that word adequately represented the view expressed in that statement.

In summary, as is often the case when scholars test new research methods, there were teething problems identified in this study, but there were many positive aspects of this data collection method as well as some that were not anticipated prior to the research. For example, in addition the three words recorded at the beginning of each interview question provided a useful anchor to draw the interviewee back if the discussion moved away from the issues of interest or if the interviewee forgot the point they were making. In an environment characterised by strong emotions this proved to be very valuable.

Another benefit was the confidentiality afforded by colour coding responses as positive or negative when reporting the results to the organisation rather than drawing attention to individual responses and quotations. Owing to the known low levels of trust within the organisation it was critical for ongoing retention and participation in the research for managers and employees to view the data collection process as transparent as possible. As with most qualitative studies it wasn't possible or sensible to reproduce the interviews in their entirety in the study report owing to confidentiality and space requirements, but the word association approach and subsequent coding meant all interviews could be represented in the report, not simply those that provided the "best" quotes. The strength of numerical values coded from the interviews provided the researchers, and indeed the case study organisation, with a clear sense of the perceptions that employees held towards the topics of interest.

Furthermore, the capacity to provide the organisation with a report containing a measurable level of satisfaction or dissatisfaction gave the partner organisation a tangible point to compare the results of forthcoming interventions. For example, looking at our question about line managers outlined in the previous section, of the 52 interviews we were given 133 codable responses. We were able to identify a high level of consistency in themes and a strong level of code-ability. At this data collection point, the responses were 83 negative, 46 positive and 10 neutral words. Clearly there was a substantial level of negativity towards line managers with almost two thirds of the responses being negative.

From a methodological point of view, the data gathered through the 50 interviews were more than enough to reach saturation based on Creswell's (2007) suggestion that a heterogeneous population would require between 25 and 30 interviews, a number supported more recently by Saunders and Townsend (forthcoming). Ultimately, the approach provided an effective platform to build on in subsequent data collection phases while still providing the rich data and depth of understanding traditionally provided with qualitative research to illuminate the issues under investigation.

TIME 2 DATA COLLECTION

After 12 months, we returned to the organisation for Time 2 data collection and an attempt to understand if the areas of interest had changed in the preceding year and if they had, the outcomes for employees. Again, we coupled the qualitative interview data with an online survey; a replication of the T1 to allow comparison with baseline data. We approached the same 50 interviewees to arrange meeting times and as a result of absenteeism, exits and people withdrawing from the project, we interviewed 24 of the same individuals, and an additional 14 new participants. The approach and interview protocol was identical, with a few minor alterations by way of deleting questions that were deemed to be not relevant at T2 for various reasons (including, for example, the timing of the enterprise bargaining cycle). In short, the T2 data collection was a replication of T1 with almost 50 per cent of the same participants in the interview process.

TIME 2 ANALYSIS

It is our contention that qualitative data can be more sensitive to context and surrounding matters, albeit at times it is more cumbersome to manage the data providing contextual explanations. When an inductive approach to a project is designed and a quantitative methodology is used, researchers are presenting their theoretically and literature informed "best guess" about what is important and how or why things have changed over time periods. By using the three word association technique, we followed an abductive approach to research design where the theoretical driven areas of investigation were nuanced by the empirically driven data provided by the research participants. We can demonstrate this by presenting and comparing two sets of data that relate to the two examples of questions given in the project in the "Time 1 Data Collection" section of this chapter. These questions were about the immediate line manager and the senior manager of the worksite. Our online survey used previously published and validated measures of satisfaction with supervisors (Spector, 1985) and loyalty to line managers and senior managers (Cook and Wall, 1980).

These results show that satisfaction with supervisors improved between T1 and T2 but no change was evident for loyalty to line managers and senior managers. We would interpret these results as indicating that

Table 3.1   Quantitative results comparing T1 and T2 data

	T1			T2			T1 − T2		
	N	Mean	SD	N	Mean	SD	N	Mean differ- ence	SE mean differ- ence
Supervisor with satisfaction	221	4.06	1.24	179	4.12	1.36	56	0.42*	0.14
Loyalty to immediate Supervisor	233	3.91	0.86	198	3.91	0.91	59	0.18	0.12
Loyalty to senior Manager	234	3.74	1.01	195	3.72	0.98	59	−0.36	0.22

Note: $* p < 0.05$.

when it comes to employees' satisfaction and loyalty with supervisor and managers there were only marginal differences between July 2013 and July 2014 (Table 3.1).

When the word association data are compared with the survey data, however, a different picture emerges. Although it is acknowledged that the numbers are not large enough to allow for statistical analysis, this is not the point of qualitative research. Figure 3.1 shows a clear reduction in negative comments when discussing managers and a small increase in neutral words. To the qualitative researcher, these results – coupled with extensive interview data (around 50 hours at each time point) – demonstrate that there have been widespread changes between the two time points in the way employees perceive their immediate supervisor.

Similar, but possibly more pronounced differences were found between the perceptions employees held towards their senior managers over the two time periods. These views, depicted in Figure 3.2, showed a dramatic increase in positive words and a concurrent decrease in negative word associations between the two time periods. Again, these results are not reflected in the quantitative study but bear out substantially in the interview study.

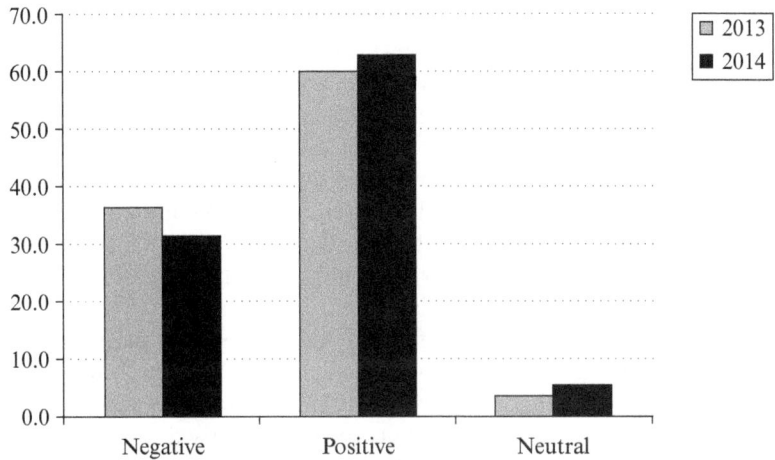

Figure 3.1   Three word results comparing T1 and T2 data – line manager

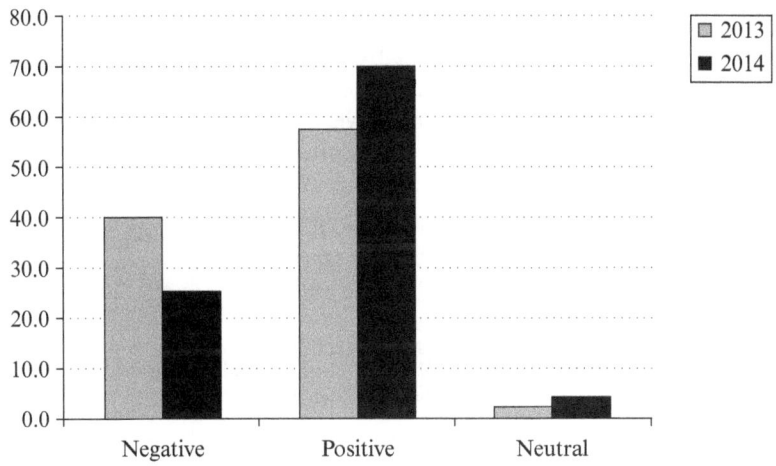

Figure 3.2   Three word results comparing T1 and T2 data – site manager

CONCLUSION

Qualitative research methods have a long and distinguished history in the social sciences. Importantly though, qualitative research methods must continue to develop alongside the needs of the modern researcher and researchers must continue to strive for rigour around data collection, analysis and, additionally, the write-up process. Experimentation with data collection methods is important, however, researchers must invest time and intellectual effort in the process of analysing the research method, not only the data collected. This chapter has described a process of data collection designed to allow recording of qualitative data of employees' perceptions of various positions, events and processes in an organisation in such a way that it could be used as baseline data to compare with data gathered at future time points in a longitudinal study. It was also designed to attempt a quantitative and, therefore, more readily comparable anchor point for the qualitative research data.

The data collection process of word association, or perhaps more appropriately, word attribution, was used in this project. Interviewees were asked to give the first three words that came to mind when various positions, events and organisational processes were raised. Interpretation, though, of both the question and the answer can be problematic when single words are given as responses. It became clear that the employees did not always interpret the question in the same manner. To minimise any potential misinformation being recorded as a result of varying inter-pretations, it proved to be very important for the researchers to fully explore what the interviewee meant by the words chosen, making sure all positive, negative or neutral attributions were accurate. Despite these challenges, the method proved to be very effective for establishing a clear baseline measure or value to take forward and evaluate subsequent periods of change within the organisation.

REFERENCES

Alvesson, M. (2011), *Interpreting Interviews*, London: Sage.
Carter, N., Daniels, M. and Zickar, M. (2013), "Projective testing: historical foundations and uses for human resource management", *Human Resource Management Review*, **23**, 205–18.
Cassell, C. and Symon, G. (2007), *Essential Guide to Qualitative Methods in Organisational Research*, London: Sage.
Cook, J. and Wall, T. (1980), "New work attitude measures of trust, organizational com-mitment and personal need non-fulfillment", *Journal of Occupational Psychology*, **53** (1), 39–52.
Cresswell, J. (2007), *Qualitative Inquiry and Research Design: Choosing among Five Approaches*, Thousand Oaks, CA: Sage.
Dick, B. (1998), "Convergent interviewing: a technique for qualitative data collection", avail-able at http://www.aral.com.au/resources/iview.html (accessed 18 March 2013).
Donaghue, S. (2000), "Projective techniques in consumer research", *Journal of Family Ecology and Consumer Sciences*, **28**, 47–53.
Galton, F. (1880), "Psychometric experiments", *Brain*, **2**, 49–162, available at http://galton.renoster.com/essays/1870-1879/galton-1879-brain-psychometric-experiments/galton-1879-brain-psychometric-experiments.pdf (accessed 6 April 2016).

Gephart, R.P. (2004), "Qualitative research and the Academy of Management Journal", *Academy of Management Journal*, **47**, 454–62.

Graves, T. (2002), *Behavioural Anthropology: Toward an Integrated Science of Human Behaviour*, Walnut Creek, CA: Roman & Littlefield.

Jepsen, D. and Rodwell, J. (2008), "Convergent interviewing: a qualitative diagnostic technique for researchers", *Management Research News*, **31** (9), 650–58.

Jung, C.G. (1904–07), *Studies in Word Association*, London: Routledge and Kegan Paul (contained in *Experimental Researches*, Collected Works of C. Jung, Vol. 2).

Lindzey, G. (1959), "On the classification of projective techniques", *Psychological Bulletin*, **56**, 158–68.

Lykke Nielsen, M. and Ingwersen, P. (1999), "The word association methodology: a gateway to work-task based retrieval", Paper presented at the MIRA 1999 Conference, Glasgow, available at http://bcs.org/upload/pdf/ewic_mi99_paper6.pdf (accessed 6 April 2016).

Pratt, M. (2009), "From the editors: For the lack of a boilerplate: tips on writing up (and reviewing) qualitative research", *Academy of Management Journal*, **52** (5), 856–62.

Saunders, M. (2012), "Choosing research participants", in G. Symons and C. Cassell (eds), *The Practice of Qualitative Organizational Research: Core Methods and Current Challenges*, London: Sage, pp. 37–55.

Saunders, M.N.K. and Townsend, K. (forthcoming), "How many participants are sufficient? An analysis of research articles using qualitative interviews in highly regarded organization and workplace journals", *British Journal of Management*, doi: 10.1111/1467-8551.12182.

Scheurich, J. (1997), *Research Method in the Postmodern*, New York: Routledge.

Spector, P. (1985), "Measurement of human service staff satisfaction: development of the job satisfaction survey", *American Journal of Community Psychology*, **13**, 693–713.

Spiteri, L. (2004), "Word association testing and thesaurus construction", *LIBRES: Library and Information Science Research Electronic Journal*, **14** (2), available at http://libres-ejournal.info/wp-content/uploads/2014/06/Vol14_I2_Spiteri_final.pdf (accessed 6 April 2016).

Van Maanen, J. (1988), *Tales of the Field: On Writing Ethnography*, Chicago, IL: University of Chicago Press.

Webb, J. (1992), *Understanding and Designing Marketing Research*, London: Academic Press.

4 Autoethnography: a novel way to study HRM

Sally Sambrook

INTRODUCTION

This chapter explores the role of autoethnography (AE) in researching highly personal aspects of human resource management (HRM). I aim to demonstrate how AE is useful for students, practitioners and researchers, whose voices are often "lost" in research. My chapter offers a novel methodology in an attempt to address this deficit. It is novel in the sense of being a new way of researching HRM – I am proposing a contemporary, and somewhat contentious, form of ethnography that weaves together the researcher's and participants' experiences to illuminate the phenomenon of inquiry. It is also novel in that the chapter is written as a story of how I have used AE to research HRM. I tell and "show" (Ellis, 2000, p. 275) how this innovative approach might help us better understand HRM in general, and the psychological contract (PC) and employee engagement (EE) in particular.

AE is a development of ethnography, an established form of qualitative research. HRM researchers are increasingly employing ethnographic methods to study EE (Arrowsmith and Parker, 2013; Jenkins and Delbridge, 2013), for example. However, there has been little consideration of the role of AE in HRM research. Perhaps due to its position "at the boundaries of accepted scholarly inquiry" (Foster et al., 2006), AE is only used sparingly. Cunliffe et al. (2009) warn that the more "'sophisticated' a qualitative methodology the more it courts a double marginalization . . . and risks telling its tales to itself" (p. 6). To address this, I wish to broaden our understanding of AE and tell my tales to others.

First, I explain AE. Next, I provide examples of the use and value of AE in researching HRM and then expose some of its challenges. I conclude that an autoethnographic approach harnesses both the experiences of those involved in HRM and the researcher's experiences and interpretations to elicit richer, layered insights. Such nuanced understanding can help facilitate more appropriate, realistic HR interventions.

AUTOETHNOGRAPHY

"An autoethnography cannot begin without some autobiography" (Taylor, 2008, p.178), so let me briefly tell you something about myself. When I was conducting my ethnographic doctoral research (Sambrook, 1998) into human resource development (HRD) in the British National Health Service (NHS), I struggled to find a way of writing that captured what I was experiencing as a researcher and connections to issues I experienced myself as a nurse (and nurse developer) in the NHS culture, some years earlier. I reluctantly settled on employing a "reflexive" approach. Years later, when I was teaching research methods at the School of Nursing, I "found" AE and this satisfied my need to link my own experiences of a given sociological phenomenon with those of participants in my ethnographic studies.

AE, founded on a postmodern – rather than traditional positivist – philosophical orientation, is a research approach that consists of "highly personalised accounts that draw upon the experience of the author/researcher for the purposes of extending sociological understanding" (Sparkes, 2000, p.21). It "lets you use yourself to get to the culture" (Pelias, 2003, p.372). The researcher selects from their personal experiences – often "epiphanies" – as well as collecting data from and about others that are analysed and constructed through the writing process to understand a wider culture (Wall, 2006). Reed-Danahay (1997, p.145) neatly defines autoethnography as research (graphy) that connects the personal (auto) to the cultural (ethnos), placing the self within a social context and the study (and story) of that. The precise nature of an AE can vary, depending on which of these three elements is in focus (Wall, 2006) and the balance between the focus on the researcher and/or the researched (Doloriert and Sambrook, 2009).

The origin of the term is unclear. Heider (1975) used the term autoethnography to refer to Dani people describing their own culture. Goldschmidt (1977) also used the term to describe studies in which cultural members provide insight about their own cultures. These do not appear to include the researcher's self. In this sense, the earliest reference to auto-ethnography (Hayano, 1979) indicated (by the hyphen) that the researcher's autobiographical was added on to the cultural story. In the more recent (and most common) AE (Ellis and Bochner, 2003), the (researcher) auto self is fully synthesised into the story. However, Ellis and Bochner (2000, pp.739–40) list a long series of terms that also embrace autobiographical research.

As a form of "reflexive ethnography", Ellis and Bochner (2000) argue the researcher's personal experience becomes the focus of inquiry, illuminating the culture under study. So, as HRM students, practitioners and researchers, we can become part of our own study, for example, investigating engagement as learners in a business school subculture or experiences of managing workplace EE initiatives, phenomena that directly affect us. Ellis and Bochner (2000, p. 754) encourage students to employ AE as "action research for the individual". I have supported doctoral students/ practitioners writing in this way (Doloriert and Sambrook, 2009, 2011, 2012; Sambrook et al., 2008, 2014; Wainwright and Sambrook, 2010). However, not all supervisors agree. Morse (2002, p. 1159) states, "With due respect to autoethnography, I usually discourage students from writing about their own experiences", fearing the threat of "broad-siding", where students' own experiences dominate and derail the study. I will show, later, how students can successfully connect the auto and ethno in doctoral research.

Writing about the "self" can expose hidden aspects of research, seldom revealed in traditional studies. As Vickers (2002, p. 609) suggests, "it is rare to find a productive scholar whose work is unconnected to his or her personal history". When I wrote my PhD, it connected to my previous nursing experience and the various questions that plagued me then: how training and development was managed; why the NHS workforce was gendered. My time as a nurse set deep seeds of inquiry relating to gender, power, justice, equality and self – why I was more motivated to learn and develop and develop others than colleagues, how this created tensions and why engaging in research was engaging with doctors (them), not for nurses (us). Despite my intention to return to the NHS as nurse manager, I remained in higher education (HE), my current organisational ethnographic home (Doloriert and Sambrook, 2012), where I write "critical" autoethnographies about workplace phenomena and struggles I encounter as teacher, researcher and manager. Humphreys (2005, p. 852) notes, it is "unusual for academics to expose their doubts, fears and potential weaknesses", yet these shape our research agendas and accounts.

Autoethnographies can be presented in a number of ways, according to our own preferences and purposes. They can be creative stories (Pelias, 2003; Sparkes, 2007), prose (Duncan, 2004); narrative (Wall, 2008), vignettes (Ellis, 1998; Humphreys, 2005) and layered accounts (Holman-Jones, 2005; Ronai, 1995). Their common feature is the desire to write about phenomena of deep concern to the author, a methodology of the heart (Pelias, 2004). Many autoethnographies are about profoundly painful experiences – death, disease, dysfunctional relationships – and, whilst personal, could also be related to employment. They are written to try to make sense of these events, to come to terms with the emotions and move forward: they provide a therapeutic journey (Haynes, 2006). They are written not only for the author but also to help others who might experience similar situations. Ellis and Bochner note that "Honest autoethnographic exploration generates a lot of fears and doubts – and emotional pain . . . there's the vulnerability of revealing yourself, not being able to take back what you've written or having any control over how readers interpret it" (2000, p. 738). King (2003, p. 10) notes that "once a story is told, it cannot be called back. Once told, it is loose in the world". This creates a conundrum: the need for transparency, honesty, revealing your self and others versus the need for anonymity relating to participants, friends, colleagues and journal reviewers.

So, a key challenge is dealing with the ethical implications for self and the ethics of I (Doloriert and Sambrook, 2009) and beyond. Clandinin and Connelly (1994, p. 423) note the vulnerability of writing one's self into the narrative, where self-disclosure enables the personal voice to be heard but leaves the researcher exposed, arguing, "The researcher is always speaking partially naked and is genuinely open to legitimate criticism from participants and from audience." Flemmons and Green (2002, p. 93) refer to this as outing and caution, "you have to decide if you are ready to be outed or to put yourself out that way and consider the impact on personal identity". Vickers (2002, p. 612) also identifies that "few have considered (psychologically, physically, materially, or emotionally) the potential harm to researchers when we write about our experiences as we go about our work". But we also have to consider our friends, family and colleagues – the concept of relational ethics (Ellis, 2007; Etherington, 2007; Medford, 2006; Vickers, 2002). To protect their identities, we can adopt a fictionalisation strategy (Humphreys and Watson, 2009) where we carefully blur individual identities and combine conversations and events to preserve anonymity.

Another challenge is deciding how to write an AE. Somewhat confusingly, the term can be used to refer to different ways of writing – whether evocative (Ellis and Bochner, 2006), analytical (Anderson, 2006), radical-political (Holman Jones, 2005) or combining any/all of these (Learmonth and Humphreys, 2012). So, we need to consider what is the purpose of our AE? What are we trying to achieve – to evoke emotions in readers, to provide theoretical analysis, to critique and effect change or a combination of each? In evocative autoethnographies, "the goal is to write meaningfully and evocatively about topics that matter and may make a difference" (Ellis and Bochner, 2003, p. 213), employing an epistemology of emotion (Denzin, 1997, p. 377). Analytical AE develops Lofland's (1995) notion of analytic ethnography, where the analytic "rescues" AE (Atkinson, 2006). Hayano (1979, p. 102) suggested, "the most fundamental dilemma raised by most autoethnographers concerns research bias and the objective/subjective polarity in collecting, interpreting and reporting information". For example, I supervised Clair's PhD and she wanted to write her thesis as a creative, analytic practice (Richardson and St Pierre, 2005) that captured her (subjective) struggles. However, her examiners sought only a polished, analytical report. Through negotiation, we eventually agreed that Clair's authentic experiences could be contained in vignettes (Humphreys, 2005), somewhat separate from the (objective) contribution to knowledge, but still in the text (Doloriert and Sambrook, 2011; Roberts, 2007). Perhaps a compromise, yet Richardson and St Pierre (2005, p.964) note that "Science is one lens, and creative arts is another. We see more deeply using two lenses."

Once our story is created, who is going to judge the quality of the writing, and how? Despite "criterialogical" concerns (Doloriert and Sambrook, 2011; Johnson et al., 2006), we need indicators to make judgements about the quality of an AE and just as there are different types of writing, there are different criteria with which to judge. For example, Richardson (2000) judges an AE on the basis of its: substantive contribution; aesthetic merit; reflexivity; impact; and expression of a reality. Bochner (2000, pp.270–71) seeks: abundant concrete detail; a past and present temporal framework; emotional credibility, vulnerability and honesty; believable journey; standard of ethical self-consciousness; and a story that moves me. Anderson (2006, p.378) stipulates: complete member status; analytic reflexivity; narrative visibility of researcher's self; dialogue with informants beyond self; and commitment to theoretical analysis. It is important to guide readers by introducing the indicators by which you would like your AE to be judged – you need to educate your reader/examiner/reviewer. As well as these challenges, there are limitations and caveats.

AE attracts savage critique, described as: a romantic construction of the self, a vulgar realism and hyperauthentic (Atkinson, 1997); self-indulgent and narcissistic (Coffey, 1999). Regarding narcissism, Hammersley and Atkinson (2007, p.204) argue that "The principle of reflexivity has been taken to a cultural extreme, in which the voice of the author is the dominant one" and then state, there is "little justification for substituting self-absorption for a thoroughgoing sociological or anthropological imagination" (p. 205). I don't wish to privilege my own voice, but conversely I am reluctant to ignore and write myself out of the text if I feel I have relevant personal experiences to share. Sparkes (2002) argues that rather than self-indulgent, AE is self-knowing and rejects claims that it is academic wank. "Self-indulgent – the word slams into my left ear . . . I want to ask him what he means by self-indulgent. Why not use different terms, such as self-knowing, self-respectful, self-sacrificing, or self-luminous? For me, the dissertation was anything but self-indulgent" (Sparkes, 2002, p. 212). So, as Holt (2003, p. 19) notes, "Researchers would be well advised to be persistent in their autoethnographic intentions, and be prepared to face rejection and critiques of their chosen genre. Resilience and conviction are required to pursue this methodology."

I have used AE to illuminate HR phenomena I have experienced within doctoral supervision and share glimpses of this work here – and in case you have any ethical concerns, I don't reveal anything that is not already in the public domain.

Doing Autoethnography in Doctoral Supervision

My first collaborative autoethnographic venture began several years ago when I had an unpleasant experience with one of my PhD students at an HRD conference (Sambrook et al., 2008). I had taught Clair in her undergraduate degree and she was an outstanding student. A few years later, Clair and I had been rehearsing our conference presentation and I suggested further practice but Clair was adamant she would be fine. Should I have asserted my legitimate power and insisted on more? After our presentation, she asked for feedback and I had to admit that it hadn't gone as well as I'd hoped but just as I was about to explain why, I was stopped by a colleague and entered into another conversation. Clair was very upset and so was I, so much so that later that evening I had a long, tearful discussion with Jim, my former supervisor, about the supervisory relationship. Was I still dependent on him? The next day, Clair and I had an emotional conversation on the journey home, working through our (auto) experiences, connecting with issues of power and emotion within the (ethno) culture of doctoral supervision, all captured in our first collaborative AE (Sambrook et al., 2008). My next example also relates to power and emotion within the psychological contract (PC).

Doing Autoethnography in a Psychological Contract

The notion of exploring the psychological contract within doctoral supervision began when I was supervising Delia's PhD. Delia managed health and social care workers in a learning disability team. I had taught and supervised Delia in the School of Nursing. After her Masters' degree, Delia was keen to study further and was particularly interested in the psychological contracts of health and social care workers. Argyris (1960, p. 22) defined the psychological contract as "the perception of both parties to the employment relationship, organisation and individual, of the reciprocal promises and obligations implied in that relationship".

Although not a conventional employment relationship, Wade-Benzoni and Rousseau (1998) argue that greater awareness of the contract-making mechanisms that operate in postgraduate education can help improve the quality of student experiences and research collaborations between faculty and doctoral students. A few months into Delia's PhD, we had an email conversation.

> Hi Delia,
> I've been thinking and wondered if there was a psychological contract in our doctoral supervisory relationship? This could run parallel with your study of the PC at work and would make a fabulous autoethnography.
>
> Hi Sally
> Interesting idea, I had actually thought about some of this when I was reviewing my reflexive notes I have been keeping about the whole research process. I have also been considering taking an autoethnographic approach.

After agreeing this, we started to keep notes of our implied expectations of and obligations to each other. In our "formal" narratives we wrote:

> Sally: I felt comfortable in our earlier academic relationship and assumed that this would continue much the same, only with a higher level of intellectual engagement. Despite this earlier relationship, and Delia's PhD research question, I hadn't even thought about our evolving psychological contract.
>
> Delia: It has evolved over time and can be "evidenced" in the way that our communication has evolved . . . Once I stated my growing interest in autoethnography the whole psychological contract seemed to start rapidly evolving, I started to question our relationship more, was our psychological contract developing because we had more shared interest? Something could happen tomorrow that changes everything about our contract. What comes next could be better or worse or just different.

Everything seemed to be going extremely well, even when I was granted a nine-month sabbatical and would be away. Delia and I discussed how we would manage this as I was her only supervisor. We agreed that I would respond to emails and provide feedback on draft chapters and this appeared to work well . . . until Delia stated that she felt her PC had been breached. This was another unpleasant experience we had to work through, and eventually decided to write a conference paper about our evolving PC (Wainwright and Sambrook, 2009).

We included excerpts from our email conversations over the previous year and our ongoing "thoughts" as we drafted the conference paper. As we began to write, we soon began to realise the risks in exposing ourselves – privately through our email exchanges and publicly in the conference paper.

Hi Sally

Hope you are enjoying the bank holiday weekend. It's back to study as usual here. I have written my AE piece which I found fascinating and am looking forward to sharing it even if it is a bit scary being so "exposed". Do you want to do this at our next meeting or do we swap before then? D

Hi D

Yes, not too bad – trying to combine some exercise and some reading (AE of course). I know exactly what you mean about the fear of being exposed. I think it might be a good idea to swap via email before our next meeting so we both have time to reflect on each other's thoughts.

And in a later email exchange, this anxiety emerges again.

Hi Sally

I have read the articles, interesting stuff. I will now have to be very careful with the composition of future emails in case we decide to analyse them.

Hi D

Yes it's a bit scary if you think what you write might be recorded and analysed, and so much of what I write is without regard for this possibility – I feel so comfortable in our supervisory relationship.

Hi Sally

I don't think it will change my emails either, I am still willing to express blind panic when appropriate, which also indicates that I too am comfortable in our supervisory relationship.

As we started crafting the paper, I became increasingly nervous and wrote in it:

Thought: I've often talked about the emotions in supervisory relationships, but when these occur in unpleasant ways – as they did for Clair and I following "that" conference presentation or now during my attempts to write this paper with Delia, it feels much more painful, and I feel very vulnerable as a supervisor – something you don't often read in academic writings.

Delia also wrote:

Thought: The above email exchange took place during the first year and reads as a mutual congratulations of our supervisory relationship success. At this time, was there an implicit mutual obligation not to test the boundaries of the relationship? I think we both understood each other's boundaries, not through explicit discussion but through an evolving understanding over time. I am unsurprised that we were comfortable, neither of us did anything to test the boundary, there was no vulnerability in the relationship as neither of us did anything to breach the comfort zone.

In recent times, and also as part of the process of producing this paper, we have perhaps for the first time become vulnerable in the process and acknowledged that we may have left a lot to evolve without setting boundaries.

I know that Sally was working flat out at that point but I still expected her to respond to me at weekends, evenings etc., there was no formal contract saying she had to do that but I knew she would, just as I made the presumption that she knew I worked hard too and that emails outside office hours were the only practicable way for me to work with her too. She expected me to contact her then and I expected her to respond. It is only now at the midway point of the process that I wonder if we had mutual expectations based on shared understandings. In a recent conversation Sally mentioned her crazy work schedule before going on sabbatical, 80-hour weeks etc. I have often also mentioned to her that my work schedule was also busy. However, when we had an explicit conversation about it, it was clear that we had different definitions of busy/crazy. A busy work schedule for me was nowhere near as busy for Sally. Had part of the implicit terms of our contract been based on a misconception on Sally's part of how busy I was? Would the terms of access/contact have been different if she had known this? Had I inadvertently deceived her about how busy I was? Does it affect the degree of trust between us if we haven't really understood each other's context?

This thought illustrates the implicit, unwritten expectations of a PC and drew our attention to the evolving nature of the contract we had not even considered. The first year presents a seemingly "rosy" view and neither of us ventured out of our comfort zone to examine our PC. This changed during the second year, following my sabbatical, with perceptions of breach, as illustrated in reflections in the conference paper.

Delia: Sally expects me to work hard and to keep going at the pace we have set. She has gone on sabbatical and, whilst not explicitly saying this, the implication is that everything will remain the same, email conversations and then tutorials when she gets back ... Sally has been constantly available during the first year and I felt that I had as much attention as I needed. In the second year I would have valued seeing her monthly like before ... I feel that I have lost momentum for not being able to have a face to face conversation with her. Has she breached my expectation? Sally explained she was going away well in advance and I would prefer to have a bit of Sally rather than more of someone else, although in reality I might not have got more of someone else ... I haven't suggested to Sal that breach has occurred and whilst I think it has I am fairly sure that it won't derail us as she will be coming back! I think the short-term effect has been that I have taken my foot off the pedal somewhat, as there are no bouncing weekend emails to encourage me on ... Does Sal think I have breached our PC? She probably expects me to be mature enough to carry on working without her being at the end of weekend emails to "hold my hand". Have I breached her expectations of me by not working as hard over the past few months? When did we agree how hard we were both obliged to work and how available we needed to be? Does she know the role she plays in keeping me motivated? I see this as a hugely significant part of our PC, "you motivate me through being available and I will try to deliver" so how would she view it, is there the element of reciprocity?

Sally: Well, this is interesting! I did feel "guilty" going on sabbatical, but I had earned it! Delia talked of me being busy/crazy at work and just before I left,

I thought I might have cracked! But, although I was going to be physically away, I always intended to retain regular email contact – and I thought I did ... But breach? That's a bit strong, but yes, I suppose Delia is not wrong to feel this. Yet, I've supervised several students "virtually" so for me, I didn't think this was going to be an issue. I thought I made a special effort to keep in touch with Delia, but I do accept that not seeing each other in person did result in her losing momentum – although she disguised it well. It's only now that I'm thinking – why hasn't she made more progress on the interview schedule? Secretly, I'm now wondering what she has exactly done over the last few months! Of course, first it was Christmas, and then she got married and then what? And another funny thing, Delia is now referring to me as Sal. That's just a recent thing! I don't encourage many people to call me Sal ... So, perhaps if there was a breach, it's healed or been resolved!

Delia: You did keep in email contact, I just didn't see you! ... When we embarked on the PhD journey I expected to meet with you regularly and for a while that didn't happen, it certainly isn't a deal breaker and I don't expect that I will stop calling you Sal or you calling me D.

Sally: No, I don't think so, either!

We concluded that being aware of each other's needs and expectations (auto) strengthened our PC, and helped Delia more deeply understand the subject of her (ethno) doctoral study. As Delia reflected towards the end of the paper:

Thought: This reads like a very sanitised account of what has been an uncomfortable and delicate process. Things have been revealed, I think pride has been hurt, but I hope trust and resilience have prevailed.

Although painful and potentially perilous, revealing expectations is important in any PC and I hope this honest account helps HR students, practitioners and researchers understand why. Another deeply personal HR concept is employee engagement (EE).

Doing Autoethnography in Employee Engagement

I recently supervised Natalie's autoethnographic doctoral thesis examining EE in the public sector in the UK (Jones, 2012). Kahn (1990, p. 700) defined engagement at work as "the simultaneous employment and expression of a person's 'preferred self' in task behaviours that promote connections to work and to others, personal presence (physical, cognitive and emotional) and active full role performances". Natalie's aim was to explore how EE was conceived, managed and experienced by a range of stakeholders: senior managers, line managers, HR specialists and non-managerial staff, including Natalie who formerly worked as a middle manager in the public sector. I should explain that the study began as a traditional ethnography. As noted in an early excerpt from her research journal, Natalie said: "I met with Sally and Clair today. Went on about autoethnography again. If they think I'm going to indulge in all that navel-gazing again, they've got another thing coming. They don't know me" (Jones, 2012). This illuminates the often sceptical perceptions and prejudices of AE. Yet, as her study developed, she expressed the intense meaning acquired in connecting (auto) personal aspects of her former managerial role and work experiences with her (ethno) findings of the wider managerial issues associated with her research topic, EE.

Natalie undertook traditional ethnographic fieldwork for almost a year in a public sector health and social care organisation implementing a management-led EE initiative. Natalie observed both the formal elements of the "in-house" engagement initiative as well as informal meetings and conversations with staff. She conducted interviews with 15 managerial and non-managerial staff, individually and in groups, regarding their under-standing of EE and their experiences of the "in-house" initiative. For her auto data, Natalie drew on recollections of five years of work experience where she had experienced both engagement with and disengagement from work. As her supervisor, it was also interesting for me to observe her engagement (and disengagement) with her research! Nevertheless, Natalie persisted with ethnographic data collection and analysis and it emerged that her earlier struggles with her own personal engagement at work had initially instigated the project. During this time, I also re-examined my own engagement with work and through our conversations we began to think more about how employees might become aware of and manage their own engagement.

Combining auto data with a traditional ethnographic study, Natalie contributed new knowledge on the dynamism and transience of EE (Bledlow et al., 2011; George, 2010), the feelings of loss and grief about losing a sense of personal engagement at work that had once been very strong and how difficult it was to connect personal attempts at rebuild-ing engagement with those being advanced by the organisation. Natalie drew upon her own experiences, not to dominate the study but offer fresh and additional insights and understandings of the other participants' accounts. EE, through these combined experiences, was nothing like the "win–win" (MacLeod and Clarke, 2009) for organisations and employees so often advanced by HR professional bodies (CIPD, 2012; Vance, 2006), government reports (APSC, 2012; UK Government, 2011) and academic literature (Harter et al., 2002).

From our own reading, personal experiences and conversations, we advocate that researchers and HR practitioners need to delve deeper than snap-shot annual surveys (see, for example, Towers Perrin, 2012) to generate more sophisticated understanding of EE, both as an individual dynamic state (the self being engaged/disengaged) and organisational device (HR and managers "doing" engagement) (Sambrook et al., 2014; Jones and Sambrook, 2016). Employing "auto" and "ethno" data enables researchers to consider both the psychological (personal) and the sociological (organisational) elements of engagement, integrating the researcher's and participants' accounts of being their selves at work, and this could be especially important with senior and middle managers who commission and deliver EE initiatives (Shuck and Sambrook, 2014). Hopefully, this will help employees consider how much of their engagement at work is of their own choice and how much is being imposed or expected, linking with the implicit PC, and assist HR practitioners design more realistic ways of capturing and supporting EE.

CONCLUSIONS

I have proposed – and hopefully shown – that autoethnographic studies are well suited to exploring highly personal HR phenomena. My aim has been to illustrate (evocatively) from personal examples how and why AE is an entirely appropriate alternative method to penetrate and illuminate otherwise neglected unique, emotional experiences of HRM. AE captures both the individual and social nature of HR concepts and enables the researcher's voice and experience to complement (but not dominate) the participants'. This synthesis elicits richer, layered, more nuanced insights that can help facilitate more appropriate, realistic HR interventions related to the PC and EE. Autoethnographic methods could also be suitable for a range of other studies of deeply personal aspects of HRM, such as workplace learning, organisational cultures, motivation to work, job satisfaction and so forth, from the various perspectives of researchers, HR practitioners, managers and employees.

Of course, AE won't appeal to everyone and budding autoethnographers will need to learn how to record their auto data, craft their tale and persevere against dominant, positivist prejudices of sponsors, examiners and editors. However, to conclude, I have shown a novel way of researching and writing that is authentic to my self. Personally, I enjoy telling, hearing stories – they help me make sense of my own and other's experiences. I hope this novel story helps you deal with your own experiences of HR phenomena, and researching/writing about them.

ANNOTATED FURTHER READING

Doloriert, C. and Sambrook, S. (2011), "Accommodating an autoethnographic PhD: the tale of the thesis, the viva voce, and the traditional business school", *Journal of Contemporary Ethnography*, **40** (5), 582–615.
This collaborative AE shows the journey of a doctoral student and her supervisor, raising issues regarding how a PhD should be presented and examined, and helps students (and supervisors) consider how to present their research for formal assessment in an environment unfamiliar with autoethnographic approaches.
Wall, S. (2006), "An autoethnography on learning about autoethnography", *International Journal of Qualitative Methods*, **5** (2), Article 9, available at https://www.ualberta. ca/~iiqm/backissues/5_2/HTML/wall.htm (accessed 22 January 2015).
Written by a doctoral student, in a very accessible style (as you might expect!), this shows how she grapples with and comes to understand AE, its varieties, strengths and criticisms.

REFERENCES

Anderson, L. (2006), "Analytic autoethnography", *Journal of Contemporary Ethnography*, **35** (4), 373–95.
APSC (Australian Public Service Commission) (2012), "Employee engagement", in *State of the Service Report 2011–2012*, chapter 4, available at http://www.apsc.gov.au/about-the-apsc/parliamentary/state-of-the-service/2011-12-sosr (accessed 21 January 2015).
Argyris, C. (1960), *Understanding Organizational Behavior*, Homewood, IL: Dorsey Press.
Arrowsmith, J. and Parker, J. (2013), "The meaning of 'employee engagement' for the values and roles of the HRM function", *International Journal of Human Resource Management*, **24** (14), 2692–712.
Atkinson, P. (1997), "Narrative turn in a blind alley?", *Qualitative Heath Research*, **7**, 325–44.
Atkinson, P. (2006), "Rescuing autoethnography", *Journal of Contemporary Ethnography*, **35** (4), 400–404.
Bochner, A.P. (2000), "Criteria against ourselves", *Qualitative Inquiry*, **6** (2), 226–72.
Bledlow, R., Schmitt, A., Frese, M. and Kuhnel, J. (2011), "The affective shift model of work engagement", *Journal of Applied Psychology*, **96** (6), 1246–57.
CIPD (Chartered Institute of Personnel and Development) (2012), *Employee Engagement in Context*, available at http://www.cipd.co.uk/hr-resources/research/employee-engagement-context.aspx (accessed 21 January 2015).
Clandinin, D.J. and Connelly, F.M. (1994), "Personal experience methods", in N.K. Denzin and Y. Lincoln (eds), *The Handbook of Qualitative Research*, London: Sage, pp. 413–27.
Coffey, A. (1999), *The Ethnographic Self: Fieldwork and the Representation of Identity*, Thousand Oaks, CA: Sage.
Cunliffe, A., Linstead, S. and Locke, K. (2009), "Telling tales: guest editorial", *Qualitative Research in Organizations and Management: An International Journal*, **4**, 5.
Denzin, N. (1997), *Interpretive Ethnography: Ethnographic Practises for the 21st Century*, Thousand Oaks, CA: Sage.
Doloriert, C. and Sambrook, S. (2009), "Ethical confessions of the 'I' of autoethnography: the student's dilemma", *Journal of Qualitative Research in Organizations and Management*, **4** (1), 27–45.
Doloriert, C. and Sambrook, S. (2011), "Accommodating an autoethnographic PhD: the tale of the thesis, the viva voce, and the traditional business school", *Journal of Contemporary Ethnography*, **40** (5), 582–615.
Doloriert, C. and Sambrook, S. (2012), "Organisational autoethnography", *Journal of Organisational Ethnography*, inaugural issue, **1** (1), 83–95.

Duncan, M. (2004), "Autoethnography: critical appreciation of an emerging art", *International Journal of Qualitative Methods*, **3**, 1–14.

Ellis, C. (1998), "What counts as scholarship in communication? An autoethnographic response", *American Communication Journal*, **1** (2), 1–5, available at http://ac-journal.org/journal/vol1/Iss2/special/ellis.htm (accessed 25 March 2016).

Ellis, C. (2000), "Creating criteria: an ethnographic short story", *Qualitative Inquiry*, **6** (2), 273–7.

Ellis, C. (2007), "Telling secrets revealing lives: relational ethics in research with intimate others", *Qualitative Inquiry*, **13** (3), 1–28.

Ellis, C. and Bochner, A.P. (2000), "Autoethnography, personal narrative, reflexivity: researcher as subject", in N.K. Denzin and Y.S. Lincoln (eds), *The Handbook of Qualitative Research*, 2nd edn, Thousand Oaks, CA: Sage, pp. 733–68.

Ellis, C. and Bochner, A.P. (2003), "Autoethnography, personal narrative, reflexivity: researcher as subject", in N.K. Denzin and Y.S. Lincoln (eds), *The Handbook of Qualitative Research*, 3rd edn, Newbury Park, CA: Sage, pp. 199–258.

Ellis, C. and Bochner, A.P. (2006), "Analyzing analytic autoethnography: an autopsy", *Journal of Contemporary Ethnography*, **35** (4), 429–49.

Etherington, K. (2007), "Ethical research in reflexive relationships", *Qualitative Inquiry*, **13**, 559–616.

Flemmons, D. and Green, S. (2002), "Stories that conform/stories that transform: a conversation in four parts", in A. Bochner and C. Ellis (eds), *Ethnographically Speaking: Autoethnography Literature, and Aesthetics*, New York, AltaMira Press, pp. 87–94.

Foster, K., McAllister, M. and O'Brien, L. (2006), "Extending the boundaries: autoethnography as an emergent method in mental health nursing research", *International Journal of Mental Health Nursing*, **15** (1), 44–53.

George, J.M. (2010), "More engagement is not necessarily better: the benefits of fluctuating levels of engagement", in S.L. Albrecht (ed.), *The Handbook of Employee Engagement: Perspectives, Issues, Research, and Practice*, Cheltenham, UK and Northampton, MA, USA: Edward Elgar, pp. 253–63.

Goldschmidt, W. (1977), "Anthropology and the coming crisis: an autoethnographic appraisal", *Anthropologist*, **79** (2), 293–308.

Hammersley, M. and Atkinson, P. (2007), *Ethnography: Principles in Practice*, 3rd edn, London: Routledge.

Harter, J.K. Schmidt, F.L. and Hayes, T.L. (2002), "Business-unit-level relationship between employee satisfaction, employee engagement, and business outcomes: a meta-analysis", *Journal of Applied Psychology*, **87** (2), 268–79.

Hayano, D.M. (1979), "Auto-ethnography: paradigms, problems and prospects", *Human Organization*, **38** (1), 99–104.

Haynes, K. (2006), "A therapeutic journey? Reflections on the effects of research on researchers and participants", *Qualitative Research in Organizations and Management*, **1** (3), 204–21.

Heider, K.G. (1975), "What do people do? Dani auto-ethnography", *Journal of Anthropological Research*, **31**, 3–17.

Holman Jones, S. (2005), "Autoethnography: making the personal political", in N.K. Denzin and Y.S. Lincoln (eds), *Handbook of Qualitative Research*, Thousand Oaks, CA: Sage, pp. 763–91.

Holt, N.L. (2003), "Representation, legitimation, and autoethnography: an autoethnographic writing story", *International Journal of Qualitative Methods*, **2** (1), 1–22.

Humphreys, M. (2005), "Getting personal: reflexivity and autoethnographic vignettes", *Qualitative Inquiry*, **11** (6), 840–60.

Humphreys, M. and Watson, T.J. (2009), "Ethnographic practices: from 'writing-up ethnographic research' to 'writing ethnography'", in S. Ybema, D. Yanow, H. Wels and F. Kamsteeg (eds), *Organizational Ethnography: Studying the Complexities of Everyday Organizational Life*, London: Sage, pp. 40–55.

Jenkins, S. and Delbridge, R. (2013), "Context matters: examining 'soft' and 'hard' approaches to employee engagement in two workplaces", *International Journal of Human Resource Management*, **24** (14), 2670–91.

Johnson, P., Buehring, A., Cassell, C. and Symon, G. (2006), "Evaluating qualitative management research: towards a contingent criteriology", *International Journal of Management Reviews*, **8** (3), 131–56.

Jones, N.L. (2012), "Full circle: employee engagement in the Welsh public service", Unpublished PhD thesis, Bangor University, Wales.

Jones, N. and Sambrook, S. (2016), "Employee engagement in the public sector", in D. Blackman, S. Teo and M. O'Donnell (eds), *Human Capital Management Research: Influencing Practice and Process*, Cheltenham, UK and Northampton, MA, USA: Edward Elgar, pp. 31–45.

Kahn, W.A. (1990), "Psychological conditions of engagement and disengagement at work", *Academy of Management Journal*, **33** (4), 692–724.

King, T. (2003), *The Truth About Stories: A Native Narrative*, Toronto: House of Anansi Press, available at http://cislit.weebly.com/uploads/2/6/1/1/26116552/the_truth_about_stories_by_thomas_king.pdf (accessed 25 March 2016).

Learmonth, M. and Humphreys, M. (2012), "Autoethnography and academic identity: glimpsing business school doppelgangers", *Organization*, **19** (1), 99–117.

Lofland, J. (1995), "Analytic ethnography: features, failings and futures", *Journal of Contemporary Ethnography*, **24** (1), 30–67.

MacLeod, D. and Clarke, N. (2009), *Engaging for Success: Enhancing Performance through Employee Engagement*, London: Department for Business, Innovation and Skills.

Medford, K. (2006), "Caught with a fake ID: ethical questions about slippage in autoethnography", *Qualitative Inquiry*, **12**, (5), 853–64.

Morse, J.M. (2002), "Writing my own experience . . .", *Qualitative Health Research*, **12**, 1159–60.

Pelias, R. (2003), "The academic tourist: an autoethography", *Qualitative Inquiry*, **9** (3), 369–73.

Pelias, R. (2004), *A Methodology of the Heart*, Walnut Creek, CA, AltaMira Press.

Reed-Danahay, D. (1997), *Auto/Ethnography: Rewriting the Self and the Social*, Oxford and New York: Berg Publishers.

Richardson, L. and St Pierre, E.A. (2005), "Writing: a method of inquiry", in N.K. Denzin and Y.S. Lincoln (eds), *The Sage Handbook of Qualitative Research*, 3rd edn, Thousand Oaks, CA: Sage, pp. 959–78.

Roberts, C. (2007), "Intraprelearning within two Welsh trusts: an autoethnography", Unpublished PhD thesis, University of Wales.

Ronai, C.R. (1995), "Multiple reflections of child sex abuse: an argument for a layered account", *Journal of Contemporary Ethnography*, **23**, 395–426.

Sambrook, S. (1998), "Models and concepts of human resource development (HRD): academic and practitioner perspectives, an ethnographic study of HRD in the British National Health Service", Nottingham Business School, Nottingham Trent University.

Sambrook, S., Stewart, J. and Roberts, C. (2008), "Doctoral supervision: a view from above, below and the middle", *Journal of Further & Higher Education*, **32** (1), 71–84.

Sambrook, S., Jones, N. and Doloriert, C. (2014), "Employee engagement and autoethnography: being and studying self", Special Issue on Employee Engagement, *Journal of Workplace Learning*, **26** (3/4), 172–87.

Shuck, B. and Sambrook, S. (2014), "Employee engagement and HRD", in R. Poell, T. Rocco and G. Roth (eds), *The Routledge HRD Companion*, Abingdon, UK: Routledge, pp. 533–41.

Sparkes, A.C. (2000), "Autoethnography and narratives of self: reflections on criteria in action", *Sociology of Sport Journal*, **17**, 21–41.

Sparkes, A.C. (2002), "Autoethnography: self-indulgence or something more?", in A.P. Bochner and C. Ellis (eds), *Ethnographically Speaking: Autoethnography, Literature and Aesthetic*, Walnut Creek, CA: AltaMira Press, pp. 209–32.

Sparkes, A.C. (2007), "Embodiment, academics, and the audit culture: a story seeking consideration", *Qualitative Research*, **7** (24), 521–50.

Taylor, J. (2008), "An autoethnographic exploration of an occupation: doing a PhD", *British Journal of Occupational Therapy*, **71** (5), 176–84.

Towers Perrin (2012), *Employee Surveys*, available at http://www.towerswatson.com/services/ Employee-Surveys (accessed 21 January 2015).

UK Government (2011), *New Task Force for Employee Engagement*, London: UK Government, available at https://www.gov.uk/government/news/new-task-force-for-employee-engagement (accessed 21 January 2015).

Vance, R. (2006), *Employee Engagement and Commitment*, Alexandria, VA: Society for Human Resource Management.

Vickers, M.H. (2002), "Researchers as storytellers: writing on the edge – and without a safety net", *Qualitative Inquiry*, **8**, 608–21.

Wade-Benzoni, K.A. and Rousseau, D.M. (1998), "Building relationships around tasks. Psychological contracting in faculty-doctoral student collaborations", Technical Paper, Heinz School of Public Policy, Carnegie Mellon University, Pittsburgh, PA, available at http://www.heinz.cmu.edu/research/19abstract.pdf (accessed 21 January 2015).

Wainwright, D. and Sambrook, S. (2009), "Working at it: autoethnographic accounts of the psychological contract between a doctoral supervisor and supervisee", Paper presented at the 4th Annual Joint University of Liverpool Management School and Keele University Institute for Public Policy and Management Symposium on Current Developments in Ethnographic Research in the Social and Management Sciences, University of Liverpool, August.

Wainwright, D. and Sambrook, S. (2010), "The ethics of data collection: unintended consequences?", *Journal of Health Organisation and Management*, **24** (3), 277–87.

Wall, S. (2006), "An autoethnography on learning about autoethnography", *International Journal of Qualitative Methods*, **5** (2), Article 9, available at https://www.ualberta. ca/~iiqm/backissues/5_2/HTML/wall.htm (accessed 22 January 2015).

Wall, S. (2008), "Easier said than done: writing an autoethnography", *International Journal of Qualitative Methods*, **7** (1), 38–53.

PART II

INNOVATIONS IN DATA SOURCES

5 Using legal research methods in human resource management research
Richard Johnstone

INTRODUCTION

This chapter considers the contribution that legal research methods may make to better understand systems at work – particularly human resource systems and their impact on employees. Human resource management (HRM) strategies and choices are bounded and, in many instances, constrained by the regulatory framework for HRM (Barry, 2010). "Regulation" is a broad interdisciplinary phenomenon (see Morgan and Yeung, 2007, pp. 1–7) but in many domains, including HRM, law plays a prominent part in shaping business decisions and processes.

For present purposes "law" may simply be defined as "those rules which will be recognised and enforced by the courts" (Chisholm and Nettheim, 2007, p. 11). In Australia there are two sources of law: legislation and common law. Legislation (also called "statutes") comprises legal rules that are directly enacted by a legislature. In the Australian constitutional systems, the legislature is parliament and a legislative enactment is referred to as an "Act of Parliament". Legislation may also be created by office holders or bodies to whom the parliament delegates law making power: for example, a minister may make "regulations", which must be approved by the governor-general or governor. This latter form of legislation is usually called "subordinate legislation".

The other major source of law is the common law, or judge-made law, which comprises a myriad of court decisions made by judges over time to incrementally develop legal rules and principles in response to the legal issues brought before the courts. When lawyers talk of "cases" they are referring to decisions, and the reasons for those decisions, made by judges in the court system.

The field of law most relevant to HRM is labour law, which principally focuses on three themes (Creighton and Stewart, 2010, p. 2):

1. The need to rationalise the relationship between workers and those who require labour for the purpose of their enterprises (employers).

2.   The need to regulate collective relations between organised labour and employers and/or the state.
3.   The need to moderate the operation of the labour market in the interests of any or all of workers, unions, employers and the public.

Labour law rules influence the way work relationships are created, the content of the work relationship and the conditions under which workers work, termination of the work relationship and the processes through which employers and employees, and their representatives, bargain collectively and approach industrial action. Labour law rules are based both in legislation (for example, the Fair Work Act 2009 (Cth), the Work Health and Safety Acts and the various anti-discrimination statutes) and in common law (for example, the rules governing the contract of employment have mainly been developed by the courts). Labour lawyers regularly read decisions of the courts interpreting labour law legislation. Other areas of law – including tort, contract, property law, administrative law and human rights law – may also affect HRM.

The relationship between law and the management of human resources suggests that it would be helpful for researchers in the field of HRM to understand the basic approaches to legal research. The next section of the chapter explains how doctrinal legal research may be used as a HRM research strategy. In particular, it outlines how legal researchers "find" the law, and draw legal rules inductively from "cases" (decisions made by judges in law courts) and interpret legislation. The chapter also recognises that HRM researchers are skilled at social science research methods, and concludes by reminding HRM researchers that they can draw on qualitative social science research methods to interrogate legal materials.

Jurisdiction – the geographical area over which legal authority extends – plays a big part in legal research. While labour law has important international and transnational dimensions, there is not space in this short chapter to discuss legal research in more than one country – so this chapter is confined to legal research within the Australian legal system.

AN INTRODUCTION TO DOCTRINAL LEGAL RESEARCH FOR HUMAN RESOURCE MANAGEMENT RESEARCHERS

An Introduction to Australian Labour Law Scholarship

Australian writing on labour law dates back to the beginning of the twentieth century, soon after the Australian federal conciliation and arbitration system was established in 1904. Most early writing was descriptive and focused on the needs of practitioners (Frazer, 2008). The "first true labour law academic", Edward Sykes, began writing on labour law in the late 1950s, although academics working in economics and commerce faculties, most notably Foęnander (1952), were also producing important studies of labour law within the industrial relations system (Frazer, 2008). It was only in the late 1970s, and more particularly the early 1980s, that labour law scholarship became well established within law schools. This early scholarship focused principally on expounding the principles of labour law, although books like Creighton et al. (1983, 1993) placed legal rules and principles in a broader historical and theoretical context. In other words, most labour law scholarship was, and much still is, firmly within the "doctrinal legal research" paradigm, an approach to legal research that was explained by the committee that reviewed Australian law schools in 1987 (Pearce Committee, 1987, vol. 3, p. 17) as:

> Research which provides a systematic exposition of the rules governing a particular legal category, analyses the relationship between rules, explains areas of difficulty and, perhaps, predicts future developments.

To be fair, since the 1980s some labour law research has also been "reform-orientated" in the sense of evaluating "the adequacy of existing rules" to recommend "changes to any rules found wanting" (Pearce Committee, 1987, p. 7), and has also encompassed "theoretical research" that "fosters a more complete understanding of the theoretical bases of legal principles and the combined effects of a range of rules and procedures that touch upon a particular area of activity" (Pearce Committee, 1987, p. 7). In the last 20 years, many, if not most, Australian law schools have accepted that "legal research" encompasses far more than these three approaches, and may include empirical research about the origins, operation and impact of law, and interdisciplinary approaches to analysing what law is and how it operates. Indeed, many legal researchers query an uncritical acceptance that "law" is only about "legal rules and principles", and argue that the boundary between law and other normative orders is blurred, should be problematised rather than assumed and that legal researchers should embrace legal, and regulatory, pluralism (Parker, 2008). This will not be news to HRM researchers, and reminds us that primary legal materials (cases and legislation) may, in addition to being interpreted through a traditional "legal research" lens, be analysed using other social science research methodologies. Indeed, Lisa Webley (2010, p. 927) reminds us that traditional legal research is similar, in at least one aspect, to qualitative social science research methods – it involves a process of using inductive theorising to interpret documents:

> Many common law practitioners are unaware that they undertake qualitative empirical legal research on a regular basis – the case-based method of establishing the law through analysis of precedent is in fact a form of qualitative research using documents as source material.

A "Primer" on Doctrinal Legal Research

How does a researcher carry out "doctrinal legal research"? One starting point is an understanding of the traditional intellectual framework – legal positivism. As a well-known legal theory textbook writer (Harris, 1997, p. 16) suggests, most adherents to legal positivism

> would subscribe to the following two propositions. First, no element of moral value enters the definition of law. Secondly, legal provisions are identified by empirically-observable criteria, such as legislation, decided cases and custom. Their contention is that there is no law but positive law . . . [W]hat law is is one thing, its goodness or badness another . . . When practising lawyers describe the law to clients, they do not give . . . their views about what the law ought to be. They look up the books, and from there state what the law is.

In short, doctrinal legal research is concerned with "what the law is", and this is discerned by finding and reading cases and legislation as well as commentaries written by law academics and legal practitioners on the area of law. As this brief explanation suggests, there are two fundamental stages to doctrinal legal research – finding the primary sources (cases and legislation) and secondary sources (textbooks, monographs, journal articles, case notes and book chapters providing commentary on the primary sources); and reading, interpreting, analysing and synthesising these primary sources and the commentary in order to discern the rules and principles.

Stage 1: Formulating the Research Question and Finding Secondary and Primary Sources

The first stage requires the researcher to select the research topic (a legal issue) and formulate a research question – for example: "When an employer engages an expert independent contractor to perform specialised work for which the employer does not have any expertise, but the contractor does have the requisite expertise, what are the legal rules and principles determining the responsibilities of the employer for the health and safety of the employer's employees, the contractor and the contractor's employees?" This research question requires the researcher to undertake doctrinal research – to find the relevant legal rules and principles that apply to the situation of an employer engaging an expert independent contractor, to analyse these and to synthesise them. A HRM researcher without training in legal research skills would be best advised to start their legal research by consulting the basic labour law textbooks (Creighton and Stewart, 2016; Johnstone and Tooma, 2012; Johnstone et al., 2012a; Johnstone et al., 2012b; Owens et al., 2011; Sappideen et al., 2011; Stewart, 2015) and to use the law electronic databases to search the law journals (for advice on how to do this, see Cook et al., 2015; Hutchinson, 2010; Watt and Johns, 2009) for relevant journal articles and case notes. The leading Australian labour law journal is the *Australian Journal of Labour Law*, and it publishes articles on all aspects of labour law. These secondary sources should explain the key principles of law, and point to the relevant legislative provisions and the most relevant and authoritative cases (the "leading" cases).

A typical academic article written within a legal doctrinal framework will introduce a legal issue and then carefully describe and analyse the legislation and case law addressing that issue and will usually try to synthesise the rules and principles into a coherent body of law. The article may also point to deficiencies in the law, and may spell out the implications of the legal rules and principles for practice.

A case note is a summary of a significant case. It usually gives the context for the decision – the broad legal issues and the actual circumstances (what lawyers call "the facts") in the dispute before the court, and then explains the court's decision. Like an article, a case note might also critically evaluate the decision, and identify the ways in which it might influence practice. Readers interested in an example of a long case note may read Freckleton (2008), which outlines the issues involved in responding to the risks of psychiatric injury for emergency services personnel, explains how the courts have developed legal principles to determine an employer's liability for psychiatric injury, and then explains and analyses in great detail the decision of the trial judge and Queensland Court of Appeal in the case of *Hegarty v. Queensland Ambulance Service* [2007] QCA 366. The case note concludes by outlining the "ramifications" of the decision of the Court of Appeal, including the implications for employers and supervisors.

HRM researchers may have research questions that require examination of primary sources – cases and legislation. For example, a research question that addresses issues about the contract of employment may lead the researcher to cases in which judges have developed common law principles about the formation, content or termination of the contract of employment. The labour law system is largely governed by the Fair Work Act 2009 (Cth), and in addition to analysing key provisions in that legislation, HRM researchers may also be interested in decisions of the Fair Work Commission that interprets and applies the Act, and of the Federal Court that determines issues litigated before it.

Cases and statutes may also be found using legal databases – see again texts such as Watt and Johns (2009), Hutchinson (2010) and Cook et al. (2015) for advice on how to use these databases. A helpful resource for the non-lawyer is the Australian Legal Information Institute (Austlii) website (http://www.austlii.edu.au/) that may be used to search for legislation and court and tribunal decisions from all the Australian jurisdictions, and is relatively easy to search. Other useful websites include those of parliamentary counsels (for legislation), courts and tribunals (for decisions of that court or tribunal) and online labour law "looseleaf" services – for example, the *CCH Australian Labour Law Reporter* and the *CCH Australian Master Work Health and Safety Guide*, which may help find key cases and statutory provisions, and recent cases and changes to legislation.

Stage 2: Interpreting Primary Sources

Reading and interpreting cases is a complex process, and the approach taken in each instance will depend on the purpose for which the case is being read: to extract the key principle from the case; to see how the court applied legal principles to the facts before it; to see the court's reasoning behind its final conclusion; and so on. Researchers reading cases need to be aware that, unlike approaches to qualitative data analysis in social science research, not all courts, and not all cases, are of equal importance. Rather, in each jurisdiction there is a court hierarchy. Very simply, at the top of each state court hierarchy is the Full Court of the High Court of Australia; followed by the Courts of Appeal/Full Courts of the State Supreme Courts; followed by single judge State Supreme Courts; followed by the Intermediate Courts (District or County Courts); followed by the Magistrates' Courts. The relative weight of a court decision is determined by the general rules of the doctrine of precedent, which may briefly be summarised as follows (Cook et al., 2015, chapter 6):

1. Each court is bound by the decisions of courts higher in its court hierarchy.
2. Only the *ratio decidendi* (the "reason for the decision") of a past case is binding. The *ratio decidendi* is the principle stated by the court to decide the case, but only where the law applicable in the case was in issue, and the court was required to make a ruling about the legal principle after hearing full argument by the parties to the case. .
3. A court does not have to follow a decision of a court in another court

hierarchy, or lower in its own hierarchy, although well-reasoned decisions may be persuasive.
4. A court is generally not bound to follow its own decisions, but will only reluctantly depart from them.
5. A precedent is no less binding just because it was determined a long time ago.

A researcher may find that the legal rules set out in the leading cases are the *ratio decidendi* of the case, are clearly stated and cover the scenario of interest to the researcher. It may be, however, that the principles in the leading cases do not provide clear answers to the researcher's research question; and the researcher will have to anticipate the way in which a high level court will determine the relevant rule or principle if the issue were to be argued before it – by using inductive, deductive or analogical reasoning (Cook et al., 2015, chapter 4). Inductive reasoning in law resembles inductive theory building in qualitative social science research, and attempts to derive a general rule from a number of specific cases where more narrowly stated rules are applied. Lawyers use deductive reasoning to apply a general rule to a specific situation. Reasoning by analogy is commonly used in law when a general rule doesn't cover a specific situation, and the court agrees that a principle applied in one situation should, by analogy, be applied in another similar situation – the two situations must be sufficiently similar for the analogy to hold.

Statutory interpretation is a complex and technical skill (see Cook et al., 2015, chapters 10–14; Pearce and Geddes, 2014), although the basic principles have been established in common law principles and in the various interpretation of legislation statutes (see, for example, the Acts Interpretation Act 1901 (Cth)). On a broad level, when interpreting legislation, contemporary courts (and lawyers and researchers) are required to consider both the meaning of the words used in the specific legislative provision and the purpose behind the legislation. The first step is always to see if the legislative provisions have a clear, unambiguous meaning – if they do, then that is the interpretation that the court will take. At this stage the court may consult dictionaries to check the meaning of key words, or court decisions interpreting words or phrases in the legislation. Only if the provisions are ambiguous does a court need to use principles of statutory interpretation to resolve the ambiguity. The court must read "the Act as a whole", including the definitions given to key terms in the legislation, when construing a particular provision. The so-called "purposive approach" means the court must give primary importance to the purpose or object underlying legislation when interpreting a provision in legislation (especially when the term is ambiguous), rather than give a narrow or

restricted "literal" meaning. If these approaches do not resolve an ambiguity, or enable the court to interpret an obscure provision, the court may
also consult secondary documents such as the Second Reading speech and
the debates in parliament when the legislation was passed, explanatory
memoranda produced by parliamentary counsel, and reports produced
by committees where the legislation was based on these reports. As a last
resort, ambiguities may be resolved by a series of "secondary guidelines"
or "maxims" – for example, that ambiguous criminal provisions must be
construed strictly; that is, in favour of an accused person.

**Examples of How Doctrinal Legal Research Methods have been Used in
HRM Research**

Two examples, both drawing on case analysis and statutory interpretation, illustrate how doctrinal legal research methods have been used to
explain the legal principles that regulate a key issue in HRM – the health
and safety of workers.

In the first example, the research question was: how do Australian work
health and safety statutes regulate the obligations of business enterprises
to different types of workers – for example, workers engaged through
labour hire, contracting, supply chain and franchise arrangements? The
Australian work health and safety statutes of the late 1970s through to
the early 1990s were enacted at a time when the standard employment
relationship – a single employer employing full-time employees on open
ended employment contracts – was the dominant paradigm. As firms reor-
ganised their work arrangements, and increasingly used labour hire, contracting and sub-contracting, supply chain and franchising arrangements,
did the general duties in the work health and safety statutes impose obligations on firms to ensure the health and safety of workers engaged through
these arrangements, and how? The research question required a close legal
analysis of the existing statutory provisions, and cases interpreting these
provisions, or the corresponding UK provisions (in the Health and Safety
etc. at Work Act 1974) upon which many of the Australian statutes were
based, as well as the key reports that shaped the statutory provisions,
and in particular the UK Robens (1972) report. The analysis (Johnstone,
1999a, 2006) showed that the main employer's duties in each statute were
broad enough to cover some of the work relationships found in these work
arrangements, and that the provisions in Victoria and Queensland covered
each type of work arrangement. A later analysis of the harmonised Work
Health and Safety Acts enacted from 2011 (Johnstone and Tooma, 2012;
Johnstone et al., 2012a, chapter 7) showed that these statutes impose the
same obligations on persons conducting businesses and undertakings to

ensure the health and safety of the workers they engage, regardless of the work arrangement used.

The second example was focused on the research question outlined earlier in this chapter – the legal obligations on firms engaging expert independent contractors for the health and safety of workers employed or engaged by the firm or the contractors. Here the doctrinal analysis (Johnstone, 2014, pp. 57–73) involved a close reading of a series of cases decided by the Supreme Court of Western Australia, the Supreme Court of Victoria and the High Court of Australia, each interpreting the work health and safety legislation in Western Australia and Victoria, respectively, in the context of prosecutions brought by work health and safety regulators against firms, and individual managers within firms, that had engaged an expert contractor in situations in which the work health and safety legislation had appeared to be breached. In each case the firm (or manager) argued that it had engaged the contractor to carry out particular activities to provide expertise that the firm did not have; and then argued that the engagement of the expert contractor was sufficient to discharge the firm's statutory work health and safety general duty. In each of these cases, the court accepted this argument. The project then analysed key provisions in the harmonised Work Health and Safety Acts, and in particular the novel wording of the "primary" general duty owed by "persons conducting business and undertakings" to "workers" (section 19); the broad principles stated in the Acts (sections 14–16), including the non-delegability of legal obligations; the new duty on all duty holders "to consult, co-operate and co-ordinate activities with other persons who have a duty in relation to the same matter" (section 46); and the new positive and proactive duty placed on officers in section 27. It argued (Johnstone, 2014, pp. 78–85) that it is likely that courts examining the issue of the principal's work health and safety obligations under the harmonised Work Health and Safety Acts will require principals to do more to actively manage the work of expert contractors to ensure the health and safety of all workers and others potentially affected by the work.

Of course, the conclusions in these two projects must be confined to analyses of Australian work health and safety law, which is probably more focused on covering the broad range of contemporary work arrangements than the corresponding legal rules and principles in other countries. If the studies were to be replicated in other countries, where the legal provisions are different, different conclusions will be drawn, and most likely the studies will show that workers other than employees are not as well protected as their Australian counterparts.

DISCUSSION

So far, this chapter has described how labour law scholars use doctrinal legal research techniques to find, analyse and describe the legal principles governing work relationships. The strength of doctrinal legal research, as I hope the discussion above has shown, is in working out "what the law is", and in predicting the way in which the law might develop and be interpreted. HRM researchers may consult secondary sources – textbooks, journal articles, case notes and book chapters – to work out which legal rules impinge upon HRM principles, process and practices, and may more closely analyse and interpret primary legal sources – legislation and cases – by following the canons of statutory interpretation and reading cases inductively to develop legal principles, although these latter activities are best done in collaboration with lawyers.

But doctrinal legal research has clear limitations – it is confined to understanding, analysing, synthesising and describing legal rules and principles. Labour law, and HRM, researchers need other methods to understand how the legal principles they have analysed and synthesised affect the theory and practice of HRM. Since at least the 1990s (see Arup et al., 2006), Australian labour law scholarship, consistent with trends in Australian legal scholarship generally, has broadened its focus to ask new kinds of research questions, to draw on other disciplines to critically evaluate legal principles and to adopt a broader range of research methods, largely drawing on methods commonly used in other disciplines – in particular, the social and behavioural sciences, and the humanities. These methods will be familiar to researchers in the field of HRM.

First, legal principles may be evaluated from an "external" perspective by drawing upon debates in another field or discipline to critically evaluate legal principles. For example, in the project on expert independent contractors described above, the second part of the study reframed the project within the principles of systematic work health and safety management (Johnstone, 2014, pp. 74–8) to show how the legal principles stated by the courts were inconsistent with the principles of systematic work health and safety management.

Second, in addition to using doctrinal legal research methods to work out relevant legal rules and principles, HRM researchers are well placed to treat "cases" and legislation as empirical data and use their usual research methods to analyse these data. For example, researchers may analyse cases and statutes using qualitative social science research methods such as hermeneutics or content analysis. Legal researchers in fields other than labour law have used "classical" or quantitative content analysis, or more qualitative approaches to content analysis (Hall and Wright, 2008; Webley,

2010, pp. 941–2) to analyse the nature and frequency of legal phenomena such as "social facts" in negligence cases in the High Court of Australia (Burns, 2012). Carolyn Sutherland (2013) has used content analysis to analyse the complexity of enterprise agreements. HRM researchers could use a similar approach to count or analyse qualitatively, how often and how, judges refer to HRM concepts (for example, systematic work health and safety management principles or particular performance management and appraisal principles) in court decisions.

Third, HRM researchers may use social science methods to analyse the origins of legal rules and the process of legal change, using a range of frameworks from pluralist "interest group" analyses, to feminist, to "political economy" explanations (see Hunter and Johnstone, 1995 for an example of how this approach was used to analyse the origins of the conciliation and arbitration legislation and the work health and safety statutes enacted in the 1980s).

Finally, HRM researchers may investigate how legal rules are operationalised by regulatory agencies, firms and other parties. Issues of regulatory compliance (see Parker, 2002) are important in HRM because of the role of law in framing many HRM processes. Using quantitative and qualitative social science research methods, HRM researchers might investigate issues such as:

1. What approaches do firms take to comply with their labour law obligations (Johnstone and Jones, 2006)? What are the lessons for human resource managers from this research?
2. How do regulators monitor compliance with, and enforce, legal requirements requiring firms to conduct and document risk assessments, and how do firms go about conducting risk assessments (Johnstone, 1999b)?
3. How do legal rules about dismissal affect HRM disciplinary procedures? What can human resource managers do to ensure fair disciplinary procedures at work?
4. How do the principles in anti-discrimination legislation shape recruitment practices and procedures? How can human resource managers structure their recruitment processes to ensure they select staff from as diverse a field of applicants as possible?

In conclusion, this chapter has introduced HRM researchers to doctrinal legal research, and shown how basic legal research techniques can be used as part of research design. But HRM researchers are not confined to using doctrinal research methods when examining legislation and cases – there are many interesting lines of enquiry when primary legal sources are treated as "empirical documents" and interrogated within social science and humanities research frameworks.

ANNOTATED FURTHER READING

Australian Journal of Labour Law.
Australia's leading labour law journal, carrying articles, case notes, notes on new legislation and reports on labour law issues.
Stewart, A., Forsyth, A., Irving, M., Johnstone, R. and McCrystal, S. (2016), *Creighton and Stewart's Labour Law*, 6th edn, Sydney: Federation Press.
This book is the leading Australian labour law text, and covers all areas of labour law in considerable detail.

REFERENCES

Arup, C., Gahan P., Howe, J., Johnstone, R., Mitchell, R. and O'Donnell, A. (eds) (2006), *Labour Law and Labour Market Regulation*, Sydney: Federation Press.
Barry, M. (2010), "The regulative framework for HRM", in A. Wilkinson, T. Redman, S. Snell and N. Bacon (eds), *Handbook of Human Resource Management*, London: Sage, pp. 71–83.
Burns, K. (2012), "The Australian High Court and social facts: a content analysis study", *Federal Law Review*, **40**, 317–48.
Chisholm, R. and Nettheim, G. (2007), *Understanding Law: An Introduction to Australia's Legal System*, 7th edn, Sydney: Lexis-Nexis Butterworths.
Cook, C., Creyke, R., Geddes, R., Hamer, D. with Taylor, T. (2015), *Laying Down the Law*, 9th edn, Sydney: Lexis Nexis Butterworths.
Creighton, B. and Stewart, A. (2010), *Labour Law*, 5th edn, Sydney: Federation Press.
Creighton, W., Ford, W. and Mitchell, R. (1983), *Labour Law: Materials and Commentary*, Sydney: Law Book Company.
Creighton, W., Ford, W. and Mitchell, R. (1993), *Labour Law: Text and Materials*, 2nd edn, Sydney: Law Book Company.
Foenander, O. de R. (1952), *Studies in Labour Law and Relations*, Melbourne: Melbourne University Press.
Frazer, A.D. (2008), "Reconceiving labour law: the labour market regulation project", *Macquarie Law Journal*, **8**, 21–44.
Freckleton, I. (2008), "Employer's duties for reasonably foreseeable psychiatric injuries", *Psychiatry, Psychology and Law*, **15** (1), 17–24.
Hall, M. and Wright, R. (2008), "Systematic content analysis of judicial opinions", *California Law Review*, **63**, 63–122.
Harris, J.W. (1997), *Legal Philosophies*, 2nd edn, Oxford: Oxford University Press.
Hunter, R. and Johnstone, R. (1995), "Explaining law reform", in R.C. Hunter, R.S. Ingleby and R.S. Johnstone (eds), *Thinking About Law: Perspectives on the History, Philosophy and Sociology of Law*, Sydney: Allen & Unwin, pp. 135–56.
Hutchinson, T. (2010), *Researching and Writing in Law*, 3rd edn, Sydney: Law Book Company.
Johnstone, R. (1999a), "Paradigm crossed? The statutory occupational health and safety obligations of the business undertaking", *Australian Journal of Labour Law*, **12**, 73–112.
Johnstone, R. (1999b), *Evaluation of Queensland Construction Safety 2000 Initiative*, Sydney: National Occupational Health and Safety Commission.
Johnstone, R. (2006), "Regulating occupational health and safety in a changing labour

market", in C. Arup, P. Gahan, J. Howe, R. Johnstone, R. Mitchell and A. O'Donnell (eds), *Labour Law and Labour Market Regulation*, Sydney: Federation Press, pp. 617–36.

Johnstone, R. (2014), "Engaging expert contractors: the work health and safety obligations of the business or undertaking", *Australian Journal of Labour Law*, **27**, 57–85.

Johnstone, R. and Jones, N. (2006), "Constitutive regulation of the firm: OHS, dismissal, discrimination and sexual harassment", in C. Arup, P. Gahan, J. Howe, R. Johnstone, R. Mitchell and A. O'Donnell (eds), *Labour Law and Labour Market Regulation*, Sydney: Federation Press, pp. 483–504.

Johnstone, R. and Tooma, M. (2012), *Work Health and Safety Regulation in Australia: The Model Act*, Sydney: Federation Press.

Johnstone, R., McCrystal, S., Nossar, I., Quinlan, M., Rawling, M. and Riley, J. (2012a), *Beyond Employment: The Legal Regulation of Work Relationships*, Sydney: Federation Press.

Johnstone, R., Bluff, E. and Clayton, M. (2012b), *Work Health and Safety Law and Policy*, 3rd edn, Sydney: Thomson International.

Morgan, B. and Yeung, K. (2007), *An Introduction to Law and Regulation*, Cambridge: Cambridge University Press.

Owens, R., Riley, R. and Murray, J. (2011), *The Law of Work*, 2nd edn, South Melbourne: Oxford University Press.

Parker, C. (2002), *The Open Corporation: Effective Self-regulation and Democracy*, Cambridge: Cambridge University Press.

Parker, C. (2008), "The pluralization of regulation", *Theoretical Inquiries in Law*, **9**, 349–69.

Pearce Committee (1987) (Pearce, D., Campbell, E. and Harding, D.), *Australian Law Schools: A Discipline Assessment for the Commonwealth Tertiary Education Commission*, Canberra: AGPS.

Pearce, D. and Geddes, R. (2014), *Statutory Interpretation in Australia*, 8th edn, Sydney: Lexis Nexis.

Robens (1972), *Report of the Committee on Safety and Health at Work 1970–72*, London: HMSO.

Sappideen, S., O'Grady, P., Riley, J. and Warburton, G. (2011), *Macken's Law of Employment*, 7th edn, Sydney: Thomson.

Stewart, A. (2015), *Stewart's Guide to Employment Law*, 5th edn, Sydney: Federation Press.

Sutherland, C. (2013), "Mapping complexity in Australian enterprise agreements: a multidimensional approach", *Australian Journal of Labour Law*, **26**, 50–74.

Watt, R. and Johns, F. (2009), *Concise Legal Research*, 6th edn, Sydney: Federation Press.

Webley, L. (2010), "Qualitative approaches to empirical legal research", in P. Cane and H.M. Kritzer (eds), *The Oxford Handbook of Empirical Legal Research*, Oxford and New York: Oxford University Press, pp. 926–50.

6 The use of news media as a data source in HRM research: exploring society's perceptions
Sheryl Ramsay, Sara Branch and Jacqueline Ewart

INTRODUCTION

Few studies of public representations of human resource management (HRM) issues via the news media have been undertaken. Although HRM topics are well represented in the news media, little is known about the content, perspectives or impacts of such stories. This chapter focuses on the important, innovative contribution that news media research can make to the field of HRM. We refer to our exploratory study into workplace bullying, a key HRM concern, to exemplify main points throughout. The chapter provides a context for HRM research, discusses the contribution of the news media as a data source, strengths and limitations of the method and makes recommendations for future research.

CONTEXT FOR HRM RESEARCH

HRM, defined broadly as the management of people within the employment relationship, is comprised of networks of public and private actors, making it a complex area to study (Greenwood, 2013). Accordingly, the meaning and significance of various research approaches to HRM continue to be debated (Harley, 2014; Marchington, 2015; Van Buren and Greenwood, 2013). For example, a widely considered aspect is HRM's perceived lack of strategic influence within organisations. By positioning itself more with senior management in driving performance goals and shareholder value, it may be argued that HRM is narrowing its focus, with the risk of overlooking key stakeholders and roles (for example, employee advocates) and contributions to society (for example, ongoing development of fair, inclusive and sustainable processes) (Marchington, 2015).

HRM methodological approaches have also been questioned, with

Greenwood (2013) suggesting there are three different approaches that can add particular value. First, mainstream HRM research tends to focus on the organisation, employees and HR practices, often using positivist empirical methods of inquiry. This use of positivist methods, which is becoming increasingly dominant, has led to calls for more methodological pluralism to allow for expansion of HRM knowledge and understanding (Harley, 2014; Van Buren and Greenwood, 2013). Second, critical HRM, in seeking to question the espoused values of HRM and examine its actual impacts on stakeholders, draws on a variety of methodologies and therefore can provide greater depth to the field (for example, see literature review on work intensification in Mariappanadar, 2014). It has been argued that the third approach, which favours a conceptual style of analysis and focuses on the organisation, society and multiple other stakeholders (for example, organisations, government, employers, employees, occupational groups) (termed ethical HRM by Greenwood, 2013), can provide even more in-depth perspectives.

This multiple stakeholder perspective is used as a framework in this chapter as it is relevant to the news media's portrayal of complex social phenomena. The news media plays a key role in people's knowledge and appreciation of current issues, and the illumination of normative boundaries that are acceptable within the particular society (Stanley et al., 2014). Analysis of news stories has shown great promise in explaining social phenomena (for example, stigma associated with so-called "dirty work" occupations such as stockbrokers; Stanley et al., 2014) and, arguably, some sections of the news media can play an important role in surfacing, discussing and legitimising or otherwise, management theories and practices that are relevant to society. Accordingly, the role of the news media is "worthy of a deeper historical and social exploration" (Mazza and Alvarez, 2000, p. 584).

Furthermore, the interplay of theory and practice has long been emphasised in HRM education, with reality brought to the classroom in many guises, including current, topical issues in the news media. For example, Latham, an internationally recognised academic and MBA teacher, describes his method of presenting a class with a headline and story from a newspaper, which students then analyse theoretically and practically (Charlier, 2014). Likewise, case studies are used to bridge the theory/practice gap. The Enron case, for example, has been widely reported and analysed in the media, as well as in academic forums. Interestingly, many of the toxic behaviours ascribed to leaders in Enron (Marchington, 2015) could be conceptualised as workplace bullying, and therefore well within the remit of HRM.

NEWS MEDIA AS A DATA SOURCE

We note that the news media has not been used as a focus of research into HRM to any extent and, in making the argument for its potential as an innovative approach, we draw on our exploratory study of workplace bullying, conceptualised academically as "a situation in which one or more persons systematically and over a long period of time perceive themselves to be on the receiving end of negative treatment on the part of one or more persons, in a situation in which the person(s) exposed to the treatment has difficulty in defending themselves against this treatment" (Matthiesen and Einarsen, 2007, p. 735). From these interactions, workplace bullying unfolds as a complex, and very costly phenomenon that negatively affects individuals, organisations, multiple stakeholders and wider society (Beswick et al., 2006; Hoel et al., 2011), for which many unanswered theoretical and practical questions remain (Branch et al., 2013). Likewise, HRM research in general is confronted by complexities, as well as frequently unclear definitions and constructs that provide impediments to research (Klein and Delery, 2012). We therefore contend that taking innovative methodological approaches to HRM research can be useful in highlighting different perspectives, and showing a way forward, which can ultimately lead to greater understanding, knowledge and clarity in the field.

Our focus on using print-based news media as an innovative data source in HRM research involves several important considerations, including the context of newspaper publishing itself. First, in relation to the news media's role in presenting complex social phenomena, debate continues about the many conflicting forces, such as the required speed of delivery, the need for journalists to become subject experts quickly, decisions on how events will be presented and from which perspectives, and a requirement to make sure the public support and see value in the news media. Compounding these issues is the stress for those who work in the news industry, with growing job insecurity and multiple changes (Ekdale et al., 2015). Second, there has also been extensive discussion about how the news media and in particular newspapers can distort reality. When such distortions are accepted as reality by the public, there may be severe ramifications for public policy and appropriate distribution of resources (Spitzberg, 2002). For example, Turkewitz's (2010, p. 3) analysis of the media's representation of the crime of rape suggests that we need to "be critical of how newspapers represent their narratives", including their potential biases and any narrowing of "the public's understanding of crime, and the actors involved". Thus, the news media including newspapers can shape and direct their messages, influencing societal culture

(Peelo et al., 2004). Third, the choices of journalists and editors as to what is reported often places an emphasis on (more engaging) individual factors related to the phenomenon, which "essentially ignores the economic and social underpinnings of the problem" (Johnstone et al., 1994, p. 870) and could reduce the potential for a well-informed public.

Interestingly, the role of newspaper reports has been discussed in relation to workplace bullying. Lewis's (2001) survey research suggests that most respondents identified hearing about workplace bullying through the news media (when compared to other sources such as unions). Some within the workplace bullying field have warned that an increase in news media attention may result in counter-effective responses. For instance, creating a sense of fear or "moral panic" may have led to an increasing tendency to use the term "workplace bullying" as a way of capturing a sense of distress or resentment (McCarthy, 2004) and voicing dissatisfaction about more general organisational issues such as change and management style (Liefooghe and Davey, 2001). There are certainly questions about how workplace bullying is understood by the public and whether this impacts on their behaviour in any way (Branch et al., 2013). In this chapter, we illustrate how workplace bullying is conceptualised and portrayed within the news media, and how this may differ from academic representations, with the aim of contributing to knowledge about the value of using news stories as data in HRM research.

NEWS MEDIA METHODS AND WORKPLACE BULLYING EXAMPLE

Turning to specific details of the method itself, there are several factors to consider. For the actual newspaper selection, broad readership is an important consideration. In our study, we selected two newspapers (both in broadsheet format at the time); *The Australian* (published by News Limited) is the national daily newspaper for Australia and *The Sydney Morning Herald* (published by Fairfax), which covers national events in addition to its primary base in Sydney, and is considered to provide a counter to the conservative perspective of *The Australian*. To identify our data set, we undertook a delimited search of the two newspapers with the news database Factiva, used by researchers to search individual or groups of newspapers from around the world using keywords and date ranges (in our case from 1 July 2010 to 30 June 2011).

With newspapers composed of many sections, it is important to be clear about the types of articles that are included in a data set. We limited our search of news articles to general news stories, that is, those appearing in the news section of these newspapers and inclusive of feature articles (that is, extended in-depth articles focused on a topic), as well as journalists' opinion pieces and editorials (that is, published pieces that reflect the writer's opinion, rather than relying on traditional journalistic devices). These make up the majority of the newspaper and are produced by paid employees considered to be authoritative in their content and approach (that is, we excluded certain published pieces such as "letters to the editor"). The search term also has to be carefully considered. For example, we found in our initial search that "workplace bullying" was a rarely used term, so our search was based on the broader terms of: "bully", "bullies", "bullying" or "bullied" (referred to as "the term" in this chapter). Our final data sample consisted of 225 articles. Table 6.1 contains a summary of the articles and the number of references to the term. As shown, the number of general news articles exceeded opinion articles, as would be expected. A high percentage of articles with singular references to the term (62 per cent general news articles and 65 per cent opinion pieces) occurred, with the number of references to the term decreasing as each article continued.

Following these simple frequencies, the 225 articles were content and thematically analysed using the software program NVivo, which enables data to be managed, coded and categorised (NVivo, 2012). Analysis commenced by assessing and categorising each of the 225 identified articles against the key aspects of the academic definition of workplace bullying presented earlier (Matthiesen and Einarsen, 2007). This is not to indicate that the academic definition would be superior to a more "lay" definition but rather to give us a starting point. Thus, each article was assessed against the four main criteria within the definition: evidence of inappropriate behaviour; repeated inappropriate behaviours; behaviours occurred over a period of time; and evidence that the target felt unable to defend his or herself. We also coded for a number of other elements that could be considered important within a newspaper, including the page number of each newspaper story (to determine the prominence given to stories about bullying), the contents of the headline, frequency of usage of the term within paragraphs and the overall story, and use of related terms (for example, sexual harassment) within articles.

Another important consideration within newspaper reporting is that of sources (also known as voices), defined as "any named individual to whom a reporter attributed news-story information" (Ewart and Massey, 2005, p. 101). That is, the source(s) is important to identify in the research and, depending on the issue being explored, may be a significant variable on which to base analysis. For instance, in relation to a research topic, comparisons could be made between elite sources (for example, those in public office) and non-elite sources (for example, lay people). In our case,

Table 6.1   Summary of 225 articles identified during Factiva search

	The Australian	The Sydney Morning Herald	Total sample
Total number of articles	119	106	225
Number of general news articles	102	75	177
1 reference to the term	65	47	112
2 references to the term	16	15	31
3 references to the term	8	3	11
4 references to the term	5	1	6
5 references or more to the term	8	9**	17
Number of opinion articles	17	31	48
1 reference to the term	10	21	31
2 references to the term	2	5	7
3 references to the term	3	4	7
4 references to the term	1	1	2
5 references or more to the term	1*	–	1
References within the headline	21	14	35
References within the 1st paragraph block[a]	56	50	106
References within the 2nd paragraph block	44	45	89
References within the 3rd paragraph block	29	27	56
References within the 4th paragraph block	21	21	42

Notes:
*   8 or more references; ** 8 articles with 8 or more references.
[a]   A paragraph block includes 5 paragraphs.

we coded each article for both direct and indirect quotes. Direct quotes, which speak to the reader without interpretation by the article writer, are considered to be more powerful than indirect quotes and paraphrases that do not represent a source's own words. Our analysis identified voices of targets, perpetrators, the judiciary, spokespeople, third parties, author's voice (found only in opinion articles, for example, "Everyone knows that the minister is a bully, so this latest incident is of no surprise") and author's contextualisation (no direct evidence of anyone in the story using the term, indicating an author's description).

Typical of research of this type, it is most important to have experienced researchers conducting the analysis, and having quality checks in place. In our case, an experienced research assistant conducted the initial analysis of the data with the close guidance of the research team. At the half way point of the initial analysis, one of the chief investigators, who had experience with the coding of newspaper articles and with news framing analysis undertook a check of a sample of the articles coded by the research assistant. The analysis was approached using Gitlin's (1980, p. 7) definition of news frames as "persistent selection, emphasis, and exclusion" that enables journalists to process and package large amounts of information quickly". While consistency in coding was at an acceptable level, to ensure a rigorous approach, the research team then reviewed the entire process with the research assistant prior to completion of the analysis.

Following further consideration of the content and frequency of the various categorisations associated with the definition and source, we moved to a more open, inductive approach to examine the data more deeply and to identify themes to give us more holistic information (that may or may not be present in the academic literature). As Semetko and Valkenburg (2000) indicate, inductive framing involves analysis of news stories that maintains "an open view to attempt to reveal the array of possible frames" (p. 94). This involved several passes of the data, identifying themes and linkages, reflecting on the articles over a period of time and referring back and forth to the more numerical analysis already conducted. Thus, thematic analysis was conducted to identify aspects of the articles such as the context/topic of each article, which was then considered in light of the definition and source categories already identified (Joffe and Yardley, 2004).

As can be seen, many perspectives may be gained from using newspapers as a data source in HRM research. The following demonstrates the types of information that can be gathered, including the depth that some stories achieve, and how the data itself can generate further questions. For instance, in order to address one aspect of our research interest, we attempted to discern whether or not the identified newspaper articles used the term in a way that accorded with the academic definition. Initially, we focused on the nine articles that used the phrase "workplace bullying". Two of the articles met the academic definition of workplace bullying, four did not meet the definition and three either partially fulfilled the definition or were considered to have insufficient evidence to meet the definition (Table 6.2).

One of the articles that met the definition focused on a case of sexual harassment and discrimination (Box 6.1) and clearly demonstrates the similarities and overlaps between the behaviours associated with repeated sexual harassment and workplace bullying. In this case the term was used regularly in conjunction with the words discrimination, harassed and/or abuse.

One of the articles that partially met the definition was mainly based on the references to inappropriate behaviour (Box 6.2). In this case the article

Table 6.2   Articles with the term "workplace bullying"

Article	Headline	Definition met
21 September 2010 *The Sydney Morning Herald*	Intimidation and fear: welcome to agency charged with stamping out *bullying*	Insufficient
08 June 2011 *The Sydney Morning Herald*	*Bullied* at work and it's not just the boss to blame	Partial
24 July 2010 *The Australian*	Bulldogs dismiss *bullying* claims – JOHNSON HITS BACK AT AKER	No
29 July 2010 *The Australian*	Air controllers claim sexual bias	Yes
01 October 2010 *The Australian*	Cops say recording ban lets *bullies* off	No
10 February 2011 *The Australian*	Nuclear reactor under investigation	No
08 April 2011 *The Australian* [Opinion]	Legislation not needed to tackle work *bullies*	Yes
09 April 2011 [3] *The Australian*	Courts cannot catch every workplace *bully*	No
25 May 2011 *The Australian*	Nuclear agency safety culture "stuck in 70s"	Insufficient

Note: Italics added.

reported the results of a national survey. Again the term was used in conjunction with the word discrimination, with other words such as abuse or intimation also used throughout the article.

One of the articles that did not fulfil the academic definition (Box 6.3) used the term only once. The article itself related to the operation of a nuclear reactor, and focused on allegations of workplace bullying and harassment allegedly not being investigated. While only used once, the term was used in conjunction with the word harassment.

Turning to the use of the broader term, interestingly, the majority of articles that did not meet the definition had a singular reference to the term (119 of 164) (only 3 articles that did not meet the definition had more than 8 references to the term). These three articles discussed the usefulness of bullying legislation (24 references to the term), the reporting of research linking social skills and bullying (15 references) and an example of a bullying prevention effort within schools (10 references). While not meeting the academic definition we consider the term was used appropriately in these three articles. Interestingly, the one article that met the definition,

BOX 6.1　EXAMPLE OF AN ARTICLE THAT MET THE DEFINITION OF WORKPLACE BULLYING

Date: 29 July 2010
Publication: *The Australian*
Headline: Air controllers claim sexual bias
Claims of "extreme" sex discrimination and *bullying* heard in court.
TWO female air traffic controllers are seeking more than $1 million each from their government-owned employer, alleging they endured years of *workplace bullying*, discrimination and abuse.
Among the allegations in the Federal Court action against Airservices Australia is that the two Melbourne controllers, Jacki Macdonald and Kirsty Fletcher, were exposed to pornography circulated by email by a manager.
On one occasion, a manager allegedly told a pregnant Ms Macdonald that her pregnancy did not suit the roster and that he had a "coat hanger in the back of his car".
When she complained about the comment, she was allegedly told the manager was "having a bad day".
The women's lawyer, Maurice Blackburn principal Josh Bornstein, said that while the women loved their jobs, he claimed they had faced "extreme" sex discrimination and *bullying* over five years.
The women allege they were refused access to professional development and training; abused and belittled for being pregnant, and told that part-time employment was not welcome.
"Australia may have its first female prime minister but the attitudes and behaviour of managers at Airservices is light years away from what a workplace should be in the 21st century," Mr Bornstein said.
Ms Macdonald, who fought back tears as she spoke to the media yesterday, said she had been an air traffic controller for 18 years but "enough is enough" and she did not want other young women to be exposed to such a workplace culture.
"What people don't realise when you are *bullied* and harassed is how belittling it makes you feel, how small it makes you feel and how inadequate and undervalued," she said. "Eighteen years I have been an air traffic controller and it's counted for nothing."
The women allege the circulation of the pornography continued even after a number of staff complained. The manager allegedly circulating the material was warned by a superior to desist "because the last thing you need is that stuff to get into the wrong hands". Despite the warning, the material continued to circulate.
Mr Bornstein said the manager who allegedly *bullied* the women had been sacked but was claiming unfair dismissal and seeking reinstatement.
In a brief statement, Airservices said it was aware of the issues raised yesterday.
"The matter is being taken seriously by Airservices management," the statement said.
"Our investigations have only just been completed and the matter is in the hands of respective legal advisers."

Note:　Italics added.

BOX 6.2   EXAMPLE OF AN ARTICLE THAT PARTIALLY MET
THE DEFINITION OF WORKPLACE BULLYING

Date: 8 June 2011
Publication: *The Sydney Morning Herald*
Headline: *Bullied* at work and it's not just the boss to blame
Bullying and discrimination are still rife in the workplace, with a national survey finding little improvement in the past three years.
Almost a third of workers claim to have been *bullied* in the workforce, with a quarter having experienced *bullying* in the past two years.
Almost half of the 5100 workers surveyed said they had also witnessed a colleague being *bullied* or discriminated against.
More than one in 10 workers claimed they had been the victim of systemic workplace abuse or intimidation.
But the boss is not necessarily to blame, with the unwelcome behaviour just as likely to come from colleagues as superiors.
The results, which come on the tail of Victoria becoming the first state to legislate against *workplace bullying*, are similar to those found three years ago in an earlier study.
Tania Evans, the manager of WorkPro, which commissioned the study, said employers refusing to address the issues were underestimating their risk of liability over future occupational health and safety claims.
"It comes down to lack of education. Employers are assuming that because the issue has gained more media attention in the past few years everyone is aware of what is and what is not acceptable in the workplace," she said. "But the Australian workplace is a melting pot, and a lot of the *bullying* and discrimination which is taking place is crosscultural."
Racial and religious conflict appeared to be at the heart of the problem, she said, with inappropriate jokes, unwanted physical approaches and deliberate exclusion from social events all common complaints.
The survey also found widespread confusion in the workplace over what the correct channels were for reporting complaints, while some felt their workplace culture discouraged reporting incidents at all.
Ms Evans said employers needed to be proactive about making sure employees got the information they needed to understand their rights and responsibilities at work.
"They need to ensure employees feel they can report inappropriate behaviour," she said.
Last week the Victorian Parliament passed legislation making *workplace bullying* a criminal offence, with offenders facing sentences of up to 10 years' jail.

Note: Italics added.

BOX 6.3   EXAMPLE OF AN ARTICLE THAT DID NOT
MEET THE DEFINITION OF WORKPLACE
BULLYING

Date: 10 February 2011
Publication: *The Australian*
Headline: Nuclear reactor under investigation
SCIENCE Minister Kim Carr has launched an investigation into the safety and operation of Australia's nuclear reactor.
Senator Carr yesterday asked department officials to work with the independent safety regulator – the Australian Radiation Protection and Nuclear Safety Agency – to examine occupational health and safety practices in place at the radiopharmaceutical product facility at the Australian Nuclear Science and Technology Organisation at Lucas Heights in Sydney.
The move follows a report by the ABC's Lateline revealing damning details of an earlier investigation conducted by Australia's workplace regulator, Comcare.
The Comcare report found that ANSTO broke federal laws involving safety breaches and failed to investigate allegations of *workplace bullying* and harassment arising from the breaches.
"I take allegations such as those aired last night very seriously," Senator Carr said. "I have been closely monitoring these events for a considerable time."
In one such event investigated by ARPANSA and cited in the Comcare document, a staff member dropped a vial of radioactive molybdenum 90.
According to the ARPANSA report, obtained by The Australian, radiation levels near the dropped vial were "abnormally high".
"This is 100 times what would have been expected," said the inspectors, who further concluded that facility staff were poorly trained and did not know how to report incidents. Staff received no feedback about safety concerns following the incident.
The inspectors found while similar accidents had occurred over the years, the situation was not corrected. "ARPANSA inspectors noted that ANSTO acknowledged the . . . facility is more akin to a research facility than a production facility," the report states. That means problems will continue, it warns.
Officials at ANSTO pointed *The Australian* to a media release claiming the Comcare report was "flawed".
A spokesman for Comcare said it stands by its report.

Note: Italics added.

but only had one reference to the term, was about a person who was a whistleblower, where the use of the term related to the behaviours the whistleblower experienced. This example shows the range of ways the term is used within the newspapers, and led us to reflect on the practical usefulness of the academic workplace bullying definition and the possible overuse of the term in general.

Indeed, our exploration of the data identified for us a substantial number of articles with only a single reference to the term (143 of the 225 articles; 64 per cent). This led us to explore in more depth this sub-set of the data. Often the majority of singular references occurred in articles identified as those that did not meet the definition of workplace bullying (119 of the 143 articles). Similarly, when the thematic analysis for the context/topic of the article was considered, 140 articles (of 143) were identified as discussing topics other than bullying (for example, the topic of the article was considered to be about business because it was about an industrial dispute) and having one reference to the term. When we removed the articles whose topic was considered to be related to bullying (for instance, bullying legislation or a related issue such as sexual harassment) from the 143 articles with a singular reference, 87 remained. That is, 39 per cent of the 225 articles had one reference to the term and the topic of the article had no relation to bullying or inappropriate behaviour. As noted, this seemed a possible overuse of the term and led us to question how the term was used in this specific group of articles.

Broadly speaking, there were two main topics within this group of articles; politics and business. Interestingly, the majority of references to the term occurred at the beginning of the article (indicating its possible news worthiness), and the term was often related to, or used in conjunction with, the word intimidation. Examples include: Political intimidation – "Bullied into silence by Kevin Rudd, the captains of industry are fearlessly speaking out" (9 October 2010 – *The Australian* – first sentence of article) and Business intimidation – "Australians are sick of watching large profitable companies bullying government for special treatment" (6 January 2011 – *The Sydney Morning Herald* [Opinion] – second sentence of article). When the use of the term was further explored within the business theme we found the term was often used in relation to a broad-based group, such as a particular country or organisation, as highlighted by the following selected quotes: "India has further enhanced its bully boy status with a series of extraordinary acts in relation to other nations' cricket in the past few days" (22 June 2011 – *The Australian*); "Like all bullies, the Knights don't know when to stop" (28 October 2010 [3] – *The Sydney Morning Herald* [Opinion]); "PAG has accused API of bullying and has threatened to take its 400 members, generating about $600m in revenue, and walk" (20 April 2011 – *The Australian*); "He accused Australia's Media, Entertainment and Arts Alliance and New Zealand Actors Equity of trying to bully the production into illegal collective bargaining" (22 October 2010 – *The Sydney Morning Herald*); and " . . . last year accused British American Tobacco of attempting to bully and intimidate his family by warning that their Cranbourne home could be sold to recover the tobacco giant's costs" (1 April 2011 – *The Australian*). The analysis gave us new insights into usage of the term in the public domain, and will be discussed in more detail later in the chapter.

Turning to the question of sources within the 225 articles, 109 articles were identified where the author paraphrased a spokesperson, target, third party, perpetrator or judiciary, although it was unclear if the original source used the term (that is, "bully", "bullies", "bullying" or "bullied") or not. Direct quotes where the term was used were only identified within 77 articles. In the case of opinion pieces, the journalist appeared to use the term themselves within 34 articles (from 48). For 87 general news articles, no direct evidence that anyone in the story had actually used the term was found, indicating the author had chosen to use the term. When reflecting on this data, especially in relation to the possible overuse of the term (that is, singular use of the term) and the use of the term early in the articles, we concluded there may be a willingness by the author to choose the term for its news value. This may be because conflict is a key news value and journalists may perceive that readers are more likely to engage with a story that features conflict. Additional research using interviews with journalists who wrote the stories would determine whether this is the case.

CONTRIBUTIONS, STRENGTHS AND WEAKNESSES OF THE METHOD, AND FUTURE DIRECTIONS

Our chapter aimed to contribute to knowledge about the value of using news stories as data in HRM research, with the particular example of the portrayal of workplace bullying. We consider that the approach is innovative and has a number of strengths, including the provision of important and interesting HRM data that can augment that already in the field. First, the method gives deep insights into the way the public accesses information about a HRM issue. From a frequency point of view, our study indicates that the term "bully" can be readily found in newspapers, suggesting the public would be well aware of the topic and its broad relationship with societal difficulties. Lewis's (2001) research would support this. We also examined how the term was used, and can see that, while the reporting rarely reflects the academic definition, the general meaning is communicated in a reasonably accurate way at times. In fact, the necessary brevity of many newspaper articles means that it is usually impractical to impart a long and complex definition and nuances of meaning.

Nevertheless, having a well-informed public is important as they can contribute to debate and communication that can ultimately build a stronger society, with well-developed policies that can be augmented with appropriate resources on the basis of public support and understanding. As well as imparting information appropriately (for example, introduction of anti-bullying legislation), the use of the term appeared to have various other aims, including to emphasise problematic situations (for example, paired with another descriptive word such as "bullying and intimidation") and to gain attention or dramatic effect (for example, the term used in the headline where a substantive story on the topic did not follow). Indeed, for a large percentage of the articles it appeared that the author had chosen to use the term in this way. Some uses therefore appear to have the potential to detract from the public's understanding of the serious nature, impacts, costs and complexity of bullying, which is an important HRM perspective in relation to the community information.

Another strength of the method is that totally new perspectives can arise. Interestingly, as indicated earlier, bullying was often depicted as emanating from a broad-based group, such as a particular country, organisation, government structure, occupational group, political alliance, union or sporting team, and directed towards an equivalent entity or, more often, a smaller party (for example, individuals and families). While this is perhaps a convenient, "shorthand" way of communicating, it does have the effect of depersonalising perpetrators and ascribing to them an overwhelming sense of power. In comparison, academic usage is more focused on processes that occur between individuals and/or small groups where effects and complexities of power are potentially more identifiable (as indicated in the definition provided in this chapter). Indeed, for academics, there tends to be tacit agreement that bullying is carried out by people (not entities), and it is only people who can devise policies and procedures and enact behavioural norms within contexts and processes that can encourage or could reduce bullying. However, within the literature there is certainly recognition that bullying is not isolated from its context (for example, Einarson et al., 2011), highlighting its occurrence within, and influence by, particular organisational processes, leadership styles, norms and, more recently, national cultures (Branch et al., 2013; Escartin et al., 2011; Ramsay et al., 2011). Thus, the present research has highlighted how a HRM topic can be portrayed in newspapers, allowing some comparisons between academic conceptualisations and more publically accessible communications, which can ultimately serve to produce higher quality information on the topic.

The method described here can contribute to HRM research in several ways. Importantly, a strength of the method is that newspapers provide a rich source of data on HRM topics that is readily available via newspaper databases, such as Factiva, at low cost, and can be analysed from a wide range of perspectives with programs like NVivo. Accordingly, researchers have the opportunity to reflect on how a particular HRM phenomenon is portrayed to the general public, which allows insights into matches or mismatches across different informational arenas (for example, academic writings and newspapers in the public domain). This can generate important insights into future research questions that could bridge perceived gaps between academic and public understandings of a complex phenomenon. Thus, researchers have an important opportunity to reflect on their own role as academics in bridging any identified gaps, which can ultimately contribute to new research directions and, in turn, theoretical and practical developments. In the study presented, many stakeholders are clearly involved, including society, various groups and individuals, the newspaper itself and journalists, and the identified sources. Such an analysis allows researchers insights that can guide actions, which have the potential to develop a more informed public (for example, offering to write informed feature articles or communicate with interested journalists about professional development in an area of HRM), and to contribute to teaching in higher education.

While a strength of the method is the level of detail provided (as exemplified in Boxes 6.1–6.3) that can be readily accessed, a limitation is the static nature of the data in that we cannot add to what is there or clarify it any further (for example, as in an in-depth interview). Also, we offer a note of caution here in relation to the effect news media has on its audiences in that research has shown that news media audiences do not uncritically accept what they see, read or hear (Scheufele and Tewksbuy, 2007), which highlights the need to examine the actual reactions of the public to stories. Therefore, one approach to overcome this limitation, would be to use more interactive data that could be sourced from the internet (for example, comments on news stories). Branch and Murray (2015) recently used an evolving conversation on social media to demonstrate the differing reactions individuals had to a case of workplace bullying. In essence, this review identified two groups of people, those who thought the alleged perpetrator was justified and the target needed to toughen up and another who felt the alleged perpetrator was a bully and something needed to be done to support the target. The methodology could also be applied to other forms of news media such as broadcast and online news sites or blogs, although analyses of television in particular would require consideration of images that accompany stories about workplace bullying.

As with any research there were challenges and shortcomings to our study. While the methodology and approach we selected did illuminate public representations of workplace bullying, we recognise limitations in relation to, first, the form of media studied and, second, to what we have termed the "multiple-perspectives" of those involved in these news stories. In relation to the first point, our study only involved two broadsheet newspapers. With some amendments to the methodology described here, further examinations of how workplace bullying is represented in broadcast, online and social media and the impacts of that coverage could enhance understanding of HRM issues.

In relation to the second limitation of our study, the need for multiple perspectives about workplace bullying stories, it would be useful for researchers to investigate the perspectives of journalists about the workplace bullying stories they write. This could be done within the context of the restrictions that are imposed by news production and practices and journalists' understandings of what workplace bullying means both in practice and in relation to academic and legislative definitions of it. The views of those cited or quoted in stories about workplace bullying, in relation to how they were represented and how the issue of workplace bullying was covered, would also be instructive in terms of improving journalistic practice and public understandings of workplace bullying. Because the perspectives of news media audiences are often overlooked in research about news media, a more nuanced approach to understanding how news media audiences respond to representations of HRM issues such as workplace bullying would be instructive, particularly in relation to any attempts that might be made to change the way such stories are reported. The impacts of citizen journalism such as alternative news media and blogs on audiences' understandings of HRM issues would also add to our understanding of the impacts of this kind of reportage.

An alignment with the multiple stakeholder approach to HRM discussed at the beginning of the chapter can be seen in this study (for example, the range and types of sources), and the methodology could be applied to other HRM research areas, as well as to comparisons of stories over time (for example, revisiting these two newspapers in the future to identify any shift in the way workplace bullying stories are reported). Other areas of HRM that could be examined include the public's access to information about workplace stress, workplace accidents, discrimination and cultural diversity; all examples of areas that would benefit from application of this innovative method to uncover important information, and build new approaches to understanding various stakeholders in the complex area of HRM. Alternatively, as recommended by Hauptmann and Steger (2013), social media can be especially helpful to HRM in terms of facilitating recruitment, organisational learning processes and the development of culture through communication, and is therefore an important future research opportunity.

In conclusion, this approach has emphasised the multiple perspectives of organisations, stakeholders and society on a complex phenomenon as conveyed by the news media. The research has contributed to greater understanding of the use of news media in terms of HRM, and specifically more knowledge as to how the public may perceive workplace bullying. The strengths of the methodological approach include the generation of new insights, including gaps in the portrayal of HRM topics, as exemplified by the workplace bullying study presented, between publically accessible media and academic approaches to the issue. Reflection on the aforementioned issues may ultimately contribute to greater theoretical and practical insights in HRM. As we begin to catch up with advances in technology and as technology continues to develop, the use of online media may provide HRM researchers and practitioners with fertile ground for future research of this kind.

REFERENCES

Beswick, J., Gore, J. and Palferman, D. (2006), "Bullying at work: a review of the literature", Working paper WPS/06/04, Health and Safety Laboratory, Harper Hill, Buxton, Derbyshire.

Branch, S. and Murray, J. (2015), "Workplace bullying: is lack of understanding the reason for inaction?", *Organizational Dynamics*, **44** (4), 266–72.

Branch, S., Ramsay, S. and Barker, M. (2013), "Workplace bullying, mobbing and general harassment: a review", *International Journal of Management Reviews*, **15** (3), 280–99.

Charlier, S.D. (2014), "Incorporating evidence-based management into management curricula: a conversation with Gary Latham", *Academy of Management Learning Education*, **13** (3), 467–75.

Einarsen, S., Hoel, H., Zapf, D. and Cooper, C. (2011), "The concept of bullying and harassment at work: the European tradition", in S. Einarsen, H. Hoel, D. Zapf and C. Cooper (eds), *Bullying and Harassment in the Workplace: Developments in Theory, Research, and Practice*, 2nd edn, London: Taylor & Francis Group, pp. 3–40.

Ekdale, B., Tully, M., Harmsen, S. and Singer, J.B. (2015), "Newswork within a culture of job insecurity", *Journalism Practice*, **9** (3), 383–98.

Escartin, J., Zapf, A. and Rodriguez-Carballeira, A. (2011), "Workers' perception of workplace bullying: a cross-cultural study", *European Journal of Work and Organizational Psychology*, **20** (2), 178–205.

Ewart, J. and Massey, B. (2005), "'Local (people) mean the world to us': Australia's regional newspapers and the 'closer to readers' assumption", *Media International Australia*, **115**, 94–108.

Gitlin, T. (1980), *The Whole World is Watching: Mass Media in the Making and Unmaking of the New Left*, Berkeley, CA: University of California Press.

Greenwood, M. (2013), "Ethical analyses of HRM: a review and research agenda", *Journal of Business Ethics*, **11**, 355–66.

Harley, B. (2014), "The one best way? 'Scientific' research on HRM and the threat to critical scholarship", in *International Labour Process Conference Proceedings*, Vol. 4, London: Kings College, pp. 355–66.

Hauptmann, S. and Steger, T. (2013), "'A brave new (digital) world'? Effects of in-house social media on HRM", *German Journal of Research in Human Resource Management*, **27** (1), 26–46.

Hoel, H., Sheehan, M., Cooper, C. and Einarsen, S. (2011), "Organisational effects of workplace bullying", in S. Einarsen, H. Hoel, D. Zapf and C. Cooper (eds), *Bullying and*

Harassment in the Workplace: Developments in Theory, Research, and Practice, 2nd edn, London: Taylor & Francis Group, pp. 129–48.

Joffe, H. and Yardley, L. (2004), "Content and thematic analysis", in D.F. Marks and L. Yardley (eds), *Research Methods for Clinical and Health Psychology*, London: Sage, pp. 56–68.

Johnstone, J., Hawkins, D. and Micener, A. (1994), "Homicide reporting in Chicago dailies", *Journalism Quarterly*, **71** (4), 860–72.

Klein, H.J. and Delery, J.E. (2012), "Construct clarity in human resource management research: introduction to the special issue", *Human Resource Management Review*, **22**, 57–61.

Lewis, D. (2001), "Perceptions of bullying in organisations", *International Journal of Management and Decision Making*, **2** (1), 48–64.

Liefooghe, A. and Davey, K. (2001), "Accounts of workplace bullying: the role of the organization", *European Journal of Work and Organizational Psychology*, **10** (4), 375–92.

Marchington, M. (2015), "Human resource management (HRM): too busy looking up to see where it is going longer term?", *Human Resource Management Review*, **25** (2), 176–87.

Mariappanadar, M. (2014), "Stakeholder harm index: a framework to review work intensification from the critical HRM perspective", *Human Resource Management Review*, **24**, 313–29.

Matthiesen, S. and Einarsen, S. (2007), "Perpetrators and targets of bullying at work: role stress and individual differences", *Violence and Victims*, **22** (6), 735–53.

Mazza, C. and Alvarez, J.L. (2000), "Haute couture and prêt-a-porter: the popular press and the diffusion of management practice", *Organization Studies*, **21**, 567–88.

McCarthy, P. (2004), "Costs of occupational violence and bullying", in P. McCarthy and C. Mayhew (eds), *Safeguarding the Organization Against Violence and Bullying*, Basingstoke: Palgrave Macmillan, pp. 38–58.

NVivo (2012), Qualitative data analysis Software, QSR International Pty Ltd, Version 10.

Peelo, M., Francis, B., Soothill, K., Pearson, J. and Ackeerley, E. (2004), "Newspaper reporting and the public construction of homicide", *British Journal of Criminology*, **4**, 256–75.

Ramsay, S., Troth, A. and Branch, S. (2011), "Workplace bullying: a group processes framework", *Journal of Occupational and Organizational Psychology*, **84** (4), 799–816.

Scheufele, D.A. and Tewksbury, D. (2007), "Framing, agenda setting, and priming: the evolution of three media effects models", *Journal of Communication*, **57**, 9–20.

Semetko, H.A., and Valkenburg, P.M. (2000), "Framing European politics: a content analysis of press and television news", *Journal of Communication*, **50** (2), 93–109.

Spitzberg, B.H. (2002), "The tactical topograph of stalking, victimization and management", *Trauma, Violence & Abuse*, **3** (4), 261–88.

Stanley, L., Mackenzie Davey, K. and Symon, G. (2014), "Exploring media construction of investment banking as dirty work", *Qualitative Research in Organizations and Management: An International Journal*, **9**, 270–87.

Turkewitz, J. (2010), "All the news that's fit to print? A content analysis of newspaper's portrayal of rape and sexual assault", Honors thesis, Wesleyan University, Connecticut.

Van Buren, H.J. and Greenwood, M. (2013), "Unitarist ideology in HRM: challenging the dominant framework using epistemological analysis", *Academy of Management Proceedings*, Vol. 13, No. 1, Academy of Management, p. 144–65.

7 Netnographical methods and the challenge of researching hidden and secretive employee social media practices
James Richards

INTRODUCTION

The use of social media appears ubiquitous in modern society. Generation Y is perhaps the greatest user of social media, yet it is apparent that older generations also make plenty of use of social media. It is apparent that organisations are increasingly using social media as marketing or recruitment tools. Even governments have attempted to inform and influence the public through the application of common social media tools, such as Facebook and Twitter. However, in human resource management (HRM) terms, the ubiquity of social media, that is, employers and employees applying the same communication technologies for often quite different purposes and to achieve quite different ends, means something quite distinct. For example, McDonald and Thompson (2016) believe social media has led to a major reshaping of the public/private boundaries in the employment relationship. What this means is social media has the potential to amplify and create a new place for tensions in the employment relationship. Social media is itself a contestable terrain as employers, unlike in the case of company emails and notice boards, do not have any direct right to control employee use of such communication technologies. Such tensions, moreover, regularly and continue to feature in the popular press, typically taking the form of employees "badmouthing" employers, managers, colleagues or customer/client groups on Facebook, and often leading to many a headache for HR departments across the land.

The focus of this chapter is an unfunded research project conducted circa 2005 at a time when social media was relatively new, yet beginning to attract the attention of both employers and employees. The research project in question represents what was then the most emergent and newsworthy form of social media – blogs. Employee blogs and blogging, while attracting a certain degree of popular media attention at the time, however, remained an often hidden and secretive practice. This was mainly because the media picked up on selective examples of such practices and employees, fearing being disciplined by their employer, often took steps, such as blogging under a pseudonym, to avoid direct association with their blogging practices.

As such, the research project in question was very much focused on the shifting terrain for employee–employer conflict expression brought about by new ways in which employees and employer could communicate and express their interests to a rapidly expanding Internet-located audience. More specifically, this chapter concerns a discussion of the methodological details of a research project characterised by a novel sample, method, research ethics and recruitment of participants, focused on employee bloggers, or employees who write online diaries about their work (Schoneboom, 2007). A further key focus of the chapter is the application of conventional methods, such as questionnaires, adapted to conduct a netnographical-styled study of online communities and cultures (Janta and Ladkin, 2013) – in this instance, communities of employee bloggers. The main aim of the chapter, however, is to provide a personal or "behind the scenes" account of a novel and innovative research project, representing, in effect, the trials and tribulations of researchers that rarely make it into journal articles. It is important to provide such an account for two key purposes: first, social media appears to be here for the long term and, second, conflict in the employment relationship remains a perennial feature of HRM research practice. The chapter should be helpful for the researcher interested in exploring in-depth, employee use of social media in relation to work and employment.

In order to delve into and discuss the methodological details often omitted from journal articles, the chapter is structured as follows. The chapter starts with a discussion of the emergence of employee blogging and how employee blogging can be distinguished from employee Internet misbehaviour. In the second section the methodological challenges and dilemmas faced by the researcher and the details of the eventual research strategy used to research the employee blogger are presented. The third section highlights the realities of researching hidden and secretive Internet phenomena. The final discussion section of the chapter sums up all the key points.

THE EMERGENCE OF EMPLOYEE BLOGGING

Wide interest and awareness of employee blogging emerged circa 2004 on the back of a range of international news stories reporting employees disciplined for posting views about their jobs, interactions with employers, colleagues and customers, to blogs, which were then new and emergent social networking platforms. In this instance, however, employee blogging quickly became branded by the popular business-friendly press as a form of deviant or anti-business behaviour. Examples of such partisan views include employee attempts to cause harm to employer reputations (Spencer, 2005), create inconsistency with business mission statements (Joyce, 2005) and exposing employer brands in a way not possible just a short time ago (Phillips, 2008).

However, it quickly became evident that employees blogging about their jobs was something quite different from employee misuse of the Internet at work, a quickly growing sub-field of HRM scholarly research. Indeed, simply observing employee blogs reveals a distinct difference between acts such as "cyberloafing" (for example, see Blanchard and Henle, 2008; Lim and Teo, 2005) and "cyberslacking" (for example, see Block, 2001; Garrett and Danziger, 2008) on work time and on work premises, and acts involving employees keeping an online diary in their own time, using their own information and communications technology (ICT) equipment and deploying a range of strategies, such as writing under pseudonyms, in order to avoid the distinct possibility of disciplinary action by employers (Richards, 2008).

As a consequence of these events and realities, it became apparent that HRM academics wishing to research employee bloggers faced a range of challenges. These challenges included designing methodologies that go beyond popular and emergent views of employee bloggers, but more importantly, designing methodologies to gain access to employees suspicious of outsiders and not accessible through conventional research gatekeepers, such as HR managers and other senior employers of work organisations.

OVERCOMING CHALLENGES AND DILEMMAS TO RESEARCH EMPLOYEE BLOGGING

The research project in question began late 2004, at the tail end of a PhD ethnographical research project on traditional forms of workplace employee misbehaviour and resistance. The impetus for the research project in question was the emergence of a new form of employee Internet behaviour that had begun to attract the attention of the popular media. As such, a decision was made to launch an unfunded side research project on employee blogs. The onset of the research project, however, came with a range of key methodological challenges and dilemmas that included scoping out the blogosphere, choosing research methods, how to act in an ethical fashion when conducting the research, as well as how best to recruit participants. Collectively, this section concerns a wider research challenge, that of overcoming the common difficulty of acquiring sufficiently high quality responses to allow research objectives to be met. This section is, as such, critical to unpicking the innovative methodology of the research project on employee blogs, as well as offering guidance on further research on employee uses of social media.

Scoping Out the Employee Blogging Blogosphere

The first key challenge was to define an "employee blog", as a definition was needed in order to determine who to recruit to the research project. A test for inclusion, however, was quickly developed in terms of being a blog that contains strong reference to matters of work, particularly in terms of providing accounts of working or customer relationships. Blogs of a highly technical or specialised nature were not considered for the study, neither were blogs where work was a passing or fleeting matter.

While the main priority of the research project was to establish employee views of their blogging practices, it was also necessary, to a point, to establish the scale of such practices. Given the limited time and resources available to conduct the research project, a priority, however, was finding sufficient quantities of employee blogs to make a study of employee practices worthwhile.

At first employee blogs were identified through following up media news stories using Internet search engines. However, such an approach helped identify only a very limited number of employee blogs. What allowed further and many more employee blogs to be identified was the use of blogrolls (lists of blogs, with hyperlinks, found on a blog and typically representing blogs that the keeper recommends or is connected to in some way). It quickly became apparent that employee bloggers typically forged links with other employee bloggers and in particular employee bloggers from similar jobs, occupations or professions. Blogrolls, as such, significantly eased the challenge to find many more employee blogs.

By early 2007 a database of approximately 750 employee blogs had been created (Table 7.1), with the 750 blogs categorised by broad occupational themes. Table 7.1 suggests that various health professionals, police officers and educators dominate the employee blogosphere. Most of such blog titles reflected in some way a feature of the job or profession of the blog keeper. For example, "Life in the law abiding Midlands" (UK police officer), "Universal solider" (a US soldier based in Iraq) and "75 degrees south" (a UK scientist based in Antarctica). The database also denoted the origin of the blog – most blogs collated were written by US employees, but the database also accounted for approximately 200 blogs written by employees from the UK, Australia, Canada and New Zealand. The

*Table 7.1   Employee blogs by broad occupational or professional
categorisation*

Employment category	Number	Example blog titles
Education (high school)	98	Report card
Nurse	93	The NHS confessional
Police	68	Life in the law abiding Midlands
Medic	62	Musings of a disheartened doctor
Office and manager	59	Thoughts of a terminally bored office worker
Emergency services	49	Confessions of a fire control operator
Education (HE)	36	A lecturer's life
IT, technical and craft	29	That's not a bug, it's a feature
Retail	29	Don't blame me! I'm just a sales assistant
Airline	27	Sorry, I don't have peanuts
Hotel and restaurant	25	Pizza Hut team member
Miscellaneous	25	Walking the streets (traffic warden)
Taxi	25	All in a day's work
Librarian	24	Loopy librarian
Call centre	22	Call Center Purgatory
Scientist	15	75 degrees south
Law	11	The magistrate's blog
Military	11	Universal soldier
Transport	11	Bus driving
Education (FE and TEFL)	10	Daily TEFL grind
Sex worker	9	A day in the night of a stripper
Actor and film industry	6	Diary of a Chicago actor
Total	744	

database in question took the form of a blog, kept by the researcher, which listed employee blogs by job/occupation/profession. The research blog in question continues to be publicly accessible via the following web address: http://workblogging.blogspot.co.uk/.

Research Methods and Researching Employee Bloggers

The second key challenge was to consider what was the most efficient research method to get high numbers of and high quality responses from employee bloggers? A wide range of conventional data collection methods were considered in order to explore the employee views of employee blogging practices. For example, ideal methods associated with ethnography, such as participant observation, were ruled out because they were highly impractical or take too long for a small, unfunded research project that was already proving to be time-consuming in terms of scoping out the employee blogosphere. Interviews with employee bloggers were also considered, yet rejected at this stage because of unsuitability in terms of the number of participants required for the project, the time-consuming nature of arranging and conducting interviews and the costs and practicalities associated with conducting interviews on a global scale (this was a time before Skype and the widespread availability of low cost broadband Internet connection). Further, interviews were judged at this stage of research development to be too intrusive and off-putting to prospective research participants.

The eventual decision was to adopt what was then an emergent data collection tool – an electronic qualitative questionnaire. An electronic qualitative questionnaire was deemed efficient in this scenario because it: (1) came with a permalink, making it very efficient to distribute in the Internet domain; (2) complemented the nature of what was being researched, that of employees highly engaged with emergent forms of Internet-based communication technologies; (3) was non-invasive, allowing employee bloggers the time and space to decide whether they wished to take part in the study or not; (4) was free to use, mainly because its design did not require the advanced premium features associated with more contemporary electronic questionnaire platforms, such as SurveyMonkey; and (5) the data to come from the questionnaire was easily and quickly downloadable in a format that made for efficient and speedy data analysis.

The platform used to host the electronic qualitative questionnaire was my3q.com, one of the first providers of such services on the Internet. Other than being a research project based on a novel sample, the research method used is defined by an age when little research had been published in HRM journals based on gathering data via electronic qualitative questionnaires. Furthermore, qualitative questionnaires are also quite rare in HRM research, mainly because it is much harder to gain meaningful cooperation from research participants compared to the use of quantitative-based questionnaires.

In order to acquire the necessary qualitative data to widely explore employee blogging practices the eventual electronic qualitative questionnaire was formulated on a range of self-reporting and open-ended questions covering the subject of personal employee blogging practices. Questions used in the questionnaire included: Why do you specifically blog about work? What is the purpose of your blog? What motivated you to start blogging about work? What motivates you to continue blogging about work? Who is the audience of your blog? However, to avoid being overly intrusive and to maintain high levels of participant cooperation, no personal details were requested as part of the electronic qualitative questionnaire exercise. A key issue in mind at the time was that electronic qualitative questionnaires do not offer the same degree of flexibility as interviews or observations, such as the opportunity to rephrase or reorder questions. The researcher is also not present and this also greatly reduces the chances of the participant seeking clarification concerning any of the questions. It was decided to pilot the electronic qualitative questionnaire on a small number of employee bloggers. Piloting was not expected to be conducted in a conventional fashion, such as requiring direct feedback from participants on the questions set. Instead, it was decided that evaluating the quality of data received from the first batch of questionnaires would be the deciding factor in any changes to the electronic qualitative questionnaire. After approximately 20 responses it was evident that the questions were understood as intended and answers typically came in the form of 2–3 sentences per question.

Research Ethics and Researching Employee Bloggers

A third challenge concerned a key research issue, that of preventing harm coming to participants, ensuring wherever possible participants gave informed consent to take part in the research and protecting each participant's right to privacy. Research ethics were particularly critical because at the time debates were emerging about the ethical implications of conducting research in a domain that might well be technically accessible yet the vast majority of employee blogs were unlikely to be on the radar of most Internet users. In other words, conducting research on employee blogs would be, for example, similar to a stranger suddenly appearing in a private social setting where sensitive issues are being discussed, and expect to be accepted into the group with open arms. Further, it was necessary to factor into the study design the negative impact the popular business press had already had on employee blogging communities, such as the heightened fear of employee bloggers facing exposure to the wider world and the possibility of employer-led disciplinary action due to publishing unofficial accounts of work organisations on the Internet. The researcher might risk being taken as an undercover reporter or employer official. Extra care and consideration was needed not to cause any harm and instead create researcher-researched relations based on trust and mutuality, necessary in order to present a rich account of employee blogging practices. More generally, acting in an ethical fashion was likely to help overcome a key weakness of electronic qualitative questionnaires, that of gaining high levels of cooperation from prospective participants.

What this entailed is summarised as follows. At the most general level it involved joining a range of employee blogging communities, representing a further novel aspect of the research project. Having set up a blog in order to keep track of employee blogs it also seemed a sensible strategy to become an active blogger and use the research blog as a means to further develop trusting relations with employee bloggers. Central to the ethics strategy was to establish trusting relations between researcher and employee bloggers, or at the very least present a means by which the researcher could establish his credentials should a potential research participant question the status and motives of the researcher. This part of the research strategy quickly evolved over the first year of the life of the research blog (April 2005 to March 2006), but continued for many more years afterwards. The strategy used was that all contact and research interest details of the researcher were placed on the blog, with a description of the research project (in lay terms) presented there too. Over time draft papers on employee blogging were posted on the research blog. During this time the researcher also blogged about how employees were making use of a wide range of social media, especially blogs, but increasingly, for example, Twitter, Facebook and LinkedIn. The researcher thus became a hub of informal activity surrounding employee blogs and wider social media, with the research blog regularly linked through the blogrolls of employee bloggers. The research blog also attracted a wide range of interest from the popular media, leading to the researcher being interviewed several times by national newspapers, from several countries, on the subject of employee blogging. This unexpected bonus no doubt further strengthened the credentials and reputation of the researcher in employee blogging circles.

The Recruitment of Employee Bloggers

A fourth key challenge involved the recruitment of sufficient participants to the research project. Additional steps were needed to gain high levels of cooperation from research participants due to the use of an electronic qualitative questionnaire. This aspect of the research also required an innovative approach. Attempts to recruit for the study began before it was decided to no longer continue adding to the blog-based database of employee blogs. The recruitment process began in April 2005 when approximately half of the eventual total of employee blogs had been identified and categorised. Data gathering using the electronic qualitative questionnaire began in April 2005 and ended in October 2005. During that time 520 questionnaires were distributed to employee bloggers, with 207 or 40 per cent of distributed questionnaires returned during the seven months of actual fieldwork.

Based on the ethical principles outlined in the previous subsection, employee bloggers were recruited in two ways. First, observations of employee blogs revealed email contact details of the employee blogger, although email addresses in nearly all such cases rarely revealed any identifying features of the blogger. In this instance a friendly and respectful email was sent to the employee blogger outlining brief details of the study and an invitation, including a web link to the electronic qualitative questionnaire, to take part in the research project. The email also contained a web link to the research blog in order to verify the credentials of the researcher and the research project, as well as details of how to contact the researcher regarding questions related to the research project. Second, where an email address was not available on an employee's blog, a message similar to the email described above was left as a comment on the latest post/diary entry made by the employee blogger. To avoid being overly intrusive, employee bloggers were only contacted once during the recruitment process.

THE REALITIES OF RESEARCHING EMPLOYEE BLOGGERS

Despite a great deal of thought going into the design of the research methodology, the execution of the research with employee bloggers was not without expected and unexpected challenges, although the purpose of this section of the chapter is not to simply comment on the downsides of such a research project. Before conducting a broader discussion of the key points to take from this chapter, it is important to present and discuss a range of important lessons to arise from the study, which are likely to have broader applicability.

Time Taken to Conduct a Netnographical Study

As the study was unfunded and an experimental side research project, the time taken to complete the project was neither anticipated nor recorded as it unfolded. However, a retrospective estimate suggests the research design and data collection stage accounted for ten or possibly more hours per week for nearly a year. In other words, the equivalent of what is typical of the fieldwork associated with a PhD, or at least a modestly funded research project. In this instance, however, the research project was mostly conducted outside regular office hours, often in the evening and at weekends. Having said that, the research project was exploratory, focused on a range of phenomena about which little was known at the time. So, to replicate such a study is unlikely to take as long or be as labour intensive as the research project discussed in this chapter.

Addictive Nature of Netnographical Study

Despite reporting the time-consuming nature of the project, it would be quite misleading to suggest it was an onerous task. If anything, the whole process was quite engrossing and most of the time it did not feel like work at all. As most people are all too aware, social media or just surfing the Internet more generally can be absorbing, time passes quickly, and this was certainly the case in this instance. Anyone contemplating a similar study should be careful to consider how researching Internet phenomena of this kind could easily intrude on other job roles and wider commitments.

Convenience of Netnographical Study

Compared to the researcher's previous experience of a more conventional form of ethnographic-styled research, also based on hidden and secretive forms of employee behaviour, the fieldwork proved to be a very different experience to observing and talking to employees in the physical work setting. However, the researcher did not speak with, let alone ever meet, a single employee blogger during the course of the research project. What made such a study markedly different from a traditional ethnography was that traditional HRM-related ethnography is usually conducted in a physical work setting, with the researcher having some sort of physical presence in that work setting. Having no physical presence required careful thought on how electronic interaction with employee bloggers could be perceived, especially if there was potential for interactions to be misconstrued. Further key differences are that a netnographical-styled research project is unlikely to require a large amount of time spent on finding a way into the organisations, or time and expense travelling to and from a traditional ethnographical setting, as well as having to overcome the mistrust often apportioned to ethnographers who gain access to research participants via the help and consent of senior managers. In this instance, it was possible to conduct the entire fieldwork involving employees from five countries, spanning many time zones from North America, Europe and Australasia, from the researcher's personal computer, or wherever an Internet-connected computer could be accessed, anytime of the day and any day of the week. The study was even portable, that is, the fieldwork went wherever the researcher went, in this instance, at home, at work, Internet cafes, airport lounges and using personal computers when visiting friends. A research project of this kind opens up a range of possibilities for researchers who may have a disability or a work–life situation that may preclude to some extent undertaking a conventional ethnography. It also opens the door to ethnographers who wish to study a demographic group different from their own, such as based on geographic location, age, ethnicity and gender. Indeed, the study in question allowed the researcher to conduct ethnographical research at a time when it would otherwise have been impossible to do so.

Quick and Efficient Collection of Netnographical Data

An important lesson – as is often the case with research involving difficult to access research participants – is that good and thoughtful research design can pay handsome dividends. In other words, research design and implementation quickly turned into a steady and efficient pipeline of data, detailing the many (at the time) unknown angles on employee blogging practices. Far more data than could possibly be used was acquired, yet it is perhaps best to have too much data when researching an unknown HRM phenomenon.

DISCUSSION

The aim of this chapter has been, first, to describe an important study of early employee use of social media and the relation of such behaviour to work and employment, with such developments representing a very new challenge to both HR researchers and practitioners. A second key purpose of the chapter is to consider social media in relation to HR research and practice, the focus being on what is now a less prominent form of social media – the blog. However, the decline of employee blogs and blogging does not suggest there is a need to turn away from considering researching social media in relation to employee behaviour. Far from it. In more recent times there has been a massive increase in both employee and employer use of more emergent forms of social media, such as Facebook and Twitter, with each social media platform representing unique challenges in terms of getting access to participants willing to offer insider accounts of such practices. The main aim of this chapter, via an insider account of conducting a netnographical-styled study, is to serve as a guide, or at least a broad template, for more HR research on social media and employee behaviour. However, as the research project under the spotlight was both experimental and resource intensive, it is important to end the chapter with a reflection on the extent to which the research approach led to a credible, alternative account of employee blogging practices.

In short, the research findings did shed a very different light on employee blogging practices (see Richards, 2008 for more details). Central to the findings was evidence to suggest such practices were for the most part a means for employees to vent genuinely held everyday frustrations with employers, managers, colleagues and customers, although almost none of the data gathered indicated that the main aim of venting frustrations concerned attempts to harm the interests of employers and businesses. In fact, just two respondents out of 207 stated employer-directed defiance as the primary aim of their blog. However, the findings also revealed further angles on employee blogging, including as an important means for employees to explore skills not required in most forms of employment, such as storytelling. A further key finding from the research project is that blogs allowed employees to connect and forge important networks with employees with similar jobs. Indeed, the findings related to employees forging important networks through blogs spurred follow-up research on employee blogs. The networking possibilities of employee blogging were later further explored by the researcher through the use of semi-structured interviews (see Ellis and Richards, 2009; Richards and Kosmala, 2013 – both in the Annotated Further Reading section).

However, as any scholarly researcher would expect, the research project (and follow-up research) did not reveal everything about employee blogging, nor did the research project in question cater for the fact that people and technology evolve and what is relevant and true now may not be even a few years down the line. Indeed, there has been a range of further research aimed at exploring employee blogging practices (for example, Pedersen et al., 2014; Schoneboom, 2015), as well as research on Facebook as a means to connect many thousands of aggrieved non-unionised workers (for example, Wood, 2015). A range of innovative methods are used in order to explore hard to reach employee groups typified by a common application of social media-based communication technologies. It should also be acknowledged that new challenges face HRM-aligned researchers wishing to research employee Internet behaviour, with the popular business press regularly reporting on employees' creative use of social media (for example, Richards, 2012 in the Annotated Further Reading section and the research blog mentioned earlier in the chapter). Indeed, employee use of social media represents a vast range of exciting, yet challenging opportunities for the contemporary HRM researchers. Employee blogging, as discussed, is much more than misbehaviour and it is important to consider how methodologies can be designed to overcome the challenges of identifying the many nuances of employee uses for social media. It is also important to rise to the challenge of finding new and innovative ways to access and gain the cooperation of groups of employees who make collective use of communication technologies. In order to explore such nuances there will need to be large-scale investment in the design and execution of innovative methodologies. However, small-scale/low budget studies of the kind detailed in this chapter, especially if the researcher is willing to be creative in the use of research methodologies, remain viable options if substantial funding is hard to come by.

ANNOTATED FURTHER READING

In addition to Schoneboom (2007) and Richards (2008) there is a good, yet far from exhaustive range of research looking at employee blogging, from various perspectives, as well as deploying a range of innovative research methodologies.

Ellis, V. and Richards, J. (2009), "Creativity connecting and correcting: motivations and meanings of work-blogging among public service workers", in S. Bolton and M. Houlihan (eds), *Work Matters: Reflections on Contemporary Work*, London: Palgrave, pp. 250–68.

Using semi-structured interviews with employee bloggers, this book chapter looks at how blogging practices allow employees a wider opportunity to share details of what they do at work beyond that of colleagues and family.

Richards, J. (2012), "What has the Internet ever done for employees? A review, map and research agenda", *Employee Relations*, **34** (1), 22–43.

Using a literature review and empirical analysis of contemporary media accounts of employee use of the Internet, this journal article evaluates employee blogs, as well as a wide range of other forms of ICT and social media as means to empower employees.

Richards, J. and Kosmala, K. (2013), "'In the end, you can only slag people off for so long': employee cynicism through work blogging", *New Technology, Work and Employment*, **28** (1), 66–77.

Using semi-structured interviews with employee bloggers, this journal article suggests that blogging practices not only provide an important place to express cynical views of work but also allow employees a sense of control and attachment to their own occupational or professional community.

Schoneboom, A. (2011), "Sleeping giants? Fired workbloggers and labour organization", *New Technology, Work and Employment*, **26** (1), 17–28.

Using extracts from a high-profile employee blog, comments made on this blog by blog readers and media coverage of the same blog, this journal article explores employee blogging practices as a vehicle to communicate and organise around employee dissent.

REFERENCES

Blanchard, A. and Henle, C. (2008), "Correlates of different forms of cyberloafing: the role of norms and external locus of control", *Computers in Human Behavior*, **24** (3), 1067–84.

Block, W. (2001), "Cyberslacking business ethics and managerial economics", *Journal of Business Ethics*, **33** (3), 225–31.

Garrett, R. and Danziger, J. (2008), "On cyberslacking: workplace status and personal internet use at work", *CyberPsychology and Behavior*, **11** (3), 287–92.

Janta, H. and Ladkin, A. (2013), "In search of employment: online technologies and Polish migrants", *New Technology, Work and Employment*, **28** (3), 241–53.

Joyce, A. (2005), "When blogging gets risky," *Washington Post*, 11 February, available at http://www.msnbc.msn.com/id/6949377 (accessed 20 August 2015).

Lim, V. and Teo, T. (2005), "Prevalence, perceived seriousness, justification and regulation of cyberloafing in Singapore – an exploratory study", *Information and Management*, **42** (8), 1081–93.

McDonald, P. and Thompson, P. (2016), "Social media(tion) and the reshaping of public/

private boundaries in employment relations", *International Journal of Management Reviews*, **18** (1), 69–84.

Pedersen, S., Burnett, S., Smith, R. and Grinnall, A. (2014), "The impact of the cessation of blogs within the UK police blogosphere", *New Technology, Work and Employment*, **29** (2), 160–76.

Phillips, L. (2008), "Control, alt or delete . . .", *People Management*, 20 March, 18.

Richards, J. (2008), "'Because I need somewhere to vent': the expression of conflict through work blogs", *New Technology, Work and Employment*, **23** (1–2), 95–109.

Schoneboom, A. (2007), "Diary of a working boy: creative resistance among anonymous workbloggers", *Ethnography*, **8** (4), 403–23.

Schoneboom, A. (2015), "The romance of the lowly clerk: recognizing the tradition of office intellectualism", *Organization*, **22** (5), 832–46.

Spencer, S. (2005), "Illegal blogging: employee bloggers are loose cannons that can go off when employers least expect it", *People Management*, **27**, January, 18–19.

Wood, A. (2015), "Networks of injustice and worker mobilisation at Walmart", *Industrial Relations Journal*, **46** (4), 259–74.

8   Doing historical research in human resource management: with some reflections on an academic career
Peter Ackers

INTRODUCTION: HISTORY AS QUALITATIVE SOCIAL SCIENCE

Not many human resource management (HRM) scholars nowadays think of adopting a historical approach. Yet there are close affinities between interpretive sociology, using qualitative social science methods and the usual historical approach (see Patmore, 1998). Both share the sense that people make society and focus on what Weber termed "actors' social meanings". The main argument of this chapter is twofold:

1. history is worth doing and possible to do within the HRM field, and I use my own career as an illustration of this, but
2. history has a distinctive method of its own, which must be learned and respected, even if this can be combined with other social science approaches.

All historians recognise that understanding and interpreting the past is a complex and uncertain process (see Carr, 1961 [2002]; Evans, 1997; Hobsbawm, 1997). Marwick (2001, pp. xiii, 33) distinguishes between *The Past*, as what actually happened and *History*, as what historians research and write about that past: "What historians do is produce *knowledge about* the past". Reflection on the writing of history is termed *historiography*, and this is where the major methodological debates take place. In Marwick's view, the "collective enterprise" of professional, academic history "challenges and deflates myths" about the past, many of which are misleading and dangerous. Most history is essentially qualitative, in social science terms, because its mission is to understand better how people thought and behaved in the past. This reflects the discipline's traditional academic home in the humanities. However, economic and social history has a close relationship with the social sciences, often using economic and sociological concepts, and one specialist, quantitative branch of economic history, *cliometrics*, attempts to test theories using "hard" data from the past. For the most part, though, we can see historical research as operating across the border of the humanities and qualitative social sciences.

SOME REASONS TO CHOOSE THE HISTORICAL APPROACH

Business schools are obsessed with the present and the future, so what is the broader case for studying the past? Three rationales for taking a historical perspective stand out.

1. There is the benefit of *longitudinal* depth of analysis. Much qualitative social science research is based on a brief "snapshot", a few interviews at a given moment in time, whereas social processes are constantly developing over time. And historical perspective allows us to observe "completed" social processes, as I have in my own research, discussed in detail at the end of this chapter. Even where we carry our analysis up to the present, we can see better the road that was travelled to reach there.

2. There is greater scope to explore *context*. A major criticism of the quantitative social sciences is their neglect of context, and contemporary qualitative research strives to counter this with what Geertz (1973 [2010]) has termed "thick description". However, historians would argue that they can do contextual depth of analysis still better, because they explore real named organisations or institutions – not "BankCo", but Barclay's Bank – and real named people, in full national and cultural context, taken in real time and place. By contrast, even the best comparative or ethnographic sociology has to disguise its subject and strip away crucial information. In these terms, the past may be a better laboratory for understanding human behaviour than the immediate present.

3. Finally, history's humanities-based emphasis on *narrative and public accessibility*, as well as storytelling and literary style, holds great benefits in this era of "research impact". Social science may claim to produce hard evidence for policy-makers, but historians are much more likely to speak directly to the public on the TV or in the newspaper, whether this is Mary Beard exploring ancient Rome, Orlando Figes discussing the Russian Revolution, Simon Sharma surveying the History of England, Niall Ferguson assessing the British Empire or David Starkey comparing the Tudor Monarchy to our own. Marwick (2001, pp.45, 84) warns us against "amateurish and literary" or "auteur history", but there is no doubt that history has

the common touch and a reading and watching public. That, by itself, may be a good reason to take the historical turn.

SUITABLE TOPICS FOR HISTORICAL RESEARCH

But, as we're based in HRM, can the historical approach offer us any mileage in this specialist field of study and what sort of approaches could we adopt? The simple answer is that all the usual historical methods apply and a natural starting point is either the individual or the organisation.

1. Through *biography*, we can illuminate the key architects of the HRM world. My own Miller and Clegg studies of a trade union leader and an academic are discussed below. But there are numerous other possibilities. A current PhD student, John Kimberley (2016), is studying the life of Edward Cadbury, as a Quaker employer who developed distinctive HRM policies, especially towards women workers. We can go wider, also, exploring groups of people in the past through *prosopography* (or multiple biography), such as the Oxford School of Industrial Relations (Ackers, 2011b), Quaker employers or Communist trade unionists (see Seifert and Sibley, 2012).
2. *Organisational history* offers a great many insights into HRM processes. We might research the company history of a major business, like IBM or Marks and Spencer, which has shaped wider HRM policy; explore an influential union, like IG Metall in Germany; take a broader industry or sector, such as British banking; or investigate alternative company forms through, say, the Co-operative movement or the John Lewis Partnership (see Cathcart, 2013; and for some examples, see Burchall, 1994; Drummond, 1995; Jacoby, 1997; Smith et al., 1990). Beyond this lie more general themes of social and economic history, such as twentieth-century changes in women's working roles or the ethnic composition of the workforce. Aggregate national statistics only take us so far in capturing the changing experience of working lives, whereas an in-depth historical study of, say, the teaching profession in Australia could provide a much richer understanding.

A business and management field like HRM that is obsessed with the latest management concept – be this employee engagement, managing diversity or HRM itself – is ripe for further historical investigation. When I began my research in England in the early 1980s, none of these terms were familiar to me and some had yet to be coined; yet organisations had been managing people for hundreds of years. At the time, we still referred to personnel management, a new management function that had emerged in large companies early in the twentieth century. There are obvious questions here, which only historical research can answer. Are these just examples of relabelling and new fashionable language? In other words, is the new HRM doing more or less the same things as the old personnel management (see Legge, 2004)? Or have changes in society, such as the decline of trade unions and rising female employment, changed the role of people management? Equally, where do these terms come from? Many like HRM originated in the USA, but others such as quality circles came from Japan. Historians might answer these crucial questions about the changing nature of HRM by organisational case studies, by oral history interviews with retired personnel managers or by discourse analysis of *People Management*, the magazine of the British Chartered Institute of Personnel and Development (CIPD) – or perhaps by a combination of them all.

DIFFERENT STRANDS OF HISTORY AND THE SORT OF QUESTIONS THEY ASK

Even here, the options are very wide. *Intellectual history* pursues ideas that have shaped the world, as in Max Weber's, *The Protestant Ethics and the Spirit of Capitalism* (1905), whereas *labour history* considers worker responses to business and capitalism (see Patmore, 2010 for Australia), while *business history* looks at the development of company strategy and *gender history* assesses the changing roles of men and women (see Yeo, 2004). The British Association of Business Schools (ABS) journal ranking list privileges a myopic range of largely business history journals, but, as my own experience shows below, there is ample scope for publishing historical research in mainstream HRM and social science journals.

The current emphasis on "Varieties of Capitalism" (Hall and Soskice, 2001) demands a *comparative history*, which compares and contrasts institutions in different countries, whether these are companies, trade unions or state policies. The highly successful German "co-ordinated market economy" thrives on national neo-corporatist tripartite relations between the state, employers and union representative; sectoral bargaining between industry unions and employers' associations; a strong training regime and forms of worker co-determination in key sectors. These institutional arrangements shape HRM policies at the enterprise level; yet none exist in a comparable form in a "liberal-market economy", such as the USA.

Here "history matters", since institutions are laid down by national political, economic and social history (see Ackers and Wilkinson, 2008). For instance, many German institutions date back to the post-war reconstruction in 1945, following the defeat of national socialism. Only historical research can uncover these roots.

To summarise, any aspect of HRM can come under the purview of history and many contemporary problems are impossible to understand without recourse to historical context.

HOW TO DISTINGUISH BETWEEN PRIMARY AND SECONDARY HISTORICAL SOURCES

So, we're interested in doing original historical research in the broad field of HRM. The next question is: "how do we gather evidence"? And here it is important to recognise that there is a different distinction between *primary and secondary evidence* to that deployed in the contemporary social sciences. For the social sciences, primary is material that you have created with your research instrument, secondary is most other published literature on the subject. So, for example, many qualitative social scientists dismiss any published material as "secondary" and make a fetish of techniques such as interviews and observation. The historian's view is rather different:

> it is only through the primary sources, the relics and traces left by past societies, that we have any knowledge of them ... *primary sources were created within the period studied*, secondary sources are produced later, by historians studying that earlier period and making use of the primary sources created within it. (Marwick, 2001, p. 156, emphasis added)

Thus, an old academic textbook, such as Clegg's (1979) *The Changing System of Industrial Relations in Great Britain*, is a *primary source* for my research on the history of British academic industrial relations (see Ackers, 2011b). On the other hand, a recently published academic book, novel or film from outside the period studied is not. Once more, Marwick (2001, pp. 166–72) explains this well and in Box 8.1 I have included some examples from my Miller and Clegg biographical projects – described later – as illustrations.

Finally, it is worth noting that in an era when research funding is hard to get, especially for large-scale qualitative projects, archives like the British Modern Records Centre (Warwick University) and National Archive (London) offer huge amounts of research material for free.

BOX 8.1   MARWICK'S TAXONOMY OF PRIMARY SOURCES

1. *Documents of record*
   Union and church minutes (Miller), birth, death and marriage certificates (both)
2. *Surveys and reports*
   1968 Donovan Royal Commission on Trade Unions and Employers Associations (Clegg)
3. *Chronicles and histories*
   Amateur union histories (Miller) and church histories (both)
4. *Family and personal sources*
   War-time letters (Clegg) and newspaper cuttings scrapbook (Miller)
5. *Polemical, hortatory and prescriptive documents*
   Draft speeches, church magazines, confessions of faith (Miller)
6. *Studies of customs and folklore and other academic works; textbooks, works of sociology and so on*
   Academic and other publications, profile in *New Society* 1968 (Clegg)
7. *Guides, handbooks, directories and other works of reference*
   Maps, Local Town Directories (Miller)
8. *Media of communication and artefacts of popular culture*
   Photos (both), cartoons (Clegg), DVD interview (Clegg)
9. *Archaeology, industrial archaeology, history on the ground and physical artefacts*
   Visits to old school (Clegg), old houses and chapels (Miller)
10. *Literary and artistic sources*
    Films and novels about coalmining or industrial relations *produced in the period* (set in the period is not the same)
11. *Processed sources*
    Quantitative data (didn't use)
12. *"Oral history" and oral traditions*
    Interviews with family and colleagues, emails and letters (both)
13. *Observed behaviour, surviving customs, technical processes*
    Visiting a coalmine, attending a religious service (Miller)

THE SORT OF EVIDENCE HISTORIANS USE AND HOW TO APPROACH IT

This raises some broader questions about the nature of historical evidence. In the first place, historians mainly *discover evidence* rather than create data – though there are exceptions, such as oral history. In crude terms, whatever is left lying around from the past, you pick up! Academic history is a jig-saw with most of the pieces either lost or scattered around the house. Second, and for these same reasons, historical research is *multi-method and opportunistic*. You can't write good history without sources, and rich personal papers or a company or trade union archive lays the basis for a historical project. For my PhD research on Miller, church records at the Selly Oak Colleges Archives (now Birmingham University), union records at Lancashire County Records and family papers and interviews provided these essential sources. With my recent Clegg research, his published work, family papers, interviews with family and colleagues and *archives*, such as Kingswood School (Bath), Oxford University Press, the National Archive, the Mass Observation Archive and the Modern Records Centre, have produced a great plenitude of material.

Often, the problem is where to start and when to stop. You can get buried in too much material; and, however thin or thick the potential sources every historical project requires a *research strategy* (Marwick, 2001, p. 163). While historians rarely engage in simple hypothesis testing – the real world is too complex – you still need *research questions* grounded in the secondary literature and the issues you want to address arising from that. In this sense, the historical approach is little different from that found in the rest of the qualitative social sciences. Yet historians do need to understand *the nature of the primary material* they are handling. Certain types of evidence are much stronger than others for a particular topic, as Marwick (2001, pp. 172–85) points out in "Witting and unwitting testimony" and "Catechism for the analysis, evaluation and use of primary sources". The authenticity of sources and accurate dating also matters, as scandals like the faked "Hitler Diaries" demonstrate. So too does chronology or "what happened first" when we are making claims about historical causation. For instance, the British Labour politician, Anthony Crosland was widely regarded as a major influence on Clegg's writing on industrial democracy but I have demonstrated that Clegg published some of his ideas before Crosland's key work (Ackers, 2007).

DISTINCTIVE FEATURES OF THE *HISTORICAL* APPROACH TO STUDYING SOCIETY

History draws on and is divided by all the major social science theories, including Marxism, political pluralism, post-modernism, neo-classical economics and so on (see Burke, 1992). Yet, at the same time, "history is an autonomous discipline with its own specialised methods" (Marwick, 2001, p. 17). And this distinctive historical perspective cuts across the customary ideological boundaries in the sense that even a post-modernist or Marxist historian isn't quite the same creature as a post-modernist or Marxist sociologist. History, as an academic discipline, has developed its own modus operandi and range of debates. Social and economic historians pioneered the application of social science theories of capitalism and class to history, but as E.P. Thompson (1976, p. 387; see also Thompson, 1968 [2013]) once commented:

> Sociologists complain, at times, that social historians are insufficiently self-conscious as to their own conceptualization, and that they tend to offer their findings as particular findings, relevant only to their particular context, and are excessively cautious in making extended generalization. And social historians, of course, offer exactly the converse criticism: they sometimes find that sociologists are over-anxious to derive from particular evidence generalizations and typologies which are then translated to inappropriate contexts.

And there are certain shared historical concepts, theories and debates that are distinctive to the historical approach. Here are five of the best known:

1. *Anachronism* is the cardinal historical sin. This means applying ways of thinking and behaving to the past that wouldn't have made sense to actors at that time. Here the test is: does your argument reflect how people thought and felt at that time and place and what was possible then? Historians' favourite literary quote is: "The past is a foreign country; they do things differently there" (L.P. Hartley, *The Go-Between*, 1953). This is similar to the sociologist's call for cultural sensitivity, but perhaps more absolute, since the past is further removed from us than other contemporary societies in our globalised, joined-up world.

2. *Contemporary history* is the study of the very recent past, of times that overlap with those that we are still living in. This begs the question, when can we begin to write history, or when do we have enough distance or perspective? In brief, when does the Past become History? Many historians operate as a rule-of-thumb with the idea of *a generation* that has passed, or about 20 years. Nearer than that lies the province of politics and sociology. In my own case, I often think of *modern history* as ending roughly when my adult life began, around 1979, the year I finished my first degree, but also conveniently the year Mrs Thatcher came to power. Some prefer still greater distance and often Indian historians have restricted themselves to the periods before independence in 1947 – nearly 70 years ago (see Sarkar, 1997). There is no simple answer to the question of when history begins; rather there is an interesting debate about the benefits and problems of personal contact with the past. In short, does "having been there" provide insight or merely bias (see Ackers, 2014b; Hobsbawm, 1994)?

3. *Counterfactual history* asks whether historical events could have turned out differently and can we isolate a key cause at a certain point in time (see Ferguson, 2011)? So "what if" Mrs Thatcher had not become the leader of the Conservative Party in 1975, after the defeat of Edward Heath at the hand of the unions, or Prime Minister in 1979, following the "Winter of Discontent" strikes that brought down a Labour Government? This question is central to my own research. To extend the scenario, would British HRM have developed in the way it has since then if our trade unions had reached an accommodation with the state in the 1970s and the "social democratic consensus" had continued into the 1980s – as in many other north European countries?

    The obvious danger here is anachronism. Are we asking "what if" about things that were not considered realistic possibilities at the time, such as Britain having the tidy German union structure? There were many failed attempts at neo-corporatist arrangements between the British state, employers and trade unions in the 1960s and 1970s, so perhaps we can regard these as a "suppressed historical alternative" (Fox, 1985) that might have happened with, say, more astute trade union leadership (see Ackers, 2014c). This sort of controversy relates to the familiar social science debate about the balance between structure and action in social processes and the relative importance of short-term versus long-term causes. In the words of Karl Marx (1852 [2004], p. 85):

    > Men make their own history, but not of their own free will; not under circumstances they themselves have chosen but under the given and inherited circumstances with which they are directly confronted. The traditions of the dead generations weigh like a nightmare on the minds of the living.

4. *Periodisation* is a central device of historians. In order to make sense of the past, historians have to order it, above all chronologically. Traditionally, general histories are often organised by centuries or decades, but since social processes don't correspond to such arbitrary time categories, this is always problematic; and it raises the question: when were the key *turning points* in historical development? Thus, Hobsbawm's (1994) great European history speaks of the "long nineteenth century" because he wants to track development from the 1789 French Revolution to the 1914 outbreak of the Great War; and the "short twentieth century" because there is a sociological and political unity to the period between the Russian Revolution and the collapse of Communism in 1989. Marwick (2001, p. 9) describes

periodisation as "simply an analytical device", but often where these lines are drawn is a major source of ideological and theoretical debate. For example, were British employers always closet neo-liberals and Mrs Thatcher inevitable? In which case, while 1979 was a political turning point, it was less profound in socio-economic terms. Or was perhaps the real industrial relations turning point 1985, when the defeat of the miners marked the end of union power?

5. *Teleology* is the claim that history has some clear, immanent sense of direction, which can be discerned by scholars or political activists. The idea that history has some moral purpose or "direction" originates in Christian ideas of God working out his plan on earth. However, there are many secular variations on what Karl Popper (1957 [2002]) dubbed "historicism", all claiming some sense of historical human *progress*, towards communism (Marx and Engels, *The Communist Manifesto*, 1848) or liberal democracy (Francis Fukuyama, *The End of History*, 1989). This is an old but tenacious heresy described, in one moderate, liberal version, by Herbert Butterfield (1931 [1973]) as "The Whig Interpretation of History". All historians look back on the past from their own times and, thus, are in danger of highlighting those developments that they approve of and apparently lead towards where they now stand. The danger with teleology is not only that we make fanciful predictions about the future, but also that we impose an anachronistic pattern on the past. Historians with strong "presentist" ideologies are most prone to this error. Marxist historicism has died a death, but not the nationalist version, while *progressive* liberal "identity history" is alive and kicking. The danger, once more, is that we search the past selectively to create narratives that support our chosen normative teleology.

ADDING SOME HISTORICAL DIMENSIONS TO A CONTEMPORARY SOCIAL SCIENCE PROJECT

There is no brick wall separating history from the social sciences. As we have seen, there are many overlapping approaches and issues, as well as some distinctive angles on HRM research. When sociologists speak of "longitudinal research", tracking social processes across time, they are moving onto the historical terrain. And historians of the post-war period often draw on classic social science studies of the time to grasp what it was like to live then – as with Goldthorpe et al.'s (1968) *The Affluent Worker* studies of 1960s Vauxhall car workers. So, yes, as I have demonstrated in my own work on partnership and voice, if you want to track developments over time, as well as comparisons between or within organisations, a historical angle may add something extra to a conventional piece of contemporary social science research.

All this said, it is important to remember that history is an academic *discipline*, with its own long explorations in theory and methodology, but also *a craft*. To research and write good history you need to read history (from all periods) and immerse yourself in it. Methods articles like this can hope to point you in the right direction, but history is best understood as a practice, best uncovered through important historical studies.

SOME PERSONAL HISTORY: BEING A HISTORIAN IN THE BROAD FIELD OF HRM

Historical methods are outside the mainstream of HRM, but perhaps the best way to make a case for doing historical research in this business school field is to demonstrate that an academic research career can be built on this basis. My own published research over nearly 30 years illustrates the scope for taking a historical perspective on industrial relations (IR) and HRM and the range of journals this can be published in. I completed my Warwick MA in IR in 1981, just as dramatic changes were sweeping through the British world of work. Mrs Thatcher had been elected in 1979 on a neo-liberal programme to reduce trade union power, and thus my subsequent academic career has been devoted to observing and understanding dramatic changes in British IR and personnel management. "Change" has been the central focus and a new language of "employment relations", "HRM" and "employee involvement" has emerged, with IR itself being re-labelled "employment relations". All this naturally drew me into historical debates about *why* change was taking place since this demanded some understanding of *what* we were changing from, and *when* and *how* this change had begun.

In the first place, two HRM studies arose directly from conventional qualitative case study research. My 1988 MPhil thesis, "Changes in workplace industrial relations in West Midlands manufacturing industry in the 1980s", compared two large, long-established companies, one in carpets, the other one in locks. This began as a qualitative sociological case study comparison, using interviews. But with ancient companies and long-service workforces these soon blurred into oral history. Both firms had been paternalist employers located in a specialist industry town, so the theme of "change" necessitated some historical exploration of where the company had come from and how its approach to HRM was changing (see Ackers and Black, 1991).

Next, I joined a large collective study, funded by the British Employment Department, *New Developments in Employee Involvement* (Marchington et al., 1992). In the first phase, there was little historical angle to this contemporary study of 25 case studies, though we did track change at my carpet company. However, when a similar group was funded to study, *Management Choice and Employee Voice* (Marchington et al., 2001), we deliberately included a longitudinal sub-sample of organisations from the original 1992 study (see Ackers et al., 2005).

By the end of the 1980s, it was clear that the "labour movement" I had encountered as a young Marxist, studying politics and philosophy (PPE) at Oxford University in the late 1970s, was ceasing to exist. Following the defeat of the 1984/85 miners' strike, trade unions were in dramatic decline and becoming increasingly marginal organisations in British society; while following the 1989 collapse of Communism, the Labour Party was busy jettisoning redundant socialist ideas. For me this was a personal intellectual crisis, with these developments suggesting that I had not adequately grasped the real history of the British labour movement. To test this, I completed a history PhD in 1993, "Christian brethren, union brother: a study of the relationship between religious nonconformity and trade union leadership, in the life of the coalmining deputies' official, W.T. Miller (1880–1963)". Miller is my great grandad and this study helped me to recover the moderate, constructive mainstream of the British trade unionism and break with the rather lurid Marxist mythology I had imbibed as a young man (see Ackers, 1994).

With this shift in theoretical perspective, away from Marxism and towards Weberian sociology and IR pluralism, I became deeply engaged in the late 1990s British partnership debate, which proposed a moderate trade union strategy of co-operating with progressive management. This was fuelled by both my contemporary employee involvement research with other colleagues and my PhD. A two-year project on *social partnership* with Jonathan Payne extended the coalmining historical evidence into the post-war nationalised industry, "Before the storm" of industrial conflict in the 1970s and 1980s, to explore the roots of co-operation. At the same time, we published on contemporary British partnership, just as this was becoming a major theme of Tony Blair's "New Labour" (see Ackers and Payne, 1998, 2002). Once more I was trying to integrate contemporary public policy research, historical perspectives and theoretical developments.

My current historical project, which began a decade ago, is a biographical study of *Professor Hugh Clegg and the Oxford School of Industrial Relations*. At the start of the new century, I'd begun formulating a "neo-pluralism" that would stand as a theoretical alternative in HRM to the radical (Marxist) "class conflict" thinking of the Left and simplistic managerial or Unitarist "win–win" ideas (see Ackers, 2014a, 2014b). Ackers and Wilkinson (2003), *Understanding Work and Employment*, opened with a historical essay on the development of IR as an academic field. The Clegg project has taken me back before the crucial 1979 "turning point" to consider what historical conditions enabled "the old" IR to emerge, thereby illuminating the pluralist and social democratic ideas of those who first built the employment relations field and exploring the role expected of trade unions and why they failed to fulfil this (Ackers, 2007, 2011a, 2011b, 2014c). Johnstone and Ackers (2015), *Finding a Voice at Work?* has returned to a familiar contemporary HRM theme, with my own essay, "Trade unions as professional associations" (Ackers, 2015) once more linking a proper grasp of the past to an adequate sociological theory and then both to a suggested public policy strategy.

To borrow Eric Hobsbawm's expression, I have lived through "Interesting Times" as far as HRM and employment relations are concerned. Often these have been quite distressing times as once cherished institutions, such as trade unions, have seen rapid decline and bad employers have got away with HRM slogans. But the point of this excursion into my own past is to demonstrate that it is possible to publish historical research on HRM and that whenever there is "change" – which also raises the question of "continuity" – some historical perspective becomes crucial. In short, understanding the past is essential to any serious social science grasp on the present and offers great insight into likely future trends. And for me this search continues (see Ackers and Reid, 2016).

REFERENCES

Ackers, P. (1994), "Colliery Deputies in the British coal industry before nationalization", *International Review of Social History*, **39** (3), 383–414.

Ackers, P. (2007), "Collective bargaining as industrial democracy: Hugh Clegg and the political foundations of British industrial relations pluralism", *British Journal of Industrial Relations*, **45** (1), 77–101.

Ackers, P. (2011a), "The changing systems of British industrial relations, 1954–1979: Hugh Clegg and the Warwick sociological turn", *British Journal of Industrial Relations*, **49** (2), 306–30.

Ackers, P. (2011b), "Finding the future in the past? The social philosophy of Oxford industrial relations pluralism", in K. Townsend and A. Wilkinson (eds), *Research Handbook on the Future of Work and Employment Relations*, Cheltenham, UK and Northampton, MA, USA: Edward Elgar, pp. 45–66.

Ackers, P. (2014a), "Rethinking the employment relationship: a neo-pluralist critique of British industrial relations orthodoxy", *International Journal of Human Resource Management*, **25** (17–18), 2608–25.

Ackers, P. (2014b), "Gramsci at the miners' strike: remembering the 1984–1985 Eurocommunist alternative industrial relations strategy", *Labor History*, **55** (2), 151–72.

Ackers, P. (2014c), "Game changer: Hugh Clegg's role in drafting the 1968 Donovan report and redefining the British industrial relations policy-problem", *Historical Studies in Industrial Relations*, **35**, 63–88.

Ackers, P. (2015), "Trade unions as professional associations", in S. Johnstone and P. Ackers (eds), *Finding a Voice at Work? New Perspectives on Employment Relations*, Oxford: Oxford University Press, pp. 95–126.

Ackers, P. and Black, J. (1991), "Paternalist capitalism: an organisation culture in transition", in M. Cross and G. Payne (eds), *Work and the Enterprise Culture*, London: Falmer/BSA, pp. 30–56.

Ackers, P. and Payne, J. (1998), "British trade unions and social partnership: rhetoric, reality and strategy", *International Journal of Human Resource Management*, **9** (3), June, 529–50.

Ackers, P. and Payne, J. (2002), "Before the storm: the experience of nationalization and the prospects for industrial relations partnership in the British coal industry, 1947–1972 – rethinking the militant narrative", *Social History*, **27** (2), 184–209.

Ackers, P. and Reid, A.J. (2016), *Alternatives to State Socialism in Britain: Other Worlds of Labour in the Twentieth Century*, London: Palgrave (forthcoming).

Ackers, P. and Wilkinson, A.J. (2003), "Introduction: the British industrial relations tradition – formation, breakdown, and salvage", in P. Ackers and A.J. Wilkinson (eds), *Understanding Work and Employment: Industrial Relations in Transition*, Oxford: Oxford University Press, pp. 1–27.

Ackers, P. and Wilkinson, A.J. (2008), "Industrial relations and the social sciences", in P. Blyton, N. Bacon, J. Fiorito and E. Heery (eds), *Sage Handbook of Industrial Relations*, London: Sage, pp. 53–68.

Ackers, P., Marchington, M., Wilkinson, A.J. and Dundon, T. (2005), "Partnership and voice, with or without trade unions: changing UK management approaches to organisational participation", in M. Stuart and M.M. Lucio (eds), *Partnership and Modernisation in Employment Relations*, London: Routledge, pp. 23–45.

Burchall, J. (1994), *Co-op: The Peoples Business*, Manchester: Manchester University Press.

Burke, P. (1992), *History and Social Theory*, Cambridge: Cambridge University Press.

Butterfield, H. (1931), *The Whig Interpretation of History*, London: Penguin, reprinted in 1973.

Carr, E.H. (1961), *What is History?*, 3rd edn reprinted in 2002, London: Palgrave.

Cathcart, A. (2013), "Directing democracy: competing interests and contested terrain in the John Lewis Partnership", *Journal of Industrial Relations*, **55** (4), 601–20.

Drummond, D.K. (1995), *Crewe: Railway Town, Company & People, 1840–1914*, London: Scholar.

Evans, R. (1997), *In Defence of History*, London: Granta.

Ferguson, N. (ed.) (2011), *Virtual History: Alternatives and Counterfactuals*, 2nd edn, London: Basic.

Fox, A. (1985), *History and Heritage: The Social Origins of the British Industrial Relations System*, London: Allen & Unwin.

Geertz, C. (1973), *The Interpretation of Cultures*, New York: Basic Books, reprinted in 2010, London: Fontana.

Hall, P. and Soskice, D. (2001), *Varieties of Capitalism*, Oxford: Oxford University Press.

Hobsbawm, E.J. (1994), *The Age of Extremes: The Short Twentieth Century, 1914–1991*, London: Weidenfield & Nicolson.

Hobsbawm, E.J. (1997), *On History*, London: Weidenfield & Nicolson.

Jacoby, S.M. (1997), *Modern Manors: Welfare Capitalism since the New Deal*, Princeton, NJ: Princeton University Press.

Kimberley, J. (2016), "Edward Cadbury: an egalitarian employer and supporter of working women's campaigns", in P. Ackers and A.J. Reid (eds), *Alternatives to State Socialism in Britain: Other Worlds of Labour in the Twentieth Century*, London: Palgrave (forthcoming).

Legge, K. (2004), *HRM: Rhetorics and Realities*, London: Palgrave.

Marchington, M., Goodman, J., Wilkinson, A.J. and Ackers, P. (1992), *New Developments in Employee Involvement*, Research Series No. 2, London: Employment Department.

Marchington, M., Wilkinson, A.J., Ackers, P. and Dundon, T. (2001), *Management Choice and Employee Voice*, London: Chartered Institute of Personnel and Development.

Marwick, A. (2001), *The New Nature of History: Knowledge, Evidence, Language*, London: Palgrave.

Marx, K. (1852), "The Eighteenth Brumaire of Louis Bonaparte", in K. Marx and F. Engels (2004), *The Communist Manifesto*, London: Penguin Books – Great Ideas, p. 85.

Patmore, G. (1998), "Digging up the past: historical methods in industrial relations research", in K. Whitfield and G. Strauss (eds), *Researching the World of Work*, Ithaca, NY: ILR Press, pp. 213–26.

Patmore, G. (2010), "Australia", in J. Allen, A. Campbell and J. McIlroy (eds), *Histories of Labour*, London: Merlin, pp. 231–55.

Popper, K. (1957), *The Poverty of Historicism*, reprinted in 2002, London: Routledge.

Sarkar, S. (1997), *Writing Social History*, New Delhi: Oxford University Press.

Seifert, R. and Sibley, T. (2012), *Revolutionary Communist at Work: A Political Biography of Bert Ramelson*, London: Lawrence and Wishart.

Smith, C., Child, J. and Rowlinson, M. (1990), *Reshaping Work: The Cadbury Experience*, Cambridge: Cambridge University Press.

Thompson, E.P. (1968), *The Making of the English Working Class*, London: Pelican, reprinted in 2013, London: Penguin Modern Classics.

Thompson, E.P. (1976), "On history, sociology and historical relevance", *British Journal of Sociology*, **27** (3), September, 381–402.

Weber, M. (1905), *The Protestant Ethic and the Spirit of Capitalism*, reprinted in 1976, London: Allen & Unwin.

Yeo, E. (2004), "Working class masculinities in Britain, 1850 to the present", Special Edition, *Labour History Review*, **69** (2), August.

9 Thinking about philosophical methods in human resources

Kerrie L. Unsworth and Matthew T. Hardin

INTRODUCTION

Much has been said about the lack of new or surprising theory in the management sciences (see, for example, Cornelissen and Durand, 2014) and the situation may be even more dire in the field of human resource management (HRM). Although our work in this field is not lacking a theoretical basis, a great deal of it has come from simply applying theories from other disciplines to our own (for example, translating the resource-based view of the firm from strategic management). Developing theories in HRM could improve the field and give new insights in how best to apply it but how does one create new and exciting theory? A special issue in the *Academy of Management Review* in 2011 identified a number of tools (for example, Alvesson and Sandberg, 2011; Corley and Gioia, 2011; Okhuysen and Bonardi, 2011; Suddaby et al., 2011), but at the heart of this problem is the need to engage in theorising for theorising's sake. In other words, we need philosophy. In this chapter, we outline the philosophical method, explain some specific techniques and apply them to HRM. By doing so, we hope that others can see the benefits and usefulness of philosophical methods in HRM.

A great deal of HRM knowledge is based on empirical research; and the preference for empiricism over theorising alone is apparent in what is published in the key HRM journals. There is nothing wrong with this approach, however, we suggest that conceptual methods and "armchair research" are valid and illuminating in and of themselves; they can be used to broaden our understanding of the world of HRM. In this chapter we describe and show how the methods of the discipline of philosophy can be used to gain understanding. Given that "the aim of philosophy, abstractly formulated, is to understand how things, in the broadest possible sense of the term, hang together, in the broadest possible sense of the term" (Sellars, 1962 [1963], p. 35), this seems like an appropriate avenue for HRM at this stage in the discipline's development.

Table 9.1   Philosophical methods, example references and HRM examples

Method	Reference	Example in HRM
Conceptual analysis – constituents in argument	Dachler and Enderle (1989)	"Human" "Resources"
Conceptual analysis – logical analysis	Russell (1986)	Employees are resources
Conceptual analysis – connective mapping	Banicki (2012)	Concept mapping of HRM journal articles
Conceptual analysis – searching for "truth"	Audi (1983)	Examining managers' meaning of "efficiency"
Dialectic inquiry and dialogue	Hegel, cited in Russell (1945)	Point/counterpoint in journals
Doubt about accepted belief	Descartes, cited in Newman (2014)	High levels of employee identification are a good thing
Phenomenological reduction	Husserl, cited in Beyer (2013)	How is identification experienced?
Thought experiments	Brown and Fehige (2014)	What if we lived in a world without pay?

THE PHILOSOPHICAL METHOD

So what are philosophical methods? As Plato said in Theaetetus 155d, "philosophy begins in wonder", so is it simply sitting in an armchair and pondering the world of work? While "thinking" is certainly the major component of any philosophical method, there are a number of different types and means of approaching this thinking. There is an entire stream of literature that discusses the history of philosophical method and argues both the meaning of the methods and their appropriateness and effectiveness (see, for example, Margolis and Laurence, 2014). We shall not discuss these finer points but instead discuss the methods themselves before outlining our experiences in using these methods (Table 9.1).

CONCEPTUAL ANALYSIS

Concepts are "the constituents of thoughts" (Margolis and Laurence, 2014) and conceptual analysis is using these concepts in different ways to get at a deeper level of meaning. At a very basic level, conceptual analysis is simply concerned with the meaning of a particular concept in the general population (or linguistic community) (Sytsma, 2010). Dachler and Enderle (1989) examine this within the context of HRM by analysing the term "resources":

> First of all, if humans are resources in the same sense as we understand material resources, then there must be somebody that uses, that buys and sells these resources. Clearly, the term human resource makes sense in its wide use, because it is an euphemism for identifying those people who are used as resources as contrasted to people who use the resources. This implied meaning, however, is usually ignored at the explicit level. The human resources of an organization embraces all members and stakeholders in general, be they "workers", managers, owners or suppliers and clients. It is worth asking how meaningful an implicit distinction is between people as resources and people as users of human resources. (p. 598)

A lot of conceptual analysis is also conducted via reductionism – breaking something complex down into its constituent elements (Strawson, 1992) and logically, often mathematically, determining their relationship (Anderson, 1993). Bertrand Russell is perhaps the most well-known logical analyst, coining the term logical atomism. An example of his work is described by Irvine (2014):

> Statements such as "There are at least two books" would be recast as statements such as "There is a book, x, and there is a book, y, and x is not identical to y." Statements such as "There are exactly two books" would be recast as "There is a book, x, and there is a book, y, and x is not identical to y, and if there is a book, z, then z is identical to either x or y."

In the context of HRM, one could investigate the logics of the concept that "employees are resources"; for example, does this mean that "all employees are resources" as implied and, if so, are they all equal in resource value or not? Many of the assumptions within HRM could be more explicitly and more aggressively analysed through this logical approach.

Third, connective conceptual analysis is a holistic map used to describe a system or a language (Wittgenstein, 2009). Banicki (2012) shows how it can be used in psychology to provide an understanding of the "grammar" of psychological constructs and languages. By making these "grammatical rules" explicit, the researcher is made aware of the fundamental assumptions of the field in question as well as being able to see connections to other fields. Within HRM, the work by Dachler and Enderle (1989) exemplifies this approach as they identify the implicit assumptions that we hold as researchers and practitioners. Alternatively, an interesting study would be to cognitively map the existing HRM research to identify assumptions and "grammar".

The final type of conceptual analysis that we consider here is the acknowledgement that "truth" often depends upon the viewpoint one takes. Critical HRM has often been concerned with the concept of "truth" and acknowledging the different truths that are held by different stakeholders (for example, Ferrary, 2009). Audi (1983) describes an application for conceptual analysis based on searching for "truth" that is very applicable to our discussion of HR and philosophy. He considers the meaning or "truth" of the concept of efficiency and safety as determined by managers; there will be obvious and differing repercussions if injuries are seen as symbolic of inefficiency (that is, that managers' meaning of a highly efficient system is one that has low injuries) compared to if efficiency is seen to mean low cost whereby injuries are only viewed as low efficiency if they cost the organisation money.

DIALECTIC INQUIRY AND DIALOGUE

A related form of philosophical methodology to conceptual analysis is that of the dialectic or dialectic inquiry. At its core, this is concerned with arguing for competing ideas and/or perspectives. The German philosopher Hegel is perhaps most associated with this method. In this method, a person comes up with a thesis, determines an anti-thesis or competing statement, idea or perspective, then works to resolve and reconcile the two until truth is arrived at (Russell, 1945).

Within the realm of HRM, dialectic appears to occur most often across people – dialogues where points and counterpoints are published. To us, the best example of where this has led to greater understanding is the dialogue between Latham, Locke and Erez regarding the role of participation in setting goals (Latham, 1992). What started as contradictory results being published and a frustrating dispute ended up with a co-authored study examining the conditions under which both original sets of authors were "right" (Latham et al., 1988).

DOUBT ABOUT ACCEPTED BELIEF

René Descartes is the key proponent of the method of doubt. He says of this method:

> Throughout my writings I have made it clear that my method imitates that of the architect. When an architect wants to build a house which is stable on ground where there is a sandy topsoil over underlying rock, or clay, or some

other firm base, he begins by digging out a set of trenches from which he removes the sand, and anything resting on or mixed in with the sand, so that he can lay his foundations on firm soil. In the same way, I began by taking everything that was doubtful and throwing it out, like sand . . . (Replies 7, AT 7, p. 537)

The key premise in this methodological approach is to not accept anything as knowledge unless it is indubitable. Every other belief, defined as an attitude we have when we accept something to be true (Schwitzgebel, 2014), can and should be questioned.

Within HRM, an example of this is the concept of who is defined as a stakeholder. Starik (1995) questions the commonly held belief that stakeholders need to be a "who" and instead suggests that they could be a "what"; he proposes that the natural environment should be a stakeholder in decisions around strategic HRM. An alternative example is that of Dale (2012) who questioned the role of employees as consumers; she identified the commodification of employees as they try to sell themselves to potential employers and highlighted the implications of this. One issue we personally have considered and started investigating is the degree to which organisational commitment and organisational identification is always a good thing; although it is often seen as positive for both the individual and the organisation (for example, Miscenko and Day, 2015), it could potentially lead to overinvolvement, workaholism, decreased creativity and ultimately decreased productivity.

PHENOMENOLOGICAL REDUCTION

Phenomenology is concerned primarily with how things (phenomena) are perceived in one's consciousness (Giorgi, 1997). Based predominantly on work by Husserl (Beyer, 2013), phenomenological reduction goes one step further by isolating the phenomenon and removing any references to "the real world" (Schmitt, 1959). In other words, we are interested in how something is experienced, not whether it exists in the real world or not. Perhaps the most well-known example of this in the world of work is Studs Terkel's book, *Working* (Terkel, 1974). In exploring how people view their lives at work, separate from any attempted "objectivity" of what it is "truly" like, Terkel is engaged in phenomenological reduction. Again, work that we are personally involved with is around what it feels like to be committed and fully identified with your organisation: is it an all-or-none phenomenon where a person always feels identification with his or her organisation or does it go through waves? Do you lose a part of yourself or does organisational identification simply "add on" to the identity you already have?

THOUGHT EXPERIMENTS

Finally, we come to perhaps one of the most well-known philosophical methods, thought experiments. Thought experiments are imaginary situations where a theory is applied. In essence, rather than testing hypotheses with visible phenomena, you are using your imagination to test the theory (Brown and Fehige, 2014). Thought experiments are used extensively not only in philosophy but in other disciplines such as maths, physics, economics and history. For example, one thought experiment was described by Lucretius. He asked people to consider the edge of the universe; if you were to throw a spear at this point then it would either bounce back (if the edge were like a wall) or it would disappear. Both of these options imply something "beyond" (either the wall or some other space beyond the end), so any edge to the universe is illusory and space is therefore infinite.

This example illustrates the purpose of a thought experiment, namely, the ability to understand something that cannot be done in actuality. Popper (1959) distinguishes between three different types of thought experiments – those that illustrate theories, those that criticise theories and those that support theories. An alternative typology differentiates between constructive and destructive thought experiments (Brown and Fehige, 2014).

Combining these typologies, we therefore find three different types of thought experiment. The first is one that is designed to illustrate situations or questions that no theory currently exists to explain. Lucretius's thought experiment about the edge of the universe exemplifies this type. The second type of thought experiment is the constructive (Brown and Fehige, 2014) or apologetic (Popper, 1959) type. Borsboom et al. (2002) cite the silicon-brain thought experiment as an example of the constructive type. In this thought experiment, you are asked to consider what would happen if all the neurons in your brain were gradually replaced by silicon computer chips one by one; you find that you would still be conscious after each one providing support for causal functionalism (Pylyshyn, 1980). As noted by Brown and Fehige (2014), the final type of thought experiment, the destructive type, can be further divided into:

1. Contradicting theory – for example, Galileo's falling bodies thought experiment wherein we imagine a heavy ball and a light ball connected to each other by a string; if the Aristotelian theory that heavy objects drop more quickly than light objects is correct, then the heavy ball should fall faster, but the system of balls and string in totality is heavier, so the heavy ball should fall slower; this inherent contradiction shows that the theory must be incorrect.

2. Showing how the theory is in conflict with other beliefs we have – for example, Schrodinger's cat thought experiment whereby a cat in a steel box with a vial of poison on a hair-trigger could be alive if the trigger has not been initiated or dead if the trigger has been initiated; when the likelihood of the trigger activating is 50:50, then we don't know whether the cat is alive or dead until we look into the box; thus, from the outside, we must assume that the cat is both alive and dead (which our intuitions tell us is impossible).

3. Undermining the central premise of the theory – for example, Thomson's (1971) thought experiment of a well-loved violinist who fell into a coma; his music fans realised that you were the only person with the appropriate blood-type and therefore kidnapped you and attached you to the unconscious violinist; the innocent violinist needs to be attached to you for nine months or he will die; and you must decide whether you will stay attached to this violinist for this time or whether you remove him. This is a thought experiment exploring the central premise of the anti-abortion argument that it is always morally reprehensible to abort an "innocent" life and suggests that there are times when it may be morally acceptable to abort.

In the context of HRM, one interesting thought experiment might be to examine a world where nobody gets paid. What would this world look like? How would anything get done? If trade and payment were banned, would something else fill that void? This is an example of the first type of thought experiment – one that describes a situation for which no theory currently exists – and demonstrates how interesting such theorising can be.

OUR EXPERIENCE OF USING THIS METHOD

Personally, we have used philosophical methods in HRM in a variety of instances. Like almost all HRM scholars, we have thought about the ramifications of various HRM factors on productivity, well-being and other outcomes. We, like all scholars, have considered aspects of the concepts as we developed our hypotheses. However, in this section we want to highlight the use of philosophical methods in and of themselves – outside the usual hypothetico-deductive paradigm. Before we discuss two particular instances, we note the following. In using these philosophical methods, we have found that we were not able to clearly distinguish between the types of methods during the process. For example, we have used doubts about accepted beliefs in creating a thought experiment; and have used logic when considering question formulation. We have found that each of the methods blends into the others and while this is certainly not a criticism of the approach, it is something to note for those wishing to follow in this endeavour. Below, therefore, we outline two examples of how we have used (and are currently using) a range of integrated philosophical methods in HRM.

For our first example, we take the concept of "creativity". It is commonly accepted, and one of us has even stated this in numerous publications, that creativity in the workplace is a necessary and positive thing (Unsworth and Parker, 2003). Indeed, a raft of research has been built identifying factors that can increase creativity among employees[1] (Axtell et al., 2000; Clegg et al., 2002; Unsworth and Clegg, 2010; Unsworth et al., 2005) and innovation at the organisational level (Sawang and Unsworth, 2006; Unsworth et al., 2012). However, is this really the case? Just as our field has considered resistance as separate to consent (see Townsend and Richards, 2011), is creativity actually separate to deviance? We can apply some conceptual analysis and thought experiments to probe this accepted belief and explore the extent to which an organisation (in its various guises) really benefits from creativity.

Consider a situation where one employee in a firm is highly creative. This person generates a lot of new ideas and implements a number of those ideas. While not all of this person's ideas are successful (the inherent risk in creativity), they are generally aimed at improving performance. If the ideas fit within the constraints of the person's job (that is, they are still able to do their "day job"), the manager's key performance indicators and the organisation's goals, and do not affect other employees in a negative way, then it is likely that the person and the organisation will reap rewards from increasing creativity. However, that list contains a lot of constraints and boundary conditions – and that is for only one employee. Let's take a look at another employee who is being creative. This person also generates and implements a lot of ideas, but they are not focused on performance. Instead, this person is highly creative at embezzling money – this is still creativity as it is novel and useful, and is still enhanced by all the factors that our current research examines, but it has very different implications for the organisation. Let's take the thought experiment one step further and consider a situation where not one, but every employee is highly creative (a situation that can be present in high technology start-ups, research-based organisations and the arts). Now you have a situation where nothing is stable, where procedures and products are being constantly changed, where it becomes difficult to know who or what is doing anything. In short, chaos reigns.

So, what can we learn from this theorising. First, we recognise that the meaning of creativity, and in particular the meaning of "useful" in the definition of creativity (Amabile, 1996), is in the eye of the beholder. Thus, defining creativity depends on whether you are a manager, an employee who is focused on helping the organisation, an employee who is focused on helping him or herself, a customer and so on. What emerges from this is the realisation that the perceiver of the idea will impose his or her meaning of creativity onto the idea – taking this in another direction, if a person believes that something must be proactive to be considered creative, then his or her perception of radicalness and creative performance will be different depending on whether the idea was initiated internally or externally (see Unsworth and Luksyte, 2015). The flip side is that he or she will also impose his or her perception of the creator, such that women will be seen as less creative than men because they do not fit the stereotype of a "creative person" (for example, Luksyte et al., 2012). Second, we realise that the consequences of creativity are not universally positive but instead depend on a range of factors that cover the intentions of the creator, the interconnectedness and characteristics of the system in which the idea is being implemented, the resources and characteristics of the organisation and so forth.

Another area where we are currently using philosophical methods to explore HRM is in the field of training and learning. We used the universal laws of thermodynamics and some of their off-shoot principles to derive a thought experiment. Below, we describe the laws and principles before taking you through the HRM thought experiment.

The first law of thermodynamics states that the total energy of a system must stay constant; it can change its form (for example, from heat to kinetic energy and thus mechanical "work") but it cannot increase or decrease within that system. On top of this, the second law of thermodynamics states that the entropy (which can be loosely interpreted as the degree of disorder) of a closed system will always stay the same or increase; this then means that energy will always flow from higher concentrations to lower concentrations. Combining the two laws shows that it is during this flow from high to low concentrations that the system will perform "work" as the energy changes form. However, if you want it to go the other way and move from low to high concentrations, then you need to add additional energy to the system. For example, a hot object will always naturally turn cold and you can use this process to heat up the air around the object (this is the work done by the system); if you want that object that is now cold to become hot again, then you must add energy to the system.

So, from these two laws, you can build a machine that: (1) heats a gas; (2) this hot gas then is cooled down and as it does so the thermal energy is transformed into work; (3) the gas is then cool; and (4) must be heated back up again before it can perform more work. This is a basic machine.

There are two big problems, however, that physicists and chemical engineers have discovered. The first is that concentrations can become so low and so "spread out" that they leak out of the system and it is not possible to have a fully 100 per cent efficient system. In fact, there is a formula, developed by Carnot, that measures the ideal machine; a formula that lets you identify just how efficient your machine could be, even if you were to eliminate all other energy dissipation sources such as friction.

The second problem is that there must be a temperature differential between the heating and the cooling in order for the system to cool down and to create work. You create this differential either by heating up the initial temperature or by cooling down the final temperature. Interestingly, Carnot discovered that you get the best results by putting proportionally more energy into cooling the final temperature rather than into heating the initial temperature.

Now, we take this brief foray into thermodynamics and use it to construct a thought experiment around learning in the workplace. We first consider the person and his or her knowledge to be the gas that is going through the system (and the system is the person's world of work including any training situations). Let us imagine this person, Patrick, attending a form of training. The training and the new information are the heat that is put into the system – this is usually done externally to Patrick at a cost to the organisation (through hiring a trainer, taking Patrick off his usual job and/or using energy provided by Patrick's colleagues as they provide explanations and help). Work is then performed (cognitively) as this new information is absorbed by Patrick and learned. The cooling process occurs when Patrick goes back to his everyday work tasks and, if the cognitive work was sufficient, transfers his training.

So far, so good. The analogy holds for our thought experiment and we can create an imaginary learning machine based on thermodynamic principles. But these philosophical methods are only important if they help us push our understanding further. We here describe four principles that we have identified by working with this thought experiment.

The first principle is that you will never get full transfer of knowledge; there will always be "leaks" in the learning and transition process. While the literature bemoans the low rates of training transfer (for example, Blume et al., 2010; Burke and Hutchins, 2007), and we recognise that these are incredibly low, we propose that there will be a theoretical limit to the amount of learning and training that can actually be performed and transferred. In factories and complex machinery, it is not uncommon to have a maximum theoretical efficiency of 75 per cent. Given that human beings are incredibly complex, it could be that our maximal learning efficiency in the workplace is of the same magnitude.

This leads us to our second point. The Carnot equation provides us with a way of working out exactly what the maximum efficiency is, given the temperatures at the heating and cooling ends of the system. We are not able to do it yet, but if at some point in the future a HRM scholar was able to measure "new information" and "old/absorbed information", then we would be able to pinpoint what the maximal learning efficiency was.

We also know from the Carnot cycle that you must cool something down before you can heat it back up again – otherwise the temperature stays the same and work is not done. Thus, a person needs to get back to thinking about their "day job" and their "old" knowledge before they can learn anything more. This is already known by many practitioners who build reflections and discussions about how this fits into people's experiences in their training sessions. However, it is less well recognised in informal learning situations and something that could bear further consideration.

Finally, and what we feel is most interesting, is Carnot's finding that you get the best results from focusing on cooling down the cool temperature rather than heating up the hot temperature. In HRM we tend to focus on how we present the new information and what new information is presented. Instead, this thought experiment leads us to consider whether we would be better placed ensuring that people know their "old" knowledge as much as possible. It's not difficult to see why this might be the case with learning – without clearly knowing what you are doing currently and why it becomes almost impossible to integrate any new information as there is nothing tangible to link it to. Thus, perhaps training should always begin by getting people to clarify, in their own heads, what they currently do.

DISCUSSION

In this chapter we have covered a range of philosophical methods and described some uses within HRM. Overall, we believe that philosophical methods provide a nice counterpart to both qualitative and quantitative research methods. Of course, there are some disadvantages to the method. The most obvious is the need that many of us have to "prove" theories with data and philosophical methods are not based on the kind of data that we (and the journals we publish in) are used to.

On the other hand, as we see it, there are two important advantages to such methods. First, and perhaps a little cynically, you do not need access to participants. It is becoming more and more difficult to gain access to working employees, particularly for in-depth qualitative research. Philosophical methods are based on the investigator's knowledge of the workplace and of the theories and so overcome this problem. Second, we are able to get a new perspective on issues that are easy to become blinded to; precisely because we have such a deep personal knowledge of the workplace we can forget to "wonder" but instead simply accept our standard view.

Philosophical methods allow us to be reflexive in our research and, we believe, hold us to a higher standard of examining what we do, not just what we are studying. Whether one uses conceptual analysis, thought experiments or simply starts doubting the accepted beliefs, philosophical methods can make us look at the world of work in a different manner; as such, it will surely lead us to some new and interesting places.

NOTE

1.   We cite our own work here to cry *mea culpa* and highlight the role that one of us has played in continuing this one-sided focus.

ANNOTATED FURTHER READING

Cornelissen, J.P. and Durand, R. (2014), "Moving forward: developing theoretical contributions in management studies", *Journal of Management Studies*, **51** (6), 995–1022.
This paper highlights the need for "better" theories in management and many of the arguments apply to HRM as well. The authors suggest a number of techniques they have found useful.
Dachler, H.P. and Enderle, G. (1989), "Epistemological and ethical considerations in conceptualizing and implementing human resource management", *Journal of Business Ethics*, **8** (8), 597–606, doi: 10.1007/bf00383028.
This is a great example of how philosophical methods can be used in HRM to create greater understanding.

REFERENCES

Alvesson, M. and Sandberg, J. (2011), "Generating research questions through problematization", *Academy of Management Review*, **36** (2), 247–71.
Amabile, T.M. (1996), *Creativity in Context*, Boulder, CO: Westview Press.
Anderson, C.A. (1993), "Analyzing analysis", *Philosophical Studies*, **72** (2–3), 199–222.
Audi, R. (1983), "The applications of conceptual analysis", *Metaphilosophy*, **14** (2), 87–106.
Axtell, C., Holman, D., Unsworth, K., Wall, T., Waterson, P. and Harrington, E. (2000), "Shopfloor innovation: facilitating the suggestion and implementation of ideas", *Journal of Occupational and Organizational Psychology*, **73** (3), 265–86.
Banicki, K. (2012), "Connective conceptual analysis and psychology", *Theory and Psychology*, **22** (3), 310–23.
Beyer, C. (2013), "Edmund Husserl", in E.N. Zalta (ed.), *The Stanford Encyclopedia of Philosophy*, Winter edn, Palo Alto, CA: Stanford University Press.

Blume, B.D., Ford, J.K., Baldwin, T.T. and Huang, J.L. (2010), "Transfer of training: a meta-analytic review", *Journal of Management*, **36** (4), 1065–105.

Borsboom, D., Mellenbergh, G.J. and Van Heerden, J. (2002), "Functional thought experiments", *Synthese*, **130** (3), 379–87.

Brown, J.R. and Fehige, Y. (2014), "Thought experiments", in E.N. Zalta (ed.), *The Stanford Encyclopedia of Philosophy*, Fall edn, Palo Alto, CA: Stanford University Press, available at http://plato.stanford.edu/archives/fall2014/entries/thought-experiment/ (accessed 28 November 2014).

Burke, L.A. and Hutchins, H.M. (2007), "Training transfer: an integrative literature review", *Human Resource Development Review*, **6** (3), 263–96.

Clegg, C., Unsworth, K., Epitropaki, O. and Parker, G. (2002), "Implicating trust in the innovation process", *Journal of Occupational and Organizational Psychology*, **75** (4), 409–22.

Corley, K.G. and Gioia, D.A. (2011), "Building theory about theory building: what constitutes a theoretical contribution?", *Academy of Management Review*, **36** (1), 12–32.

Cornelissen, J.P. and Durand, R. (2014), "Moving forward: developing theoretical contributions in management studies", *Journal of Management Studies*, **51** (6), 995–1022.

Dachler, H.P. and Enderle, G. (1989), "Epistemological and ethical considerations in conceptualizing and implementing human resource management", *Journal of Business Ethics*, **8** (8), 597–606, doi: 10.1007/bf00383028.

Dale, K. (2012), "The employee as 'dish of the day': the ethics of the consuming/consumed self in human resource management", *Journal of Business Ethics*, **111** (1), 13–24, doi: 10.1007/s10551-012-1437-9.

Ferrary, M. (2009), "A stakeholder's perspective on human resource management", *Journal of Business Ethics*, **87** (1), 31–43, doi: 10.1007/s10551-008-9868-z.

Giorgi, A. (1997), "The theory, practice, and evaluation of the phenomenological method as a qualitative research procedure", *Journal of Phenomenological Psychology*, **28** (2), 235–60.

Irvine, A.D. (2014), "Bertrand Russell", in E.N. Zalta (ed.), *The Stanford Encyclopedia of Philosophy*, Palo Alto, CA: Stanford University Press, available at http://plato.stanford.edu/archives/spr2015/entries/russell (accessed 28 November 2014).

Latham, G.P. (1992), "Resolving a scientific dispute with Dr. Miriam Erez: genesis, process, outcome, and reflection", in P.J. Frost and R.E. Stablein (eds), *Doing Exemplary Research*, Thousand Oaks, CA: Sage, pp.146–54.

Latham, G.P., Erez, M. and Locke, E.A. (1988), "Resolving scientific disputes by the joint design of crucial experiments by the antagonists: application to the Erez–Latham dispute regarding participation in goal setting", *Journal of Applied Psychology*, **73** (4), 753.

Luksyte, A., Unsworth, K.L. and Avery, D. (2012), "Gender and idea generation: do women benefit less for innovative behaviour?", Paper presented at the Academy of Management Annual Meeting, Boston, MA, 3–7 August.

Margolis, E. and Laurence, S. (2014), "Concepts", in E.N. Zalta (ed.), *The Stanford Encyclopedia of Philosophy*, Spring edn, Palo Alto, CA: Stanford University Press, available at http://plato.stanford.edu/archives/spr2014/entries/concepts (accessed 28 November 2014).

Miscenko, D. and Day, D.V. (2015), "Identity and identification at work", *Organizational Psychology Review*, doi: 2041386615584009.

Newman, L. (2014), "Descartes' epistemology", in E.N. Zalta (ed.), *The Stanford Encyclopedia of Philosophy*, Winter edn, Palo Alto, CA: Stanford University Press.

Okhuysen, G. and Bonardi, J.-P. (2011), "The challenges of building theory by combining lenses", *Academy of Management Review*, **36** (1), 6–11.

Popper, K. (1959), *The Logic of Scientific Discovery*, London: Hutchinson & Co.

Pylyshyn, Z. (1980), "Computation and cognition: issues in the foundation of cognitive science", *Behavioral and Brain Sciences*, **3**, 111–32.

Russell, B. (1945), *The History of Philosophy*, New York: Simon & Schuster.

Russell, B. (1986), *The Collected Papers of Bertrand Russell*, Vol. 8, *The Philosophy of*

Logical Atomism and Other Essays, 1914–19, ed. John G. Slater, London: George Allen and Unwin.

Sawang, S. and Unsworth, K. (2006), "An empirical study: the role of financial and non-financial performance measurement and perceived innovation effectiveness", Paper presented at the 2006 IEEE International Conference on Management of Innovation and Technology, Singapore, 21–23 June.

Schmitt, R. (1959), "Husserl's transcendental-phenomenological reduction", *Philosophy and Phenomenological Research*, **20** (2), 238–45.

Schwitzgebel, E. (2014), "Belief", in E.N. Zalta (ed.), *The Stanford Encyclopedia of Philosophy*, Spring edn, Palo Alto, CA: Stanford University Press.

Sellars, W. (1962), "Philosophy and the scientific image of man", in R.G. Colodny (ed.), *Frontiers of Science and Philosophy*, Pittsburgh, PA: University of Pittsburgh Press, pp. 35–78, reprinted in 1963, *Science, Perception and Reality*: London: Routledge & Kegan Paul.

Starik, M. (1995), "Should trees have managerial standing? Toward stakeholder status for non-human nature", *Journal of Business Ethics*, **14** (3), 207–17, doi: 10.1007/bf00881435.

Strawson, P. (1992), *Analysis and Metaphysics: An Introduction to Philosophy*, Oxford: Oxford University Press.

Suddaby, R., Hardy, C. and Huy, Q.N. (2011), "Introduction to special topic forum: where are the new theories of organization?", *Academy of Management Review*, **36** (2), 236–46.

Sytsma, J. (2010), "The proper province of philosophy", *Review of Philosophy and Psychology*, **1** (3), 427–45.

Terkel, S. (1974), *Working: People Talk About What They Do All Day and How They Feel About What They Do*, New York: Pantheon/Random House.

Thomson, J.J. (1971), "A defense of abortion", *Philosophy & Public Affairs*, **1**, 47–66.

Townsend, K. and Richards, J. (2011), "Re-examining resistance and misbehaviour", in A. Wilkinson and K. Townsend (eds), *The Future of Employment Relations: New Paradigms, New Approaches*, London: Palgrave Macmillan, pp. 101–21.

Unsworth, K.L. and Clegg, C.W. (2010), "Why do employees undertake creative action?", *Journal of Occupational and Organizational Psychology*, **83** (1), 77–99.

Unsworth, K.L. and Luksyte, A. (2015), "Is all creativity created equal? Types of creativity and their effects", in C. Shalley, M. Hitt and J. Zhou (eds), *The Oxford Handbook of Creativity, Innovation and Entrepreneurship: Multilevel Linkages* New York: Oxford University Press, pp. 279–300.

Unsworth, K.L. and Parker, S.K. (2003), "Proactivity and innovation: promoting a new workplace for the new workplace", in D. Holman, C. Wall, C. Clegg, P. Sparrow and A. Howard (eds), *The New Workplace: People, Technology and Organization. A Handbook and Guide to the Human Impact of Modern Working Practices*, Chichester: John Wiley and Sons, pp. 175–96.

Unsworth, K.L., Wall, T.D. and Carter, A. (2005), "Creative requirement: a neglected construct in the study of employee creativity", *Group and Organization Management*, **30** (5), 541–60.

Unsworth, K L., Sawang, S., Murray, J., Sorbello, T. and Norman, P. (2012), "Understanding innovation adoption: effects of orientation, pressure and control on adoption intentions", *International Journal of Innovation Management*, 16, 1, doi: 10.1142/S1363919611003593.

Wittgenstein, L. (2009), *Philosophical Investigations*, 4th edn (trans. Hacker and Schulte), Chichester: Wiley-Blackwell.

PART III

INNOVATIONS IN DATA COLLECTION METHODS

10 An experiment with "the miracle question": an innovative data collection technique in HR research*

Keith Townsend

INTRODUCTION

The field of human resource management (HRM), if we were to attempt to provide a single overarching summary, is designed to understand aspects of managing people in workplaces. Research within the field is diverse in many ways, ideological starting points, data collection techniques, units of analysis and methods of analysis. Within the HRM realm a wide variety of project designs are used. Researchers can focus on single topics, for example, recruitment, or training. Alternatively, they can examine how various elements of the HRM architecture in a firm interact together, for example, the high performance body of research. Adding more complexity to this web of research is the implied "intention" of the research – for example, is the research intended to increase efficiency in the workplace? This approach can place increased pressure on employees in an attempt to lift organisation profits and performance. Or is the research intended to improve the working lives of the employees studied?

Sometimes the problem with HR-focused research is that it can be too concerned with the organisation at the expense of the employee's views and experiences or, alternatively, too concerned with employees' individual characteristics without adequate consideration of important contextual factors within and external to the workplace. In this chapter we propose a method that we have found to assist with generating employee views of the issues that face them in the workplace. We found ourselves in a position of some freedom – we were provided with a large enough sample of qualitative interviews that we could experiment with data collection, and if the experiment failed, we would still have adequate interviews to reach the important point of data saturation as per Creswell's (2007) recommendations of around 35 interviews. Our research project aimed to understand both employee and managerial experiences of change programmes that were designed to implement high performance work systems in Australian hospitals.

In this chapter we consider the use of a data collection technique that, to the best of our knowledge, had not been used by researchers in HRM. "The miracle question" has a psychiatry origin, and we decided that there was merit in using this to frame our semi-structured interviews. We outline the development of the miracle question, followed by how we used it in our data collection approach. Importantly, the context of the research project is explained at this time. Finally, the discussion draws in some of the positives and potential limitations of this approach.

The context for this study is important to understand before we examine the innovative data collection technique. Hospitals had, for decades, been faced with increasing costs and decreased funding and state and federal governments of all political persuasions were seen to be using the hospital system for short-term political gain. Through our practitioner networks we were aware that a number of hospitals were aiming to embark on transformational change of their HR systems. We were able to negotiate access to five different hospital sites where we planned to investigate the "black box" of high performance (Purcell and Kinnie, 2007). This was in part to understand what happens between the HR manager's desk, floor staff experiences and organisational performance measures. We were cognisant of recent methodological critiques that suggested that asking HR managers whether their HR system worked was flawed (Wall and Wood, 2005). Hence, we wanted the employees' perspective as Guest (1999) rightly points out; worker's concerns are a legitimate focus of study.

Our experience as qualitative researchers in the broad field of "people management", encapsulating industrial relations and human resources, suggests that it is very easy to point to flaws in the systems that suggest the planned or intended outcomes of change programmes (and organisational policy generally) that can be a long way from the actual outcomes that employees experience. By avoiding armchair theorising and deciding what we scholars determined would be the issues employees faced, we were much better placed to understand how employees viewed their predicament in the midst of a change programme, surrounded by cost and service imperatives within the healthcare sector.

MIRACLES AND SOLUTIONS, JUST WHAT EVERY HR TEAM NEEDS

In the early 1980s within the fields of psychiatry and psychology, the miracle question developed. Made famous through its use in the Brief Family Therapy Centre (BFTC), in Milwaukee, USA, the miracle question formed part of what has become known as solution-focused therapy (SFT). A key assumption to SFT is that people attend counselling because there is some problem facing them in their lives, but furthermore, the problem that the clients raise *is* the problem (Littrell et al., 1995). But as the name implies, SFT is not so much about problems per se but more about the client's goal of finding a solution (Littrel et al., 1995). To put this another way, the therapists are emphasising with the client the constructing of solutions, not the resolution of problems (Gingerich and Eisengart, 2000).

SFT is often used with children in family counselling as it is viewed as child-friendly (Lethern, 1994). With children, according to Lethern, parents and teachers will have reached a point of "blaming" the child by the time they reach therapy sessions, hence, alternative interventions are required. SFT aims to focus on the key individuals involved in counselling (for example, a parent and child) and elicit information about their interactions. It is the non-blame approach to this method that makes it successful with children. If we were to make an over-simplification of a vast body of HR research, it would be fair to say that most research investigates the barriers, or the enablers, of performance success. Projects might be couched in ideological and methodological differences but generally research investigates what works and what does not work. So attempting a non-blame approach seemed a potentially interesting approach in data collection, and as people experience diverse experiences within the same context, allowing the employees to name their issues presented an exciting opportunity.

The traditional approach to therapy is where the "expert/analyst" decides on the "best" solution to resolving the client's problems (de Jong and Berg, 1998). With SFT though the relationship built between the therapist and client is essential as they partner towards developing collaborative solutions to the problems at hand. Depending on the level of clarity the individual has, the therapist can work with the individual to develop what the client would see as a "preferred future" that is free from the problems that have led them to seek the assistance of a therapist. There is an array of various elements that can be taken in the solutions approach; perhaps the best-known approach is the one that we used, the miracle question.

One of the principle developers of the miracle question, Steve de Shazer, explains that in his view it was a mistake to call it "the miracle question" when it was never a simple question with a simple response. Rather, it was designed "to shift the conversation quickly and easily into the future when the problems (that brought the client to therapy) were gone" (de Shazer, 2007). While there are many different forms of the question, it can be and has been shaped in various guises to investigate particular issues. The example that was initially brought to our attention was one of a counsellor working with an adolescent who presented with anger management concerns. The script read as follows:

> This is a bit of an unusual question, one that might take some imagination to answer. So imagine leaving here and going home. You're evening is typical, you do all your usual activities, you then get tired and eventually fall asleep. While you are asleep a miracle happens and you didn't know about it. All of the problems in your life have been resolved because of this miracle. But because the miracle occurred overnight while you were asleep, you didn't realise. What things would be different? How would you be able to tell that a miracle had occurred?

Ideally, this question might receive responses that refer to the client noticing that they "feel better about themselves" or that their school peers might "treat them better". The counsellor would be able to draw the reasonable conclusion that the self-esteem and peer interactions were the areas in life in which the client wanted to make improvements. At this point, the counsellor and the client have enough information to begin formulating a plan to work on solutions to these problems.

The context here is very different to that of a HR research project in the workplace. The relationship between a client and therapist is very different from that relationship found between a manager and an employee, but also between a researcher and an interview subject. We also know that some areas of problems in the employment relationship are external to the relationship altogether – for example, the economic downturn of 2008/09 would have placed significant pressure in workplaces throughout the world that lie far beyond an individual's ability to find solutions. But to ignore the capacity of individuals to change things might be regarded as fatalistic, so we examine what problems remain that the individual might resolve. There is also significant value in pursuing a technique that allows the voice of workers to be heard, putting forward their own views in a different approach to a typical interview schedule.

As we mentioned previously, this question has rarely been used in HR research but our experience is that it has a lot of value. For example, the question seems to fit with projects that aim to go beyond the "blaming" for what is not working properly, and to contribute to solutions in assisting workplaces to become more efficient and effective while not pushing increased workloads and work intensification on to lower level staff members. This method can also be used as a means of triangulating and cross-checking data – an essential process in maintaining high standards in qualitative research – by using two different methods of data collection, a solution-focused approach and a problem-focused approach to collect data from each participant. This allowed us to infer whether the differing approaches would provide data from which we could draw overlapping and supporting conclusions or perhaps different conclusions.

THE PROJECT CONTEXT

As HR researchers, we might anticipate that when we ask employees a question designed to explore their "miracle" workplace, the responses might focus on factors that would contribute to an "ideal" employment relationship. For example, issues that relate to the standard HRM practices like employee voice, remuneration, training, performance reviews. If we were to continue to investigate we might uncover areas already examined including work intensification, tensions between work and family life, real or perceived threats of violence at work, dissatisfaction with managers' preoccupation with cost control (Townsend and Allan, 2005) or a culture of bullying and intimidation in many hospitals (Wilkinson et al., 2015). But we found this technique to be particularly successful when we have the freedom to go back to the very roots of inductive techniques and start, as Neuman (2005) suggests, with a few vague concepts. This is indeed the strength of the miracle question approach in HR, the researcher is not imposing a pre-determined expectation of what the employees are facing; rather, the employees are directing the research agenda.

The potential problem associated with this method though is that this approach to data collection is not a common and accepted method in HR journals. Hence, it has not generated what Lincoln and Guba (1985) refer to as "trustworthiness criteria". So maintaining a more commonly accepted approach to data collection was critical when we began to send our research for publication. We completed over 100 interviews and were able to access a range of organisational specific data including employee satisfaction surveys, strategic planning documents and so on. As we began to receive reviewers' comments associated with the initial rejections from journals, we realised the importance of our decision to marry this method with more traditional and accepted methods.

ASKING FOR MIRACLES

While our pilot interviews demonstrated that we would be able to collect some useful data, we also realised that we were novices with this approach and that relying on this data alone would be an expensive experiment. Hence, when our interviews began we not only had the miracle question but three semi-structured interview protocols to use. These protocols were tailored for hierarchical levels within the organisation, floor staff, line managers and senior managers.

Methods research demonstrates that people's responses can be influenced by what has been said earlier in conversations (Alvesson and Skoldberg, 2000). To ensure that our problem-based research questions did not direct or influence the interviewees' responses we asked the miracle question at the start of the interview. By using such a standardised approach we increased the rigour of the research design.

The interview script for this question was as follows:

> This question is a bit of an odd question. Some people can find an answer straight away and some people find it more difficult to answer. I want you to imagine leaving work today and you go about your usual evening activities, maybe have dinner, maybe a drink, perhaps watch some TV and then eventually you go to bed and fall asleep. And while you are asleep overnight a miracle occurs. You don't realise that there has been a miracle, but when you walk in to work tomorrow the whole hospital is running superbly. The ward, the hospital, everything is just absolutely perfect. What would be different?

By setting the scene of the miracle in creating the "perfect" superbly run workplace, and finally asking "what would be different?" we were allowing the interviewees to provide a narrative that might be incomplete (Rubin and Rubin, 2005), but nonetheless gave us good clues to piece together during the data analysis. Based on what we would predict given the SFT explanation of the question and answers, an employee response would allow us to understand what is missing. For example: "I guess everything that you needed in your day would be available. You wouldn't spend time chasing things . . .". This expression of "the miracle (workplace)" indicated to us that this employee (and others) had frustrations with wasting time looking for equipment that they needed to perform their role.

Interestingly for the research project, data collected was not about "HR" at all. Certainly there was a relationship between our findings and HR systems and the impact on employees and managers, but employees were not concerned about a shift to high performance models, or recruitment systems, rather, their concerns were related to the things that affected them every moment of every day. What we were able to do with this data was to present the findings that employees consistently noticed with the miracles leading to differences in two areas – resources and relationships. In short, resources were too scarce and not present where and when they were required, and there were some fractures in relationships, typically that stemmed back to low levels of managerial training.

Another challenge with this approach was to see if we could find out how we might use the solution-based approach to establish ways to either leap or creep towards this miracle hospital environment. This typically seemed to be the most difficult part of the question for the employees to answer. This is perhaps not surprising as most people have a capacity to understand what might not be perfect in their lives but "fixing" these problems is a more difficult process. It is at this point that the attraction and growing use of the solution-based approach is more apparent (Gingerich and Eisengart, 2000; Littrel et al., 1995). The divide between "tomorrow's miracle" and what employees are facing today in effect tells the researcher what the workplace problems are. Hospital funding arrangements were recognised by employees as a key source of problems, but employees are not able to develop a solution to that problem. Increasingly bureaucratised and administratively top-heavy organisations might go some way to explain some of the resourcing problems but again they are not problems for which employees can readily find solutions.

DISCUSSION

Publishing the findings from this research proved difficult. Some reviewers simply did not see the data collection method as a legitimate technique. Other reviewers felt that by introducing a new method and claiming some value in that method we should be able to deliver results that were not available with existing methods. To some extent we disagree. We were able to get an article published in a respectable journal and we were successful in part because we were able to demonstrate that there was indeed a difference in the data collected with our solution-based question and our problem-based questions. Hence, had we not split our data collection time and energies between an "innovative method" and a more conservative, traditional method we would not have collected the data to make that comparison possible.

We generally use this data collection method when the aim is to avoid the notion of "armchair theorising" or sitting in our offices deciding that we as academics know the problems that these employees faced. For example, in our semi-structured protocol we asked, "Do you think your workload is manageable?" Then follow-up questions were asked to probe deeper and understand why that response was given, who controls the employees' workload, and examples of under what conditions workloads are more or less manageable. In contrast, the miracle question allowed employees to say if indeed workloads were an issue. We argue this provides a truer reflection on what employees think are the main concerns for them in the workplace and consequently allows the researcher a greater opportunity to uncover stories relevant to the workplace context – the workers' lived reality. This innovative approach might not be appropriate for every interview-based project, but it did yield interesting data on this occasion.

The miracle question is, according to one of the pioneers of the solution-focused approach, simple but not easy (cited in Lethern, 2002). Within academic circles innovation can be slow, and even at times resisted. However, innovation can only occur if people experiment and take risks. This chapter documents a conservative risk – we did not rely solely on the miracle question, we had our back-up traditional interview sched-ule. It does allow for an appropriate research project design, allowing a researcher to understand what the issues are for a workforce rather than imposing a pre-determined set of values or findings that, might we add, are also very legitimate means of designing research projects and data collection endeavours. We would also suggest that this method is excel-lent for preliminary data collection in consultancy research projects prior to instigating change programmes. This technique can be another tool in the researchers' kit. We would suggest that it is a tool that can be used to support other data collection techniques, perhaps in pilot studies to estab-lish what the workforce think are the issues at hand. But at this time we would not encourage researchers to use this innovative technique in place of more traditional methods of interview questions.

NOTE

*   I would like to thank Dr Allan Cameron for bringing the idea of the miracle question to our attention. Additionally, Adrian Wilkinson also played an important role in the data collection and analysis of this project.

REFERENCES

Alvesson, M. and Skoldberg, K. (2000), *Reflexive Methodology: New Vistas for Qualitative Research*, London: Sage.
Creswell, J.W. (2007), *Qualitative Inquiry and Research Design: Choosing among Five Approaches*, 2nd edn, Thousand Oaks, CA: Sage.
de Jong, P. and Berg, I.K. (1998), *Interviewing for Solutions*, Pacific Grove, CA: Brooks Cole.
de Shazer, S. (2007), "The miracle question", Brief Family Therapy Center, available at http://www.netzwerk-ost.at/publikationen/pdf/miraclequestion.pdf (accessed 27 February 2014).
Gingerich, W. and Eisengart, S. (2000), "Solution-focused brief therapy: a review of the outcome research", *Family Process*, **39** (4), 477–97.
Guest, D. (1999), "Human resource management: the worker's verdict", *Human Resource Management Journal*, **9** (1), 5–25.
Lethern, J. (1994), *Moved to Tears, Moved to Action: Solution Focused Brief Therapy with Women and Children*, London: BT Press.

Lethem, J. (2002), "Brief solution focused therapy", *Child and Adolescent Mental Health*, **7** (4), 189–92.

Lincoln, Y.S. and Guba, E.G. (1985), *Naturalistic Inquiry*, Beverly Hills, CA: Sage.

Littrell, J., Malia, J. and Vanderwood, M. (1995), "Single-session brief counselling in a high school", *Journal of Counselling and Development*, **73** (4), 451–58.

Neuman, W.L. (2005), *Social Research Methods: Qualitative and Quantitative Approaches*, 6th edn, Boston, MA: Pearson.

Purcell, J. and Kinnie, N. (2007), "HRM and performance", in P. Boxall, J. Purcell and P. Wright (eds), *The Oxford Handbook of Human Resource Management*, Oxford: Oxford University Press, pp. 533–51.

Rubin, H. and Rubin, I. (2005), *Qualitative Interviewing: The Art of Hearing Data*, Thousand Oaks, CA: Sage.

Townsend, K. and Allan, C. (2005), "Flexibility at a cost: Responding to a skilled labour shortage", in P. Stanton, E. Willis and S. Young (eds), *Workplace Reform in the Healthcare Industry: The Australian Experience*, Basingstoke: Palgrave Macmillan, pp. 197–212.

Wall, T.D. and Wood, S.J. (2005), "The romance of human resource management and business performance, and the case for big science", *Human Relations*, **58** (4), 429–62.

Wilkinson, A., Townsend, K. and Graham, T. (2015), "Fatal consequences: an analysis of the failed employee voice system at the Bundaberg Hospital", *Asia Pacific Journal of Human Resources*, **53** (3), 265–80.

11 Using photo-elicitation to understand experiences of work–life balance

Catherine Cassell, Fatima Malik and Laura S. Radcliffe

INTRODUCTION

Recent times have seen an increased use of visual methods throughout the social sciences including the management and organisational domain (Davison et al., 2012). However, the use of photographic methods in human resource management (HRM) more generally is not as evident. Yet the opportunity of generating rich qualitative data from the use of photographs, otherwise not produced using alternative methodological approaches (Clark-Ibanez, 2004, p. 1524), has great potential for HRM, organisational and management researchers (Harper, 2002; Ray and Smith, 2012; Warren, 2002, 2008). There are different ways of using photographs as part of a research study. Researchers can use photo documentary through taking their own photographs of research sites or can analyse already existing photographs, for example, those in company documents. They can also ask research participants to take their own photographs.

Within this chapter, we explore the use of participant photo-elicitation methods in studying how people manage their daily episodes or incidences of work–life balance. Participant photo-elicitation methods rely upon research participants taking their own photographs of a subject as guided by the researcher(s). In addressing this particular technique, we explore some important methodological issues for HRM researchers who seek to use these methods and explain how this type of methodology has much to offer when studying HR issues such as work–life balance. We conclude that one of the major benefits of this method is the role of photographs as a "conversational technology" (Gammack and Stephens, 1994, p. 76) in encouraging participants to talk and reflect.

The chapter is structured in the following way. We begin by briefly outlining the context of the study in terms of the work–life balance literature as a way of setting the scene for the research and our choice of participant photo-elicitation as a method. By way of background, we then explore the use of photographs in management and organisational research before outlining the research project including the design of the photo-elicitation study. Next, we provide an illustration of the kind of findings generated by the method and comment on how participants respond to it. Finally, we discuss what has been learned about the method and provide some recommendations for its use by other HRM researchers.

WORK–LIFE BALANCE RESEARCH

There is an increasing interest within the field of HRM about work–life balance and conflict and explorations have occurred from both theoretical and policy-making standpoints. The literature that considers the interactions between work and life highlights wide-ranging explanations of how one influences the other (Guest, 2002; Minnotte, 2012; Voyandoff, 2005). However, there has been some concern that the term "work–life balance" is more appropriately considered a "misnomer" due to its limitations in capturing the multi-faceted and multi-dimensional nature of the work and family domains (Guest, 2002, p. 262). Other critiques have focused upon the inappropriateness of the metaphor of balance (Cohen et al., 2009), and the normative constructions of both the terms "work" and "life" (Özbiglin et al., 2011). Moreover, it has been recognised that most research has focused upon a stereotypical view of the family as forming the "life" part of "work–life", neglecting the diversity of both individual and collective experience in this area.

Greenhaus (2008) noted that a number of reviews of the field have drawn attention to some of the methodological limitations in our knowledge and understanding of this area (for example, Casper et al., 2007). As noted by Eby et al. (2005) in their review of the work–family literature, research has tended to focus on the centrality of the work role rather than the family role in people's lives. This overemphasis on the work domain results in a limited perspective on the totality of work–family experiences. Furthermore, the focus of the majority of previous research upon a "levels" approach, where conflict is conceptualised and measured as a consolidated level, makes it difficult to capture any of the specific details of the complexities that might be at play.

An alternative approach focuses upon events and episodes. However, to date, there has been a scarcity of research that has taken an episodic approach in exploring how people manage daily work–family responsibilities. One exception is research conducted by Poppleton et al. (2008) who collected daily diary data on work/non-work events in two contrasting organisations. The authors emphasised the advantages of taking an episodic approach in terms of capturing immediate assessments of daily experiences in relation to flexible working, enabling more accurate judgements of the impact of such working arrangements, based on real and experienced events. Photo-elicitation is one example of an episodic technique amongst others such as video, which is also increasing in usage in the HRM field.

Given these concerns with current understandings of work–life balance, the research project we are currently engaged in that informs this chapter seeks to elicit the diversity of different experiences of work–life balance from different and under-researched groups (Gatrell, 2005; Gatrell et al., 2013; Voyandoff, 2005). Here, our aim through a longitudinal episodic approach was to gain a deeper understanding of the holistic nature of the work–life relationship. We chose photo-elicitation rather than video because we were keen to use episodic snapshots of the participants' experiences of work–life balance. With video the participant produces videos that are then edited by the researcher. In this case we wanted participants to also act as editors, to use the photographs to illustrate their edited snapshot versions of their work–life balance. Hence, as part of a mixed methodology approach using a range of different qualitative methods, we were keen to use a novel method in this area of research: photo-elicitation.

PHOTO-ELICITATION METHODS

There are numerous different ways of using photographs in research including researcher production of photographs and the use of photographs from archives. However, here our focus is with participant photo production as a form of photo-elicitation. Rose (2012) suggests that there are four key strengths of photo-elicitation as a data collection method. First, it enables a range of different insights into a given phenomenon from different perspectives. Second, it facilitates the exploration of everyday things that are taken for granted. Informants can reflect on everyday activities or occurrences directly as part of the data collection process. Third, this method has a positive impact on the power relationship between researchers and the researched in that the researched in choosing what to photograph are defining what is important about a given phenomenon. Fourth, Rose points to a distinctive collaboration between the researcher and the researched that is different from other methods.

Photo-elicitation can be a stand-alone method where the researcher analyses photographs taken by participants without any discussion with the participant. However, in most cases it is used alongside an interview. Harper (2002) notes the advantages of the use of photo-elicitation in this way. Here, the participant engages in dialogue in collaboration with the researcher to uncover details encapsulated within photographs taken within the field. Combining visual and verbal methods allows the researcher to disentangle social phenomena, further observing the purpose, existence and meaning of social categories, bodies and items within photographs. Warren's (2002, 2008) studies of working life further complement the "can-opener effect" (Walker and Weidel, 1985), where photo-elicitation facilitates the researcher's access to new, unexpected data providing alternative ways to talk about, reflect upon and thus understand HRM phenomena.

Other advantages are suggested by Ray and Smith (2012) who point out that photographs are a way of capturing phenomena in real time and are less restrictive than other methods of data collection. However, there are potentially also problems with the use of photo-elicitation (Rose, 2012; Warren, 2002). Complex ethical issues call into question, for example, the ownership rights of the interpretive elements of visual images that – although produced by participants – are nevertheless jointly interpreted as part of a collaborative dialogue between the researcher and participant. There is also the issue of consent when individuals are the subject of photographs.

Within HRM research, the use of photographic methods is sparse, but there are some interesting examples, most notably of the lived experience of work. For example, Slutskaya et al. (2012) conducted photo-elicitation interviews with butchers and suggested that the use of photographs encouraged working-class men who are not usually accessible to researchers to talk about various aspects of their work. Moreover, they provided detailed and expressive accounts of their everyday experiences of physical labour. Warren (2006) asked individuals working in a hot-desking environment to take photographs of their desks as part of a larger ethnographic study of workplace aesthetics. Initially being interested in why hot-desking staff sought to personalise their work environments, Warren (2006) through her interviews argues that the drivers to efficiency that underpin hot-desking may have a negative impact on employee well-being. In summary, existing studies suggest that there is much to gain from the use of photo-elicitation methods in HRM research.

USING PHOTO-ELICITATION TECHNIQUES TO STUDY WORK–LIFE BALANCE

In the study we draw upon here, photo-elicitation was one method used in a larger research project designed to explore how diverse groups experience work–life balance and conflict. We were keen to capture their daily experiences and events in an episodic way. The project is ongoing and based upon a multiple qualitative methods design including diaries, interviews and photo-elicitation. Here we are concerned with the photo-elicitation aspects of the methodology.

The instructions given to participants regarding the photographic elements of the research design are shown in Appendix 11A.1. We drew upon Vince and Warren's (2012) notion of responsible photography to underpin the instructions for the research participants as we were particularly keen to observe ethical practice in managing this process. Ray and Smith (2012) suggest that one key decision for researchers adopting this approach involves assessing how much direction to give to organisational members and they suggest piloting the wording used. In our pilot work a key issue that emerged initially when we compared the photographs generated was that the terminology used, notably "work–life balance" or "work–life conflict", had an important impact on the photographs taken. For example, one of our pilot participants had taken photographs that mainly portrayed the feeling of balance and control, whereas the other two had taken photographs that portrayed the conflict that they felt in managing work–life dynamics. We therefore realised that the terminology we used to guide our interviewees when taking their photographs needed to be both inclusive and precise. Such difficulties no doubt reflect some of the problems within the current literature in this area where a plethora of terms explaining work–life or work–family dynamics are used. We concluded after much debate that it was probably best to ask interviewees about both work–life balance and work–life conflict.

A further issue that emerged from the pilot was that the definition of a photograph was not necessarily as straightforward as we originally thought. So one participant produced screen shot messages from their mobile phone, as did one of the study participants. In both cases, we found that this type of photograph tended to be used to convey incidents when work–life relationships caused some kind of difficulty, for example, discussions of who was picking a child up from school. These snapshots, probably because they presented text, portrayed specific incidents rather than general themes, though still fitted into our preferred focus upon episodes.

The method was used in the following way. As can be seen from the instructions in the Appendix, we asked the following of our interviewees: "At the end of the two week period please email one of the researchers five of the photographs you have taken." Once a participant had submitted their photos an interview was arranged. The semi-structured interview started with the interviewer asking the interviewee about each of their photographs in turn. They were asked to talk about the photograph, what was in it and why they had taken it. They were then asked what the photograph captured about their work and life roles and episodes. Once each of the photographs had been discussed, the interview then continued with further questions probing for in-depth and detailed information about their work–life balance and conflict experiences. At the end of the interview, participants were asked a series of short questions about their experiences of taking part in the research, including their reflections of both taking the photographs and participation in the interview process. We now turn to the kind of data that this methodological approach produced.

ILLUSTRATIVE FINDINGS

In this section, by way of illustration we shall make some comments on the kinds of photographs taken and how people responded to the method more generally. We also draw upon comments made by the participants during the interviews. All names of participants have been changed to ensure anonymity.

What Kind of Photographs did People Capture?

A whole range of different photographs were sent to the researchers by the participants. Perhaps unsurprisingly there were some similarities in the photographs taken. An enduring theme was the perception that work–life balance was something that the participant needed to control, or be in control of, whereas maintaining that control was an ongoing accomplishment. A number of participants took photographs of their workspaces, either in the office or at home, and discussed them in relation to control. For example, Figure 11.1 shows Paul's desk at work.

Paul talked about this photograph in the following way:

> It just emphasises the fact that that's how work feels a lot of the time and that's why my desk looks like it does. About every year and a half I manage to clear it up. But it's that feeling of just about keeping your head above water.

Later on in the interview Paul went on to talk about how this perception of where he was with work impacted upon his home life:

> Yeah, disorganised, and I've found work quite stressful over the last two to three years and I think that [the desk] is a kind of metaphor for that stress as well, there are times when it impacts upon home life, it impacts on my kind of personal well-being and I think that level of . . . being that busy is probably not a good thing, really, to the extent where you can't find time to clear your desk.

Figure 11.1   Paul's desk

It's a bit like sinking, isn't it, sinking under a deluge of paper, or drowning in paper; that is literally drowning in paper, that desk!

On a similar theme, Ros described why she had taken this photograph of her dining room table (Figure 11.2):

R: It's chaos, isn't it?
I: Is that what you think it's about, chaos?
R: That's what it felt at the time. I think I got calmer as the week went on but that was in the middle of quite a busy week. So we'd had tea and I think I'd done a bit of James's homework and then . . . what is that? That's just work. I was looking at registers and it was just the way the table looked. We'd finished tea and I'd not cleared away my stuff, my work, and it was there waiting for me. So I wasn't in a particularly good place; work–life balance wasn't particularly good at that point in time. So it felt a bit chaotic.

The thematic analysis of the photographs enabled us to surface the concerns participants had about their work–life balance, in this instance about control.

Figure 11.2   Ros's dining room table

It is important to note that the interview was crucial in providing the contextual background in which to understand the meaning of the photographs taken. Photographs of the same subject were interpreted in different ways by our participants. For example, a number of participants took photographs of their lunch at their desks. Examples are Corrine's (Figure 11.3), Jess's (Figure 11.4) and Hilary's photographs (Figure 11.5). However, although of the same topic, these photographs were interpreted quite differently by the participants. For Jess the issue was about striving to maintain a healthy diet:

> So that photograph represents a few things, and there's some positives and negatives in there. The positives are that I've actually got the healthy lunch; probably the negatives are that I'm eating it at my desk. Again, depending on the time of year, depending on my workload, sometimes I will take more of a break at lunchtime.

Whereas for Hilary, the time-saving element was important:

> I suppose on being a parent it's like I don't have a problem with eating at my desk because the work needs to be done and I'd rather work through my lunch than work at the weekend.

Figure 11.3   Corrine's lunch

For Corrine, eating at her desk was a necessity in order to fit in with the office culture and the expectations she thought that co-workers had of her:

> Sometimes I eat it at my desk because the feeling in the office is very much that everybody else does, and if I go out for my lunch, because I'm the only one in the whole office that's gone out for lunch, just to take a sandwich to the park or something, I feel when I get back . . . it might be my paranoia but I feel really guilty and worried about it, that people think she's gone on lunch, we're really busy.

A number of the photographs were also of participants' family members and children. But here again interpretations could be quite varied. Janette used the photograph of her children to illustrate "the ferocious

Figure 11.4 Jess's lunch

boundaries" she kept between home and work; Paula used a family photograph to talk about the importance of family time; and Jess used a photograph of her son revising to talk about how she felt guilty that she couldn't be at home to help him more. Therefore, the photographs were an important way of enabling participants to talk about a variety of different aspects of work–life balance and conflict, emphasising the significance of the interview talk generated by them.

How People Responded to the Method

As part of the interview method we asked participants what they thought about using the photographic method. In summary, participants viewed the method as having considerable advantages, both practical and otherwise. The use of cameras on mobile phones meant that the method was seen to be both practical and convenient. However, perhaps the most interesting feedback we received from the participants related to their comments about how taking the photographs and the discussion about them in the interviews enabled them to reflect upon their work–life balance. The longitudinal element of the task is important here in that participants were given at minimum a couple of weeks to complete their photographs and in most cases took longer than that. It was evident that

Figure 11.5   Hilary's lunch

engaging with the task had facilitated considerable reflection on the part of the interviewees. This reflection covered a number of different angles. For some it drew close attention to daily patterns:

> It made me start to think a bit more actively about work–life balance and notice where things were creeping in or taking things home, how often it was, because often I found I was taking things home and I thought later "oh I could have taken a picture of that". (Roisin)

For others the reflections led to them evaluating their current situation:

I guess for me mostly it made me realise that again, I've got it quite good. Like I said, I do have quite a good work–life balance so I'm quite lucky. I think it's just . . . I guess the thing about taking the picture of the lunch, actually I guess again it was like I can feel sorry for myself because I always have lunch at my desk but even just talking about it, I don't have to do that. That's my decision. So that again makes you realise that these things are actually in your own control mostly. Well, they are in my situation. Yeah, I guess that again is a good thing, so definitely I've got a lot of flexibility where I work. (Nicky)

Clearly, the exercise enabled participants to have the space to think about their current circumstances and how they are managing. In several cases, this reflection led to some ideas about taking action to address concerns about work–life balance. For Roisin, for example:

It has made you reflect on it more, because I think often everything is happening so fast and you're noticing it but you're not thinking about it. So it's made me actually think actually why aren't I approaching, why haven't I pushed to have meetings with my boss? You just think maybe I shouldn't, I don't know, and then you think actually, it's probably not a big deal to just say can we meet every week. It makes you think more about it and then look for solutions or be more proactive about making things happen.

In summary, the method itself enabled reflection that we might speculate would not have come from an interview alone. The photographs acted as a talking point bringing discussions to mind that might not have occurred as part of a standard interview process. However, it is important to note that the reflections could produce both positive and negative emotions, so although producing interesting and useful data for the research team, these are important issues to consider when using this method in terms of the possible impact it may have on interviewees.

Overall, the interviewees welcomed the opportunity to reflect upon their specific work–life balance episodes, recognising that their daily busy lives rarely provided them with the time to do so.

Challenges in Using the Method

As stated earlier, a key challenge in any research using photographs is the ethical one. Participants highlighted various ethical issues associated with their use of the method, especially in relation to taking photographs of others. This was particularly the case in relation to taking photographs of children. As Jess suggested:

When I was taking a picture of something inanimate, fine, but trying to get a photograph of my 16 year old without him knowing or ask me what it was about, that was quite difficult. I had to sneak up on him and kind of click. So I felt a bit odd, it felt a bit weird.

Duncan pinpointed that cultural values surrounding child photography had changed in recent years, indicating, "I'd be very careful of taking photos of other children." This point reflects child protection legislation within the UK preventing parents from photographing even when it is their own children participating in organised professional sports (for example, football). Therefore, a concern is that although participants make the decision about which photos to hand over, other people who may accidentally be in the background will not have given their consent. We would suggest that photo-elicitation requires ongoing ethical vigilance on behalf of the researcher to ensure that ethical research practice is not compromised. It is important that any ethical concerns are dealt with clearly in the participants' briefing and the opportunity to discuss them is taken as part of the interview, in line with the notion of responsible photography (Vince and Warren, 2012).

A further challenge for the researcher is how to analyse photographic data. Vince and Warren (2012) outline content, thematic and hybrid analytic approaches although in theory any tool for qualitative data analysis can be used to analyse photographs. Here we found template analysis (King, 2012) particularly helpful.

There are also the questions that arise from any kind of qualitative approach about how we assess the quality of the data generated and the analytic process. In recognising that a range of alternative quality criteria have been posited for qualitative research (Symon and Cassell, 2012), our contention is that the criteria used should reflect the philosophical position and methodological stance of the researcher (see Johnson et al., 2006). For example, if the photographs are part of an ethnographic study we would expect quality criteria to include those typically used for ethnography, such as prolonged engagement in the field. In this case, from our interpretivist viewpoint we were keen to ensure that the analysis could be seen as transparent, hence credible and authentic.

CONCLUSIONS

The literature on the use of photographic methods more generally highlights that research participants enjoy engaging with them. As Vince and Warren (2012) suggest, taking photographs can be fun and socially inviting and people like to talk about them. The comments from our interviewees would suggest that they are indeed an excellent conversational technology (Gammack and Stephens, 1994, p.76) in that they encourage individuals to talk and impart often personal information in a non-intrusive and socially interactive manner. Indeed, Warren and Parker (2009) suggest that the photograph itself has a third-party effect in that both the researcher and the researched actually have something to talk about. From the research team's perspective, we found that the use of photographs at the start of the interviews led to the generation of some rich interview data with interviewees disclosing more openly than perhaps they may have done if we had used traditional interview methods. Their enthusiasm for communicating the different rationales underpinning their photographs enabled this. The photographs also meant that they had a role in setting the interview agenda.

Our experience is also that the use of photographs enabled diverse interpretations of the term work–life balance, suggesting that this method is particularly appropriate where the focus is upon the sensemaking of participants about particular concepts – such as work–life balance – in that it enables a variety of participant-driven definitions to surface. Within the HRM field, examples could include more individually experienced phenomena such as career or work fulfilment, job satisfaction and perceptions of leadership as well as organisationally based phenomena such as organisational culture and the management of change.

Furthermore, the method clearly provides the opportunity for participants to reflect upon pertinent issues – in this case related to work–life balance – both before and during the interviews. Qualitative researchers have long been aware that offering the opportunities for people to talk about their work and organisational experiences will potentially lead to such reflection, and photo-elicitation is an excellent example of this. In conclusion, the photographs and the interviews both provided considerable insights into our understanding of work–life balance and conflict. We would therefore encourage other HRM researchers to engage with the opportunities that photo-elicitation offers, particularly given the positive experiences reported by those engaging with the method.

ANNOTATED FURTHER READING

Ray, J.L. and Smith, A.D. (2012), "Using photographs to research organizations: evidence, considerations, and application in a field study", *Organizational Research Methods*, **15** (2), 288–315.
This paper provides a useful and comprehensive overview of the use of photographic methods in the organisational research field.
Vince, R. and Warren, S. (2012), "Participatory visual methods", in G. Symon and

C.M. Cassell (eds), *Qualitative Organizational Research: Core Methods and Current Challenges*, London: Sage, pp. 275–95.
This chapter provides a good introduction to the use of visual methods more generally in organisational research.

REFERENCES

Casper, W.J., Eby, L.T., Bordeaux, C., Lockwood, A. and Lambert, D. (2007), "A review of research methods in IO/OB work–family research", *Journal of Applied Psychology*, **92** (1), 28–43.
Clark-Ibanez, M. (2004), "Framing the social world with photo-elicitation interviews", *American Behavioural Scientist*, **47**, 1507–27.
Cohen, L., Duberley, J. and Musson, G. (2009), "Work–life balance? An auto-ethnographic exploration of everyday home–work dynamics", *Journal of Management Inquiry*, **18**, 229–41.
Davison, J., Mclean, C. and Warren, S.A. (2012), "Exploring the visual in organizations and management", *Qualitative Research in Organizations and Management: An International Journal*, **7** (1), 5–15.
Eby, L.T., Casper, W., Lockwood, A., Bordeaux, C. and Brinley, A. (2005), "Work and family research in IO/OB: content analysis and review of the literature (1980–2002)", *Journal of Vocational Behavior*, **66**, 124–97.
Gammack, J.G. and Stephens, R.A. (1994), "Repertory grid technique in constructive interaction", in C.M. Cassell and G. Symon (eds), *Qualitative Methods in Organizational Research: A Practical Guide*, London: Sage, pp. 72–90.
Gatrell, C. (2005), *Hard Labour: The Sociology of Parenthood*, Maidenhead: Open University Press.
Gatrell, C., Burnett, S., Cooper, C. and Sparrow, P.R. (2013), "Work–life balance and parenthood: a comparative review of definitions, equity and enrichment", *International Journal of Management Reviews*, **15** (3), 300–316.
Greenhaus, J.H. (2008), "Innovations in the study of the work–family interface: introduction to the special section", *Journal of Occupational and Organizational Psychology*, **81**, 343–8.
Guest, D.E. (2002), "Perspectives on the study of work–life balance", *Social Science Information*, **41** (2), 255–79.
Harper, D. (2002), "Talking about pictures: a case for photo-elicitation", *Visual Studies*, **17** (1), 13–26.
Johnson, P., Buehring, A., Cassell, C. and Symon, G. (2006), "Evaluating qualitative management research: Towards a contingent criteriology", *International Journal of Management Reviews*, **8**, 131–56.
King, N. (2012), "Using templates in the thematic analysis of text", in G. Symon and C.M. Cassell (eds), *Qualitative Organizational Research: Core Methods and Current Challenges*, London: Sage, pp. 426–50.
Minotte, K.L. (2012), "Perceived discrimination and work-to-life conflict among workers in the United States", *Sociological Quarterly*, **53** (2), 188–210.
Özbiglin, M.F., Beauregard, A., Tatli, A. and Bell, M.P. (2011), "Work–life, diversity and intersectionality: a critical review and research agenda", *International Journal of Management Reviews*, **13**, 177–98.
Poppleton, S., Briner, R.B. and Kiefer, T. (2008), "The roles of context and everyday experience in understanding work–non-work relationships: a qualitative diary study of white- and blue-collar workers", *Journal of Occupational and Organizational Psychology*, **81**, 481–502.
Ray, J.L. and Smith, A.D. (2012), "Using photographs to research organizations: evidence, considerations, and application in a field study", *Organizational Research Methods*, **15** (2), 288–315.

Rose, G. (2012), *Visual Methodologies: An Introduction to Researching with the Visual*, London: Sage.

Slutskaya, N., Hughes, J. and Simpson, A. (2012), "Lessons from photo-elicitation: encouraging working men to speak", *Qualitative Research in Organizations and Management*, **7** (1), 16–33.

Symon, G. and Cassell, C.M. (2012), "Evaluating qualitative research", in G. Symon and C.M. Cassell (eds), *Qualitative Organizational Research: Core Methods and Current Challenges*, London: Sage, pp. 204–23.

Vince, R. and Warren, S. (2012), "Participatory visual methods", in G. Symon and C.M. Cassell (eds), *Qualitative Organizational Research: Core Methods and Current Challenges*, London: Sage, pp. 275–95.

Voyandoff, P. (2005), "Work demands and work-to-family and family-to-work conflict: direct and indirect relationships", *Journal of Family Issues*, **26** (6), 707–26.

Walker, R. and Wiedel, J. (1985), "Using photographs in a discipline of words", in R. Burgess (ed.), *Field Methods in the Study of Education*, London: Falmer Press, pp. 191–216.

Warren, S. (2002), "Show me how it feels to work here", *Ephemera – Critical Dialogues on Organisation*, **2** (3), 224–45.

Warren, S. (2006), "Hot nesting? A visual exploration of personalised workspaces in a 'hot-desk' office environment", in P. Case, S. Lilley and T. Owens (eds), *The Speed of Organization*, Copenhagen: Copenhagen Business School Press, pp. 119–46.

Warren, S. (2008), "Empirical challenges in organisational aesthetic research: towards a sensual methodology", *Organisation Studies*, **29** (4), 559–70.

Warren, S. and Parker, L. (2009), "Bean-counters or bright young things? Towards the visual study of identity construction in professional accountants", *Qualitative Research in Accounting and Management*, **6** (4), 205–23.

APPENDIX 11A.1   DETAILS GIVEN TO PARTICIPANTS

Instructions for Photo-elicitation and Interviews

Over the next two weeks please take some photographs that illustrate your daily experiences of work–life conflict or work–life balance.

Taking pictures can be a personal thing – please ask any people who are subjects of your photographs for permission to show them to us (either before or after you take the picture).

You might also need to take care not to photograph anything that invades another person's privacy or contravenes your organization's confidentiality policy (for example, the visible contents of documents or computer screens). Rest assured that we can digitally obscure any identifying features of people or the company (e.g. faces, company logos, etc.) and you will be given full opportunity to have any of the pictures we discuss deleted.

Other than these common sense precautions feel free to take pictures of whatever you feel illustrates your work–life balance or conflict. We hope you will enjoy taking part in the research and we look forward to seeing the pictures you take.

At the end of the two-week period please email one of the researchers five of the photographs you have taken. We will then arrange to meet with you again for about an hour to talk about your photographs and ask you some other questions about your experiences of work–life balance and conflict.

Once again, we'd like to thank you for agreeing to participate in this research study, if you have any questions at all about the research then don't hesitate to contact any of us at:
****

12 Using qualitative repertory grid interviews to gather shared perspectives in a sequential mixed methods research design

Céline Rojon, Mark N.K. Saunders and Almuth McDowall

INTRODUCTION

In this chapter, we consider a specific example of applying mixed methods designs combining both qualitative and quantitative data collection and analysis approaches, giving particular attention to issues including reliability and validity. Human resource management (HRM) researchers, like others setting out to examine a novel or insufficiently defined research topic, frequently favour qualitative approaches to gather data during initial stages, to facilitate an in-depth exploration of individuals' notions of a subject matter and development of theory (Symon and Cassell, 2012). A variety of qualitative data gathering and analytic methods can be used to such effect, including focus groups followed by thematic analysis of data (for example, Braun and Clarke, 2006) or diary studies (for example, Xanthopoulou et al., 2009). Having made sense of gathered qualitative data, scholars may often decide to examine their chosen topic through further quantitative study, such as a survey.

To this end, we consider a specific example of using the repertory grid technique (RGT) (Kelly, 1955, 1963) as the qualitative first stage in a mixed methods design. Whilst the RGT is a popular data gathering technique in management and organisation sciences (MOS) generally and HRM research specifically, utilising it as the first stage of mixed methods research is unusual. In particular, we discuss the application of the RGT for aggregative analysis of data collected from interviewees. Such an approach to analysing RGT data is rare as, typically, the technique is used on its own within an interview study of one or more participants. Yet, it offers considerable utility to examine shared perceptions, as we illustrate from our personal experience of researching individual workplace performance amongst 25 professionals and managers. We begin our chapter by offering an outline of the RGT, which includes a discussion of its validity and caveats as well as its history of use. Subsequently, we provide details of our application of the RGT in the context of wider work performance research. Having further summarised potential challenges and shortcomings, we conclude by a discussion of the method and its usage to elicit shared perceptions within mixed methods research.

DESCRIPTION OF THE METHOD AND HISTORY OF ITS USE

Within this section, we explain the RGT's origins and history of use from a more general point of view; details regarding its operationalisation for HRM research more specifically are provided in the subsequent section outlining an application to develop a model of individual workplace performance. The foundations of the RGT lie in Kelly's Personal Construct Theory (1955, 1963), which was initially conceived in the context of family therapy, but is today no longer confined to the clinical domain. More recently, the RGT has been used for a variety of academic and practical endeavours, such as to examine organisational culture (Dick and Jankowicz, 2001) or organisational learning (Sillince and Shipton, 2013), for career counselling and coaching purposes (Brook, 1992), for professional training (Fransella and Bannister, 1977) and its evaluation (Jankowicz, 1990) or employee selection (Brewerton and Millward, 2001), amongst others. Outside the HRM/MOS field, the technique has also been used widely, with examples in product development (Goffin and Koners, 2011), business analysis (Wright et al., 2013) and marketing (Marsden and Littler, 2000).

According to Personal Construct Theory, the world is "constructed", an individual formulating their own ways of seeing the world "through transparent patterns or templates which he [*sic*] creates and then attempts to fit over the realities of which the world is composed" (Kelly, 1955, pp. 8ff.); such patterns are known as "constructs". Since individuals' constructed worlds (or their "construction systems") are based on their own unique experiences, they differ from person to person (Brewerton and Millward, 2001) and also develop and alter over time when tested against reality (Kelly, 1955, 1963). Kelly suggests that an individual's construction system is made up of a finite number of dichotomous constructs, which are bipolar (for example, ugly-beautiful), that is being formed by one relationship of similarity and one relationship of difference. The manner in which individuals speak about their construction system is indicative of how they view the world – or what the two ends of a construct mean for them. Since constructs are – often non-verbalised – abstractions of the world, Kelly introduced the notion of "elements". Elements exemplify the area that is being explored, helping individuals in thinking and talking about their constructs. They can be people, objects, places, activities or other similarly tangible representations of the area being investigated (Jankowicz, 2004).

To learn about a person's constructs, Kelly developed the "Role Construct Repertory Test" (or "Rep Test"), an idiographic technique facilitating the communication of construction systems. Although procedure and technicalities have evolved over time, the basic idea of eliciting elements and constructs to learn about an individual's "implicit theories" of the world (that is, schema-like knowledge structures individuals use to process and respond to observed stimuli; Detert and Edmondson, 2011), through which they try to make sense of it (Fransella and Bannister, 1977), remains the same. As such, the RGT is typically employed within a particular form of structured interview, the so-called repertory grid interview (RGI), "extracting personal constructs in a systematic way" (Hassenzahl and Wessler, 2000, p. 444). As part of this, an interviewer first elicits elements from the interviewee, before going on to elicit that person's constructs in relation to the area being explored. Finally, constructs are linked to elements by constructing a grid matrix. We provide further detail of the procedure of conducting a RGI in our example of using the RGT to develop a work performance model.

Questioning within RGIs focuses on individual constructs through which respondents understand the study's topic (Jankowicz, 2004), the RGT purporting to minimise researcher interference or bias in the data gathering process (Whyte and Bytheway, 1996). In practice, this means that interviewees talk about the topic in their own words, without being influenced by a researcher's predetermined questions or probes (for example, Slater, 1977). The RGT is also considered a reliable method, both regarding internal consistency as well as stability, with test-retest reliabilities (over a period ranging from one week to several months) across studies having been found to be adequate to high ($r_{tt} = 0.41 - 0.95$), for instance (Hardison and Neimeyer, 2012; cf. Adams-Webber, 1989). Finally, it has been suggested that the technique offers adequate validity (for a full discussion refer to Hardison and Neimeyer, 2012). Indeed, with regard to face validity, RGIs do well, given the process of eliciting elements and constructs is very transparent, as further detailed below.

Notwithstanding the assumption that implicit theories are unique to the individual as aforementioned, the constructs, of which these theories are composed, may be shared by individuals (Arnold et al., 2010; Kelly, 1955, 1963). Consequently, the RGT can also be used to elicit shared patterns across individuals. Having gathered data from multiple respondents via individual interviews, there are a variety of approaches that HRM researchers can choose to analyse data at the group level. These include principal components analysis (for example, Senior and Swailes, 2007), generic content analysis (for example, Purvis and Cropley, 2003) or similarity matching (Borman, 1987). Yet, an alternative analytical approach was developed over 35 years ago by Honey (1979a, 1979b). In contrast to other group analytical methods, which may neglect the complexity of elicited data in the aggregation process, Honey's approach allows aggregation of interview data in a way similar to larger-scale questionnaire analysis, whilst maximising retention of individual meaning contained in the (qualitative) grid information. His procedure entails content analysis across all respondents, this being "concerned with the accurate expression of common or shared context related constructs among collectives of people" (Hill, 1995, p. 107).

USING THE RGT TO DEVELOP A MODEL OF WORK PERFORMANCE

We used the RGT here as part of wider research on individual workplace performance. Our aim was to advance understanding of individual workplace performance in terms of how the construct can be defined, conceptualised and operationalised. Three specific objectives were addressed within a sequential mixed methods design (Tashakkori and Teddlie, 2010) consisting of three interlinked studies building on each other (Figure 12.1).

Our first study was a systematic review and psychometric meta-analysis (Hunter and Schmidt, 2004), which focused on providing an enhanced understanding of how to define, conceptualise and measure individual workplace performance. Systematic review methodology was used to review the literature, because its rigour and standardisation enable greater transparency, replicability and clarity of review findings (Briner et al., 2009; Rojon et al., 2011) in comparison to other possible literature review strategies. The second study explored working individuals' notions of performance, employing the RGT (Kelly, 1955, 1963) to inform personal interviews with a varied sample. This study focused on gathering individuals' notions of performance to provide the basis for the development of a new model of performance. Since the purpose of this study was to explore in detail individuals' thoughts and ideas pertaining to performance, a qualitative approach was more suited than a quantitative one (Saunders et al., 2016). The RGT in particular was thought to be a useful way of gaining a real-life insight into individuals' understanding of performance, because it allows interviewees to contextualise their thoughts more easily compared to other qualitative approaches (Kelly, 1955, 1963). In the final study, our objective was to test the model developed based on findings

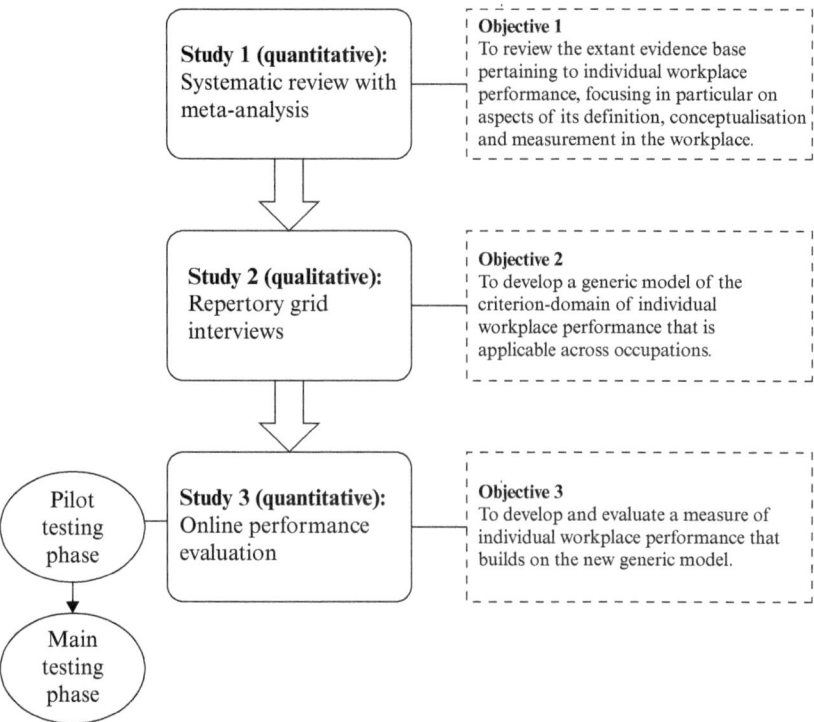

Figure 12.1   Overview of the research process

from the second study in two consecutive phases, using a newly designed multi-rater performance measure to examine the model's applicability in a wider context. Given the main focus of both study phases was to statistically evaluate the new performance model as well as its associated performance measure, a quantitative research approach was considered more appropriate, because it facilitates data collection from larger samples, which are required to perform statistical analyses (Saunders et al., 2016).

Since our chapter is concerned with using the RGT as part of a mixed methods design, we now explain in detail how we applied the technique within our research, following a systematic review and meta-analysis. We chose the RGT to help us gain a real-life insight into what working individuals who perform in organisations think about performance. Despite having gained a thorough understanding of individual workplace performance through our systematic review and meta-analysis, we were aware that this understanding was of a theoretical nature. It was therefore equally important to collect data regarding individuals' beliefs and ideas, formed through their day-to-day experience with performance-related behaviours in the workplace. The RGT offers a powerful means of learning about individuals' notions of work performance, mainly because it allows participants to contextualise their thoughts by drawing directly on experience with the people they work with. Three prior studies that had drawn on Personal Construct Theory to arrive at performance categories for specific jobs (Borman, 1987; Davis, 2005; Hedge et al., 2004) were identified through the systematic review, leading us to conclude that the RGT could also be a useful method for our own study. However, rather than looking at specific occupations, as was done by these three studies, the scope of our study was broader. As such, it aimed at developing a generic model of individual workplace performance by eliciting performance constructs from participants from a wide variety of cultural and occupational backgrounds; in other words, individuals with different jobs and varying levels of work experience and management responsibilities, from diverse industries.

Data Collection Using the RGT

Our overall approach to data collection can be summarised as shown in Figure 12.2. Having concluded that the RGT should be utilised in the initial stage of developing a new performance model, we conducted personal, face-to-face RGIs to "uncover" interviewees' performance constructs. Participants were working adults with at least three years of prior work experience to ensure they could contextualise the interviews. They were purposefully selected to represent a wide range of industries and sectors, as well as national cultures, to enable gathering a comprehensive picture of diverse individual experiences of work performance. Following expert recommendations regarding sample size and data saturation within heterogeneous populations such as ours (Brinkmann and Kvale, 2015; Creswell, 2007), we interviewed 25 individuals: participants were mostly male (72 per cent), their age ranging between 25 and 54 years ($M = 38.60$; $SD = 9.81$); 48 per cent of participants were British, the remaining individuals originating from a variety of countries (India, France, Germany, Russia, USA, China, Jordan, Switzerland); the majority of participants were highly qualified (68 per cent postgraduate degree, 28 per cent undergraduate degree) and worked in top or middle management positions (56 per cent); 24 per cent of individuals describing themselves as professionals/specialists; 36 per cent of participants had more than 20 years of work experience, 32 per cent had 10–20 years, 24 per cent had 6–9 years, with the remaining 8 per cent having had 3–5 years of work experience. They were employed both in public and private industry, with industry

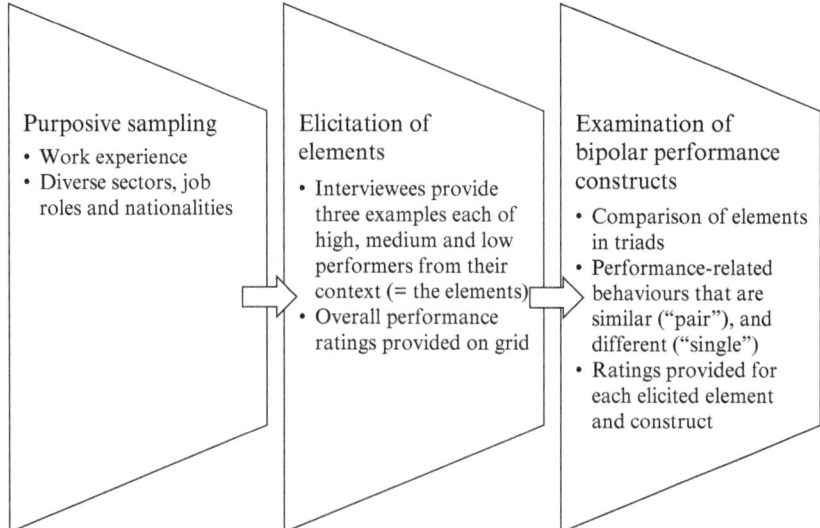

Figure 12.2   Overview of overall approach to data collection using the RGT

sectors being diverse, for example, automobile, education, finance, hospitality, local government and retail.

At the outset of each interview, we asked participants to think of nine individuals they currently (or have previously) interact(ed) with in the workplace, namely, three persons that they consider high, medium and low performers respectively. These nine individuals were the elements. The elements' names were written on one file card for each and were also entered in the nine columns at the top of a grid that was used to supplement the interview, as is customary for RGIs (see Figure 12.3 for an example of a completed grid). Each interviewee then assigned performance ratings to their nine individuals ranging from 1 (very low workplace performance) to 5 (very high workplace performance), writing these underneath the individuals' names, in the first line of the grid (the "top view") (Figure 12.3). Next, we elicited each interviewee's bipolar performance constructs. Presenting a "triad" of three individuals' name cards (that is, three elements) at a time, each interviewee was requested to pair up two individuals. These two individuals (the "pair") were required to have something in common in terms of their performance-related behaviour that differentiates them from the third individual (the "single"). Each interviewee was then asked to elaborate on the behaviours that make the individuals forming the pair similar, distinguishing them from the

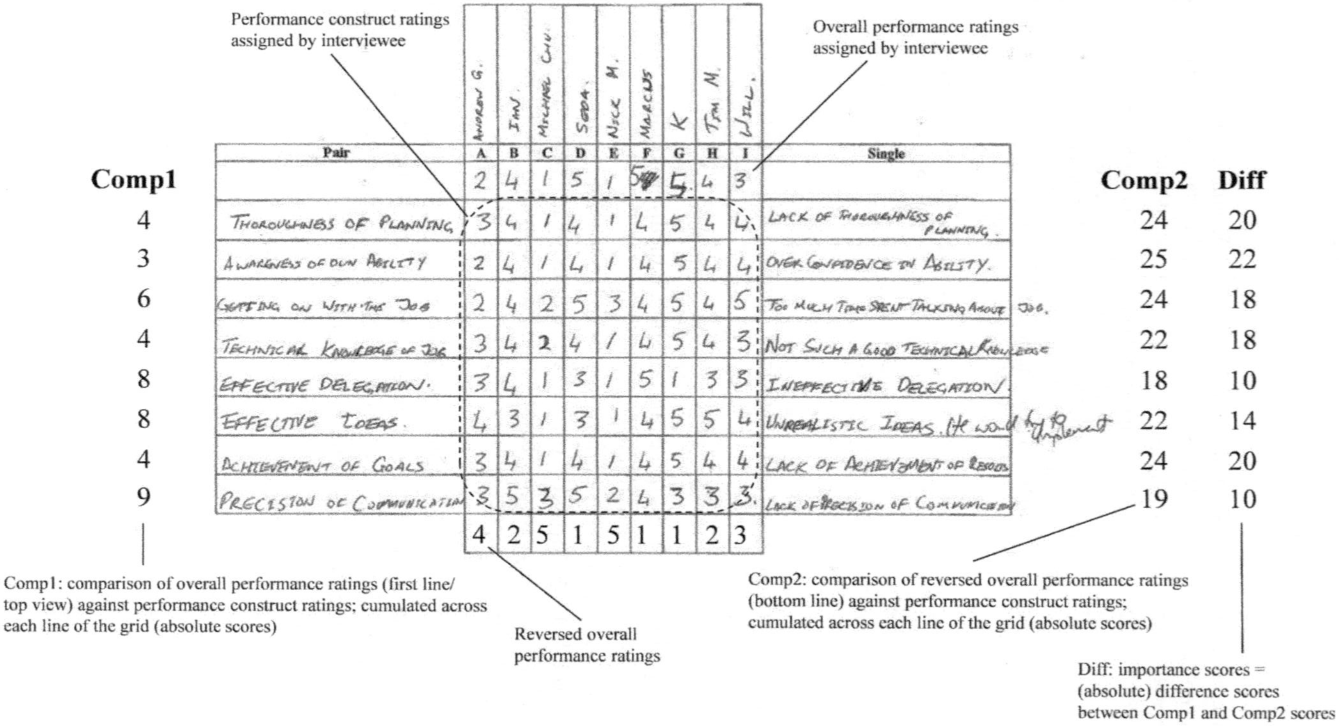

Performance construct ratings assigned by interviewee

Overall performance ratings assigned by interviewee

Comp1

Pair	A	B	C	D	E	F	G	H	I	Single	Comp2	Diff
	Andrew G.	Ian	Michael Chu	Sean	Nick M.	Marcus	K	Tim M.	Phil.			
4 Thoroughness of Planning	3	4	4	5	1	4	5	4	4	Lack of Resourcefulness of Planning.	24	20
3 Awareness of own Ability	2	4	1	4	1	4	5	4	4	Over Confidence on Ability.	25	22
6 Gets on with the Job	2	4	2	5	3	4	5	4	5	Too much time spent thinking about Job.	24	18
4 Technical Knowledge of Job	3	4	2	4	1	4	5	4	3	Not such a good Technical/Knowledge	22	18
8 Effective Delegation.	3	4	1	3	2	5	1	3	3	Ineffective Delegation.	18	10
8 Effective Ideas	4	3	3	3	4	4	5	5	4	Unrealistic Ideas, (it would by Implement	22	14
4 Achievement of Goals	3	4	1	4	4	5	5	4	3	Lack of Achievement of Goals	24	20
9 Precision of Communication	3	5	5	5	2	1	3	3	3	Lack of Precision of Communication	19	10
	4	2	5	1	5	1	1	2	3			

Reversed overall performance ratings

Comp1: comparison of overall performance ratings (first line/ top view) against performance construct ratings; cumulated across each line of the grid (absolute scores)

Comp2: comparison of reversed overall performance ratings (bottom line) against performance construct ratings; cumulated across each line of the grid (absolute scores)

Diff: importance scores = (absolute) difference scores between Comp1 and Comp2 scores

Figure 12.3   Annotated example of completed grid

single, and to write these behaviours (the constructs) in the grid (the pair description on the left-hand side, the single description on the right-hand side). This process of presenting triads was continued for each interviewee until constructs pertinent to individual workplace performance had been exhausted. The final step of the RGI, a rating procedure, involved treating the two construct poles as extremes on a continuum: On a scale from 1 to 5, each interviewee had to decide for each of their elements whether it was rather like the description of the pair or rather like the single description (5 = very much like the pair, 1 = very much like the single).

Data Analysis: Individual Level

Interviewees generated a total of 317 performance constructs (for example, "asks for permission/never asks for permission"; "makes friends and works along with others/makes enemies at work"; "takes initiative where needed/will not take initiative"). On average, 13 constructs were elicited per interviewee, with a minimum of 6 and a maximum of 18 ($SD = 3.06$).

These data were initially analysed individually and manually to determine the importance of each elicited performance construct/behaviour for the respective interviewee by deriving an importance score for each construct. This enabled insights into how each interviewee understands individual workplace performance (Brewerton and Millward, 2001). First, we compared the top view overall performance ratings for each interviewee against each set of construct ratings, noting down and summing the differences. For example, where a top view overall performance rating was "2" and a construct rating was "3", the difference was "1". Second, the top view overall performance scores were reversed and the same process was applied again, difference scores being taken down. For example, a top view overall performance rating of "2" was reversed to "4". Differences between these two sets of sums were then calculated to create an importance score for each construct. For our research, importance scores ranged from 0 to 24, the mean being 9.96 ($SD = 5.33$). Based on these scores, the constructs were ranked into descending order of importance, the higher scores being the most important constructs for an interviewee concerning their notion of individual workplace performance, the lower ones being less important, but still dominant constructs.

Data Analysis: Group Level

Honey's approach of aggregating data to the group level was then applied. First, we determined for each interviewee which of their constructs ranged in the highest third (the "top data"), the middle third (the "medium data") and the lowest third (the "tail data") amongst all their importance scores. The top data are those constructs that are linked most closely with high individual workplace performance; conversely, the tail data constructs are associated least with high individual workplace performance. Second, the performance constructs were sorted into categories (and subcategories where applicable) of two or more constructs, separately for each level of importance (top/medium/tail). Next, categories across the three levels of importance were compared. Categories that resembled each other within the three levels were grouped together (for example, categories pertaining to communicating effectively were identified in all three levels). Subsequently, the constructs comprising each of the categories and the ratio of top to medium to tail data were examined closely. Where a category consisted mostly of top-level and medium-level constructs, it was retained to form part of an initial model of individual workplace performance, this being a category interviewees believed to be an important performance indicator. Categories in which more tail constructs than top constructs were represented were discarded, because the interviewees agreed such categories were not strongly associated with performance and thus not important enough to be kept further.

The aforementioned process of sorting constructs into categories and developing a model was undertaken twice, independently by two researchers, as recommended (Honey, 1979a). As such, two independent, initial models of individual workplace performance emerged. Model A had nine categories and ten subcategories, whilst model B featured twelve categories and three subcategories. A comparison of the two models indicated that the majority of behaviours (55 per cent) had been sorted into nine conceptually identical or very similar categories. Since there was not complete overlap between the two models, we undertook an expert panel discussion consisting of five HRM scholars by way of categorising the remaining 45 per cent of behaviours. Panel members were split into two groups of two and three individuals, respectively. Each group was asked to sort half of the uncategorised behaviours ($N = 42$) into the nine categories, which, as suggested by Honey (1979a), were presented to the experts alongside three to four exemplar behaviours. This was followed by a discussion amongst all participants in which the two groups justified their sorting decisions. Any disagreements of how and why behaviours had been sorted into categories were resolved within this final panel discussion.

Findings: A New Model of Individual Workplace Performance

Discussions within the expert panel confirmed the nine performance categories that had emerged from models A and B. Moreover, a tenth category pertaining to work–life balance was added to the model, with a number of previously uncategorised behaviours relating to this concept. In addition to this, we chose to include a separate eleventh category to reflect the notion of counterproductive performance (Viswesvaran and Ones, 2000), which was found to be inherent in a number of constructs elicited from interviewees (for example, "lazy/conscientious, works hard", "motivates others/destructive") and which researchers understand as "voluntary behaviour that harms the well-being of the organization", detracting from organisational goals (Rotundo and Sackett, 2002, p. 69).

The resultant performance model has 11 categories, as described through 57 subcategories (Table 12.1). Behaviours for each of the 11 categories were elicited from, on average, 15 of the 25 study participants (60 per cent). Each individual mentioned behaviours that fell into seven of the 11 performance categories on average, the minimum being four, the maximum ten. Our new model formed the basis for a larger, survey-based

Table 12.1   Performance framework resulting from RGIs

11 categories	Examples of 57 subcategories
Demonstrating Knowledge and Skills	• Having and Applying Technical Knowledge • Thinking Analytically
Communicating Effectively	• Being Comfortable at Giving Presentations/Speaking Publicly • Showing Active Listening Skills
Demonstrating Effort and Drive	• Taking Initiative • Thinking Long Term
Leading/Managing Others	• Delegating • Assuming Responsibility
Engaging with Others	• Supporting Others • Showing Respect for Others
Showing Creativity/Openness for Change	• Generating Ideas and Strategies • Adapting to Changes
Planning and Organising	• Demonstrating Organised Working Approach • Demonstrating Thoroughness
Behaving Professionally	• Demonstrating Credibility • Acting Honestly
Displaying Self-confidence	• Coping with Criticism • Being Assertive
Balancing Work and Life	• Balancing Work and Life
Showing Counterproductive Conduct	• Being Dishonest • Displaying Rigid Attitude to Change

study, aimed at testing and refining it. We shall reflect on this further in the discussion section.

CHALLENGES AND SHORTCOMINGS

Invariably, the most pertinent challenge of using the RGT in conjunction with Honey's (1979a, 1979b) group analysis technique will arise if there are no common conceptions in the data elicited from individual RGIs, that is, if interviewees are not in agreement when it comes to the topic being researched. Whilst such an outcome could be interpreted as an inherent danger – or disadvantage – of using Honey's (or indeed any group analysis) approach to analyse RGI data, it represents an interesting finding in itself, namely, that it may not be possible to elicit a shared understanding of the topic. Rather, it may be the case that it is highly idiographic in nature, rendering the idea of developing a framework based on common notions nonsensical.

Aside from lack of consensus, a further possible disadvantage is the relatively large amount of time required for manual analysis of RGI data (Honey, 1979a; Thota, 2011). Nevertheless, analysing data manually, whilst likely being labour-intensive, enables the researcher(s) to remain close to the data collected, supporting the gaining of deeper insights compared to that gained by a software-driven analysis procedure or statistical analysis.

Concerns can also be raised regarding the feasibility of categorising data elicited from RGIs without any preconceived ideas or imposing one's own insights. Thota (2011) has given this issue some thought, concluding that even though a data-driven and researcher-led content analysis approach is advantageous in terms of any categories developed being close to the raw data, the danger of replicability of such a category system is low given the potentially idiosyncratic interpretation. Even Honey (1979a) acknowledges that there is a risk of distorting individuals' data by forcing constructs into categories. Still, according to both Honey (1979a) and Thota (2011), these issues can be remedied by asking at least two independent scholars to carry out the data analysis, by way of checking the coding scheme's consistency. In our study, we involved two researchers in the process, who independently sorted the constructs into categories; second, the category systems developed by both researchers were discussed as part of a panel meeting of further, independent scholars. Consequently, even though Honey's (1979a, 1979b) aggregative approach may not be faultless, the above highlighted actions can be taken to address the perceived issues.

DISCUSSION

In this chapter, drawing on a project examining individual workplace performance, we have outlined how the RGT can be used as the first data collection stage within a sequential mixed methods design. Following an explanation of the method, its usage in HRM and related fields, as well as its philosophical underpinnings, we noted that the RGT has been found to be reliable, valid and relatively free from bias compared to other qualitative approaches.

Although the RGT is used frequently at the individual level, we have highlighted that analysing constructs across multiple interviewees is also possible using a variety of analytical approaches. In our example study, we chose Honey's (1979a, 1979b) aggregative analysis method, allowing the granularity of individuals' data to be retained even when analysed at the group level. This enabled us to elicit shared understandings of work performance. Considering the RGT study in the context of our research project as a whole, gathering data through RGIs and analysing them using Honey's (1979a, 1979b) approach was instrumental to gaining an in-depth insight into the performance construct per se. In comparison with other qualitative data gathering strategies, the sample size required to achieve data saturation (in our case 25 interviews) is in our experience very similar. In contrast, the data collection is perhaps slightly less onerous, given that participants write down their bipolar constructs themselves, making the recording and transcribing of data unnecessary. Analysis of data is undertaken initially for each interview individually – which takes approximately the same amount of time compared to other qualitative approaches – and then at the level of the group. In our case, this latter stage worked particularly well, the manual aggregation of interviewees' constructs enabling us to stay close to the data. Whilst such an approach may be more labour-intensive compared to other ways of aggregating RGI data – or even compared to other qualitative methods – involving a number of different scholars (with and without knowledge of the research project) in the group analysis process as recommended is likely to improve validity.

Overall, employing the RGT enabled us to address our research objective of developing a new performance model based on individuals' (common) understanding of the topic. This model formed the basis for further quantitative research. However, as highlighted in our section on challenges and shortcomings, it may not always be possible to elicit common notions from interviewees, in which case alternative explanations about the topic being investigated need to be considered. To conclude, our experience shows that the RGT can be very usefully applied in the early stages of a mixed methods research project – and we hope fellow HRM scholars will also consider using it.

ANNOTATED FURTHER READING

Honey, P. (1979a), "The repertory grid in action: how to use it to conduct an attitude survey", *Industrial & Commercial Training*, **11** (11), 452–9.
Honey's article explains his new take on analysing several repertory grids at the same time to generate shared constructs.
Jankowicz, D. (2004), *The Easy Guide to Repertory Grids*, Chichester: Wiley.
This book provides an easily accessible but comprehensive introduction to using repertory grid interviews.
Kelly, G.A. (1963), *A Theory of Personality: The Psychology of Personal Constructs*, New York: W.W. Norton & Company.
One of Kelly's original books introducing the reader to his Personal Construct Theory.

REFERENCES

Adams-Webber, J.R. (1989), "Some reflections on the 'meaning' of repertory grid responses", *International Journal of Personal Construct Psychology*, **2**, 77–92.
Arnold, J., Randall, R., Patterson, F. et al. (2010), *Work Psychology: Understanding Human Behaviour in the Workplace*, 5th edn, London: Financial Times/Prentice Hall.
Borman, W.C. (1987), "Personal constructs, performance schemata, and 'folk theories' of subordinate effectiveness: explorations of an army officer sample", *Organizational Behavior and Human Decision Processes*, **40**, 307–22.
Braun, V. and Clarke, V. (2006), "Using thematic analysis in psychology", *Qualitative Research in Psychology*, **3** (2), 77–101.
Brewerton, P. and Millward, L. (2001), *Organizational Research Methods: A Guide for Students and Researchers*, London: Sage.
Briner, R.B., Denyer, D. and Rousseau, D.M. (2009), "Evidence-based management: concept cleanup time?", *Academy of Management Perspectives*, **23** (4), 19–32.
Brinkmann, S. and Kvale, S. (2015), *InterViews: Learning the Craft of Qualitative Research Interviewing*, 3rd edn, Thousand Oaks, CA: Sage.
Brook, J.A. (1992), "Use of the repertory grid in career counseling", *Career Development Quarterly*, **41**, 39–50.
Creswell, J. (2007), *Qualitative Inquiry and Research Design: Choosing Among Five Approaches*, 2nd edn, Thousand Oaks, CA: Sage.
Davis, P. (2005), "A study of the implications of applying a competency-based approach to performance management in a global organization", DBA School of Management, Cranfield University, UK.
Detert, J.R. and Edmondson, A.C. (2011), "Implicit voice theories: taken-for-granted rules of self-censorship at work", *Academy of Management Journal*, **54** (3), 461–88.
Dick, P. and Jankowicz, D. (2001), "A social constructionist account of police culture and its influence on the representation and progression of female officers: a repertory grid analysis in a UK police force", *Policing: An International Journal of Police Strategies & Management*, **24** (2), 181–99.
Fransella, F. and Bannister, D. (1977), *A Manual for Repertory Grid Technique*, London: Academic Press.
Goffin, K. and Koners, U. (2011), "Tacit knowledge, lessons learnt, and new product development", *Journal of Product Innovation Management*, **28**, 300–318.

Hardison, H.G. and Neimeyer, R.A. (2012), "Assessment of personal constructs: features and functions of constructivist techniques", in P. Caputi, L.L. Viney, B.M. Walker and N. Crittenden (eds), *Personal Construct Methodology*, Chichester: John Wiley & Sons, pp. 3–51.

Hassenzahl, M. and Wessler, R. (2000), "Capturing design space from a user perspective: the repertory grid technique revisited", *International Journal of Human-Computer Interaction*, **12** (3–4), 441–59.

Hedge, J.W., Borman, W.C., Bruskiewicz, K.T. and Bourne, M.J. (2004), "The development of an integrated performance category system for supervisory jobs in the U.S. Navy", *Military Psychology*, **1** (4), 231–43.

Hill, R.A. (1995), "Content analysis for creating and depicting aggregated personal construct derived cognitive maps", in R.A. Neimeyer and G.J. Neimeyer (eds), *Advances in Personal Construct Psychology*, Greenwich, CT: JAI Press, pp. 101–32.

Honey, P. (1979a), "The repertory grid in action: how to use it to conduct an attitude survey", *Industrial & Commercial Training*, **11** (11), 452–9.

Honey, P. (1979b), "The repertory grid in action: how to use it as a pre/post test to validate courses", *Industrial & Commercial Training*, **11** (9), 358–69.

Hunter, J.E. and Schmidt, F.L. (2004), *Methods of Meta-analysis: Correcting for Error and Bias in Research Findings*, 2nd edn, Thousand Oaks, CA: Sage.

Jankowicz, A.D. (1990), "Applications of personal construct psychology in business practice", in G.J. Neimeyer and R.A. Neimeyer (eds), *Advances in Personal Construct Psychology*, Greenwich, CT: JAI Press, pp. 257–87.

Jankowicz, D. (2004), *The Easy Guide to Repertory Grids*, Chichester: Wiley.

Kelly, G.A. (1955), *The Psychology of Personal Constructs*, Vol. 1, *A Theory of Personality*, New York: W.W. Norton & Company.

Kelly, G.A. (1963), *A Theory of Personality: The Psychology of Personal Constructs*, New York: W.W. Norton & Company.

Marsden, D. and Littler, D. (2000), "Repertory grid technique: an interpretive research framework", *European Journal of Marketing*, **34** (7), 816–34.

Purvis, L.J. and Cropley, M. (2003), "The psychological contracts of National Health Service nurses", *Journal of Nursing Management*, **11**, 107–20.

Rojon C., McDowall, A. and Saunders, M.N.K. (2011), "On the experience of conducting a systematic review in industrial, work and organizational psychology: yes, it is worthwhile", *Journal of Personnel Psychology*, **10** (3), 133–8.

Rotundo, M. and Sackett, P.R. (2002), "The relative importance of task, citizenship, and counterproductive performance to global ratings of job performance: a policy-capturing approach", *Journal of Applied Psychology*, **87** (1), 66–80.

Saunders, M.N.K., Lewis, P. and Thornhill, A. (2016), *Research Methods for Business Students*, 7th edn, Harlow: Pearson Education.

Senior, B. and Swailes, S. (2007), "Inside management teams: developing a team survey instrument", *British Journal of Management*, **18**, 138–53.

Sillince, J. and Shipton, H. (2013), "More than a cognitive experience: unfamiliarity, invalidation, and emotion in organizational learning", *Journal of Management Inquiry*, **22** (3), 342–55.

Slater, P. (1977), *Dimensions of Intra-personal Space: The Measurement of Intra-personal Space by Repertory Grid Technique*, New York: John Wiley & Sons.

Symon, G. and Cassell, C. (eds) (2012), *The Practice of Qualitative Organizational Research: Core Methods and Current Challenges*, London: Sage.

Tashakkori, A. and Teddlie, C. (eds) (2010), *The Sage Handbook of Mixed Methods in Social and Behavioural Research*, 2nd edn, Thousand Oaks, CA: Sage.

Thota, N. (2011), "Repertory grid: investigating personal constructs of novice programmers", in *Proceedings of the 11th Koli Calling International Conference on Computing Education Research*, Koli National Park, FI, pp. 23–32.

Viswesvaran, C. and Ones, D.S. (2000), "Perspectives on models of job performance", *International Journal of Selection and Assessment*, **8** (4), 216–26.

Whyte, G. and Bytheway, A. (1996), "Factors affecting information systems' success", *International Journal of Service Industry Management*, **7** (1), 74–93.

Wright, R.P., Paroutis, S.E. and Blettner, D.P. (2013), "How useful are the strategic tools we teach in business schools?", *Journal of Management Studies*, **50**, 92–125.

Xanthopoulou, D., Bakker, A.B., Demerouti, E. and Schaufeli, W.B. (2009), "Work engagement and financial returns: a diary study on the role of job and personal resources", *Journal of Occupational and Organizational Psychology*, **82**, 183–200.

13 Free verbal associations: measuring what people think about employee participation

Werner Nienhüser

INTRODUCTION

How can we gauge a person's attitudes towards a particular topic, what she or he thinks about it and how she or he values it? Osgood et al. (1971) speak about the "measurement of meaning". This question has huge practical relevance to human resources management (HRM) research. For example, measuring organisational citizenship behaviour (OCB), work satisfaction and motivation, alongside perceived corporate image, leadership style or incentive systems, entails establishing the subject's cognitive thoughts and feelings about that particular topic. An attitude construct is often used for this purpose. This chapter outlines the free verbal associations (FVA) technique and highlights the pros and cons as well as problems associated with this method, using as an example a study on the attitudes of the German public towards codetermination and employee participation.

DESCRIPTION OF THE METHOD

The basic concept behind the FVA method is that spontaneously verbalised associations (written or spoken) occurring to an individual in response to a stimulus word allow us to measure the respondent's attitudes to the object described by the stimulus word. The technique works like this. First, the subjects are presented with a sequence of words or images (stimuli) (such as employee participation, works council). The stimulus may be presented either verbally in an interview or in the form of a written questionnaire. Occasionally, a stimulus object may also be presented visually, for example, as a picture of a product or person. Respondents are asked to spontaneously verbalise their associations (responses), that is, whatever crosses their mind in that moment. They are usually asked to verbalise their association in the form of a single word. Each subject may associate up to ten words with each stimulus object. (Another option is to limit the time available and ask the subjects to associate as many words as possible in that time.) Next, the subjects are asked to rate each of the associated terms as positive, neutral or negative. If required, the importance of each association can also be graded on a scale.

The suitability of any method must be assessed both against its intended purpose and in relation to other methods. Below, I briefly outline the attitude construct and the aspects or dimensions of attitudes that should be covered. I also discuss alternative techniques for measuring attitudes. Attitudes are often interpreted as (positive or negative) valuations of objects, persons and ideas (cf., for example, Albarracin et al., 2005; Fiske and Taylor, 2013). The affective dimension, that is, the feeling-related, subjective rejection or acceptance of the object in question, is at the core of any attitude (Rosenberg and Hovland, 1960). The cognitive dimension is also important. This refers to the content of attitudes, for example, the causes and consequences people associate with an object (such as taxes). Research indicates that attitudes are not necessarily reflected in behaviour (Bohner and Dickel, 2011). The weak correlation may be partly due to the influence of other situational factors.

When measuring attitudes, we make a distinction between explicit and implicit attitudes, and the techniques used to measure them (Bassili and Brown, 2005). Explicit attitudes are consciously retrieved by the test subjects and are typically measured using scales, with the subjects being asked to give a direct valuation of a given object (Bohner and Dickel, 2011; Schwarz, 2008). In simplified terms, the response values to the individual questions are added together, and the combined total is considered indicative of the valuation. Such scales allow us to measure the affective, valuing component of attitudes. This technique is not well suited for measuring the cognitive component, that is, the person's beliefs about a topic, which may not be covered by the prescribed responses. Respondents do not always find it easy to access their attitudes introspectively (Bohner and Dickel, 2011, p. 394). Furthermore, they may be unwilling to disclose their attitudes, for example, if they fear this would give a negative impression to others. Or they may purport to have certain attitudes because they feel they are expected of them, or because they hope it will gain them an advantage. Such distortions are referred to as social desirability bias (King and Bruner, 2000). There are various techniques for measuring implicit attitudes that attempt to minimise these types of problems. One group draws on semantic differentials. A word is given as a stimulus, and the respondent is asked to indicate which opposing adjectives apply to that word, and to what extent. Free associations are not possible here. This technique gives inadequate consideration to the cognitive dimension because respondents select from a number of prescribed responses (De Rosa, 2002). A second group of measurement techniques is known as the implicit association test (Greenwald et al., 1998). These tests, which are widely used in market and consumer research, are carried out on a computer. The basic idea is that the faster a subject responds to a stimulus (word or image) on the screen by clicking a button (for example, plus or minus button), the more closely linked the two cognitive elements are in that person's mind (for example, a cognition referring to a picture of a man or woman with the evaluative cognition "positive" or "negative"). This technique likewise prescribes certain valuations or words, and fails to measure varying interpretations of the object in question.

There is therefore a need for an implicit technique that satisfies the following criteria. To allow valid and reliable measurements, the technique should be capable of identifying the deeper layers of attitudes and should incorporate both the affective and the cognitive dimension. Minimal demands should be made on the subjects (for example, in terms of computer knowledge). Furthermore, the technique should be suitable for use in larger surveys as well as small-scale studies, including the option for structured applications, for example, in telephone interviews or with structured questionnaires. The proponents of the FVA technique believe that it satisfies these requirements; in particular, it is capable of determining the cognitive dimension of attitudes, which other methods barely measure. As far as I am aware, the method has not yet been used in the field of HRM research in its narrower sense.

HISTORY OF THE METHOD'S USE

The FVA method has developed in parallel (and often in isolation) among a number of different scientific communities with different philosophical and theoretical assumptions (for an account of the historical background cf. Szalay and Brent, 1967; Szalay and Deese, 1978, pp. 9–16).

In recent decades, the FVA technique has attracted renewed interest, primarily among a group of psychologists focusing on the theory of social representation (Moscovici, 2001). They have coined the phrase "associative network analysis" (De Rosa, 2002; Kirchler, 1998). The main difference between this and the original use of the method (as in Deese, 1962) is in the elaborated data evaluation approach. Statistical techniques are used to attempt to identify networks or clusters of associations, and then to distinguish which individuals with certain features belong to which clusters or networks.

All variants work on the assumption that a spontaneous verbalisation (be it in the form of a single word or longer phrases) is considered a response to a stimulus term, and that this response expresses a person's (inner) mental state towards an (external) object – the object described in the stimulus (Szalay and Deese, 1978, p. 1). Thus, free associations with a stimulus word allow conclusions to be drawn about an individual's or group's deeper, cognitive and emotionally anchored value-knowledge structures.

RESEARCH VALIDITY AND CAVEATS

One key advantage of the FVA method is that it allows us to measure multiple dimensions of attitudes. First, the free associations provide an insight into the respondent's cognitive representation of an object. Second, the affective component of attitudes can then be measured by asking the subject to value these associations as positive or negative. One benefit of this method over others is that it measures attitudes indirectly, and therefore unobtrusively, and should therefore be largely uninfluenced by social desirability effects.

Another benefit is that the method can be used for both qualitative and quantitative, large-scale surveys. Admittedly, there are few examples in the literature of it being used with a large group of subjects (one example is the study by Moodie et al., 1995).

The fact that it is easy to use is another benefit. Even people unfamiliar with survey research (which depends to a large extent on their education and cultural milieu) will be able to state what crosses their mind when they hear a certain word, and whether the word has a positive, negative or neutral connotation for them. It is also easy to gauge its importance. The FVA research situation feels more like a natural conversation, whereas the usual scale-based questions with their structured responses create a more artificial situation.

One relative disadvantage compared with scale-based surveys is the amount of work potentially involved in preparation and evaluation of the data, especially where the survey returns large numbers of associations. Evaluation entails the processing of text strings rather than numerical values. Additionally, the researcher is required to categorise different words with the same or similar meanings. Respondents do not always follow the instruction limiting them to one-word associations, and often reply in whole sentences instead. These associations will need to be categorised, leading to a typical problem of qualitative research and the associated difficulties of preparing the data for quantitative analysis, as required with large groups of subjects.

USING THE METHOD ON ATTITUDES TOWARDS EMPLOYEE PARTICIPATION

We applied the FVA method in a research project on attitudes to employee participation among the German adult population (the project was financed by the Hans Böckler Foundation). Germany has an elaborate system of employee participation and codetermination that gives employees comparatively strong and wide-ranging rights (Fulton, 2013). This makes research into attitudes towards this system of codetermination particularly interesting because it sheds some light on the acceptance and legitimisation of this elaborate system. In a broad overview of empirical studies on employee participation, Greifenstein and Kissler (2010) conclude that the attitudes towards codetermination (*Mitbestimmung*) seem to be "diffuse positive" since its introduction after the Second World War (p. 47). A recent study of 2005 employees found very positive attitudes towards codetermination (Hans-Böckler-Stiftung and PolisSinus Gesellschaft für Sozial- und Marktforschung, 2008). All in all, we would expect the attitudes towards codetermination to be positive. However, we cannot rule out the possibility that these results were partly influenced by a social desirability bias (King and Bruner, 2000). In Germany, codetermination is an integral part of the industrial relations system, and we would expect it to be institutionalised in the sense of being "taken for granted" (Meyer and Rowan, 1977). At a superficial level, nearly everybody agrees with the advantages of codetermination, but one of our hypotheses is that at a deeper level, attitudes (on average) are much less positive. We were therefore keen to find a method suitable for measuring deeper levels and the content of attitudes, which led us to the FVA technique.

Data and Method

We used data from an Infratest Dimap telephone survey of 3203 people (87 per cent of them of working age) carried out in Germany in late 2013, and drew an age-disproportionate random sample. Because we were most interested in the attitudes of younger people, we included a larger number of respondents in the group of 15–30 year olds than their equivalent proportion in the general population.

In addition to the conventional Likert scales, we also used the indirect FVA technique to measure attitudes. The terms "participation" (*Mitbestimmung*), "employee participation" (*Mitbestimmung der Arbeitnehmer*) and "works council" (*Betriebsrat*) were used as the stimulus words. The German terms are not clearly translatable into English, particularly the word *Mitbestimmung*, which may mean both "codetermination" and "participation". If *Mitbestimmung* is used without a context, it is usually interpreted in the sense of "participation", but if used in conjunction with employees, work and companies, "codetermination" would be a more accurate translation where institutionalised, representative codetermination is concerned or "employee participation" where referring to less institutionalised, more direct participation (Page, 2011). The meaning that the respondents themselves ascribe to the German term *Mitbestimmung* is one of the research questions, and a prerequisite for being able to interpret the content of attitude measurements.

For each stimulus word, participants were asked to spontaneously associate up to five words (three associations in the case of the first stimulus word "participation"). The participants were then asked whether each of the words (or sentences) they associated with the stimuli "employee participation" and "works council" signified something positive or negative. The subject's associations with the word "participation" used in isolation were primarily used to gauge the extent to which they verbalise any workplace or company-related associations, or if their associations were limited to participation in a more general sense, for example, in connection with democracy.

This method enables us to measure three things: first, we can establish the extent of the subject's knowledge of participation. Respondents who verbalise no or very few associations are likely to be less knowledgeable than those who associate multiple words. Second, we can ascertain the content of that knowledge. What do people associate with participation? Do they associate it with work at all? And third, we can define their attitudes in a narrower sense by evaluating the content of the associated words (or sentences). In other words, we are able to measure the cognitive dimension as well as the affective or evaluative dimension of attitudes. Below are some of the results.

Extent of Knowledge about Employee Participation

The first interesting finding concerns the frequency of associations. In total, our subjects verbalised 13,367 associations in response to the three stimuli (participation: 4619; employee participation: 4129; works council: 4619), equivalent to approximately 1.6 associations per word per respondent for those who were able to verbalise at least one association.

Table 13.1 shows that 8.7 per cent were unable or unwilling to verbalise any associations in response to the stimulus "participation" (which is rather surprising, given that this is a very general word); 21 per cent and just under 18 per cent, respectively, gave no associations at all for the stimuli "employee participation" and "works council". Only around 3 per cent verbalised more than three associations. The fact that a person

*Table 13.1   Relative frequencies of respondents' answers to the association
questions (n = 3203 in each case)*

	Participation	Employee participation	Works council
No association	8.7	21.1	17.5
One association	52.9	45.4	50.8
Two associations	23.9	20.6	20.0
Three associations	14.5	10.0	8.9
Four or five associations	Not asked	2.8	2.8

is unable or unwilling to voice any associations to the two work context-
related participation stimuli is assumed to indicate the extent of their
knowledge about that topic.

Content of Knowledge about Employee Participation

To evaluate the content of associations, we rely on the development of a
system of categories. This is because many respondents associate the same
content but express it differently. Furthermore, different content can also
be summarised into general themes. We used two different systems of
categories. For the first stimulus word, we used an inductive approach, in
other words, we developed the categories from the data using a "bottom-
up" technique. Finally, we assigned the associations to four thematic
categories: "Participation in general"; "Democracy/politics", "Employee
participation", and "Other associations". Our main objective was to
identify whether the respondents' associations referred to employee or
workers' participation. For associations with the other two stimuli, we
used a system comprising a total of 98 different categories. This system of
categories was developed partly from a pre-test based on a student survey.
We also selected categories that play an important role in the political and
academic debate over employee participation. As such, we used a combination of inductive and deductive approaches.

First, let us consider the content of associations with the word
"participation". Just 21.3 per cent of respondents' associations made
reference to company-related topics and therefore referred to employee
participation. Most (30.8 per cent) responded with general words or sentences, such as "If you're in a dance group and everyone can have their
say, there's not just one person who's the boss"; 28.9 per cent verbalised
other associations, such as "helping others" or "being involved in a club";
19.1 per cent spontaneously thought of democracy and politics but not

of work-related participation – they responded with sentences such as "Everything connected to democracy (parliament, parliamentary group, political parties and so on)." Overall, this reinforces our theory that knowledge of participation in the sense of "employee participation" is not very pronounced.

What did Respondents Associate with the Next Stimuli, "Employee Participation" and "Works Council"?

In response to the stimulus "employee participation", just under 24 per cent of respondents verbalised one or more associations that we have summarised under works council or related institutions; around 21 per cent associated it with the word trade union and 14 per cent thought of working

Table 13.2   The first ten most frequent responses (categorised) associated with "employee participation" and "participation via the works council"

Employee participation		Works council	
Category	Percentage of participants with one or more associations	Category	Percentage of participants with one or more associations
Works Council or similar associations	24.3	Representation of employee interests	21.0
Trade union	20.8	Positive association	
Working hours	14.4	(e.g. "good")	13.5
Participation is very limited/does not exist	8.9	Participation in decision making	7.7
Wages	8.8	Help/support	6.5
Collective agreement	4.5	Negative (e.g. "bad")	6.0
Other associations	4.3	Company size	5.9
Working conditions	3.6	Employee rights	5.8
Participation in decision making	3.4	Other associations	5.7
Workplace/work context	3.4	Employee interests	5.4
		Election	5.1
Proportion of the ten most common responses: 61%		Proportion of the ten most common responses: 55%	

hours; 9 per cent spontaneously responded that there is no such thing as employee participation, or only in a very limited form (Table 13.2). (Because multiple responses are possible, the percentages across all categories add up to more than 100 per cent.)

For the term "works council", 20 per cent responded with a kind of definition, and verbalised associations such as "those are the employees' representatives" or similar; just under 14 per cent spontaneously voiced positive associations such as "is a good thing". The number of spontaneous explicitly positive associations was around twice as high as the negative ones (both in the sense of corresponding adjectives). Overall, we ascertained that associations were clearly concentrated on just a few categories. Ten categories cover 61 per cent and 55 per cent, respectively, of all associations; a significant proportion was distributed among the first few categories, then the numbers in each category became much smaller. On the one hand, this may reflect the weak cognitive anchoring of thoughts on participation in general, and employee participation specifically. On the other, the associations verbalised tend to be positive, and there are fewer indications of a negative assessment.

Affective Meaning of Employee Participation

The affective or evaluative dimension of attitudes to participation is derived from the respondents' valuations (Table 13.3).

The percentage of positive associations is 67.9 per cent in relation to "employee participation" and 69.8 per cent to "works council". However, it is important to remember that, particularly with regard to the stimulus "employee participation", respondents verbalised associations such as "does not exist", "little" or "sham". The same respondents subsequently valued these associations as negative. If a person states that there is insufficient participation and values this perceived status as negative, this cannot be interpreted as a negative attitude towards participation per se. We therefore rated the negative valuations of such "negative" associations as neutral in the index, and included them numerically. The percentage of negative words is relatively low (12.4 per cent and 6.7 per cent,

Table 13.3   Valuations of associations ($2384 \leq n \leq 2578$)

	Employee participation	Works council
Positive associations (%)	67.9	69.8
Negative associations (%)	6.9	11.6
Polarity index (mean)	0.65	0.59

respectively, for employee participations, and 13.5 per cent and 11.5 per cent, respectively, for works council).

We also calculated a polarity index (Polarity Index = (number of positive associations – number of negative associations)/(sum of all associations)). This index ranges from +1 to −1. The higher the index value, the more positive the attitude towards participation. The polarity index for both "employee participation" (on average 0.65) and "works council" (0.59) is very high. We can therefore conclude that the attitudes towards employee participation in general as well as works councils as concrete institutions are positive.

CHALLENGES AND SHORTCOMINGS

One initial challenge with the FVA method is that it requires a more detailed formulation and review of its measurement hypotheses. Does it really ascertain the deeper levels of attitudes, and how valid and reliable are the measurements? There has been very little research in this area. Handling the relatively large quantities of text data produced by surveys with a large number of subjects poses another challenge. When we embarked on this project, we imagined it would be possible to limit ourselves to a dictionary-based, computer-assisted analysis.

This approach was in fact used for the one-word associations (using the program MAXQDA). However, we later decided to code the multiple-word associations by hand. This necessitated training the coders and entailed a considerable amount of coordination work between them, particularly for non-matching codes. The fact that, unlike qualitative, in-depth interviews, there is little linguistic context available to aid interpretation makes it more difficult to allocate associations to one category. This is a potential source of errors.

DISCUSSION

The FVA technique offers a useful alternative or supplement to conventional, pre-structured questions, and also to qualitative interviews. It may be applied flexibly to both large and small numbers of respondents. As the number of cases increases, however, the work involved is likely to rise disproportionately. Furthermore, the demands placed on the respondents are comparatively low. If it is merely a matter of valuing a certain topic whose meaning is clear, simple assessment scales may suffice, and may even be more suitable than Likert scales or a semantic differential. On the other hand, in cases where it is unclear whether all respondents have the same understanding of a topic, the FVA technique may prove beneficial. With a complex topic like "participation", we can assume that not everyone has the same understanding of this word and the same cognitive representation. This is likely to be true of many HRM-related topics (work satisfaction, commitment and so on).

ANNOTATED FURTHER READING

De Rosa, A.S. (2002), "The 'associative network': a technique for detecting structure, contents, polarity and stereotyping indexes of the semantic fields", *European Review of Applied Psychology*, **52** (3–4), 181–200.
A good start for qualitative and quantitative researchers.

REFERENCES

Albarracin, D., Johnson, B.T. and Zanna, M.P. (eds) (2005), *The Handbook of Attitudes*, New York: Psychology Press.
Bassili, J. and Brown, R. (2005), "Implicit and explicit attitudes: research, challenges, and theory", in D. Albaracin, B. Johnson and M. Zanna (eds), *The Handbook of Attitudes*, Mahwah, NJ: Erlbaum, pp. 543–74.
Bohner, G. and Dickel, N. (2011), "Attitudes and attitude change", *Annual Review of Psychology*, **62**, 391–417.
De Rosa, A.S. (2002), "The 'associative network': a technique for detecting structure, contents, polarity and stereotyping indexes of the semantic fields", *European Review of Applied Psychology*, **52** (3–4), 181–200.
Deese, J. (1962), "On the structure of associative meaning", *Psychological Review*, **69** (3), 161–75.
Fiske, S. and Taylor, S.K. (2013), *Social Cognition: From Brains to Culture*, 2nd edn. London: Sage.
Fulton, L. (2013), "Worker representation in Europe", available at http://www.worker-participation.eu/National-Industrial-Relations (accessed 1 April 2016).
Greenwald, A., McGhee, D. and Schwartz, J. (1998), "Measuring individual differences in implicit cognition: the implicit association test", *Journal of Personality and Social Psychology*, **74**, 1464–80.
Greifenstein, R. and Kissler, L. (2010), *Mitbestimmung im Spiegel der Forschung: Eine Bilanz der empirischen Untersuchungen 1952–2010*, Berlin: Edition Sigma.
Hans-Böckler-Stiftung and PolisSinus Gesellschaft für Sozial- und Marktforschung (2008), *Arbeitnehmer-Meinungsmonitor 2008 (Datensatz und Fragebogen)*, Düsseldorf and München.
King, M.F. and Bruner, G.C. (2000), "Social desirability bias: a neglected aspect of validity testing", *Psychology and Marketing*, **17** (2), 79–103.
Kirchler, E. (1998), "Differential representations of taxes: analysis of free associations and judgments of five employment groups", *Journal of Socio-Economics*, **27** (1), 117–31.
Meyer, J.W. and Rowan, B. (1977), "Institutionalized organizations: formal structure as myth and ceremony", *American Journal of Sociology*, **83** (2), 340–63.
Moodie, E., Markova, I. and Plichtova, J. (1995), "Lay representations of democracy: a study in two cultures", *Culture Psychology*, **1** (1), 423–53.

Moscovici, S. (ed.) (2001), *Social Representations: Explorations in Social Psychology*, New York: New York University Press.

Osgood, C.E., Suci, G.J. and Tannenbaum, P.H. (1971), *The Measurement of Meaning*, 8th edn, Urbana, Il: University of Illinois Press.

Page, R. (2011), *Co-determination in Germany – A Beginners's Guide*, 5th edn, Düsseldorf: Hans-Böckler-Stiftung.

Rosenberg, M. and Hovland, C. (1960), "Cognitive, affective, and behavioural components of attitudes", in C. Hovland and M. Rosenberg (eds), *Attitude Organization and Change*, New Haven, CT: Yale University Press, pp. 1–14.

Schwarz, N. (2008), "Attitude measurement", in W. Crano and H. Prislin (eds), *Attitudes and Attitude Change*, New York: Psychology Press, pp. 41–60.

Szalay, L.B. and Brent, J.E. (1967), "The analysis of cultural meanings through free verbal associations", *Journal of Social Psychology*, **72** (2), 161–87.

Szalay, L.B. and Deese, J. (1978), *Subjective Meaning and Culture: An Assessment through Word Associations*, Hillsdale, NJ: Erlbaum.

14 Using qualitative diaries to uncover the complexities of daily experiences
Laura S. Radcliffe

INTRODUCTION

Investigating human beings, and subsequently strategies for managing people, is a somewhat difficult endeavour due to the fact that their lives, thoughts, feelings and decisions are infinitely complex. Authors across the human resource management (HRM) field have raised concerns that the most frequently used methods cannot adequately capture the complexity of the numerous interactions that are essential to our understanding of HRM (for example, Guest, 2011; Kiessling and Harvey, 2005). The everyday realities of people take place in an uncertain and changeable world where moods, experiences and behaviours fluctuate daily, or perhaps more frequently (Ohly et al., 2010). It is this daily element that many frequently used data collection methods are less able to capture (Radcliffe, 2013). This chapter aims to highlight the importance of capturing, and understanding, complex daily practices and experiences and, therefore, of more HRM researchers considering the use of qualitative research diaries; a method that has the ability to capture this complexity and dynamism.

The chapter begins by providing an overview of research diaries and how they can be utilised before introducing my own qualitative diary study, which explored how people deal with daily work–life conflict. It then continues by addressing some of the key challenges of utilising qualitative research diaries, whilst also providing some practical considerations with regards to dealing with these challenges. Additionally, it highlights the important benefits that can be achieved by persevering with this approach. In order to more effectively illustrate these practical issues and benefits, I have made reference to my own experiences of using qualitative diaries throughout. Finally, the chapter concludes by highlighting how this methodological approach can help move HRM research forward by gaining fresh and original insights into important issues that affect people in the workplace on a daily basis. It is hoped that this will encourage other HRM researchers to take on the challenges of this rich methodological approach in order to reap the research rewards.

QUALITATIVE DIARIES: AN OVERVIEW

A diary can be referred to as "a frequently kept, often daily, record of personal experiences and observations in which ongoing thoughts, feelings, and ideas can be expressed" (Travers, 2011, p.204). Whilst diaries are something with which we are all familiar in terms of recording our daily events and experiences, they are infrequently used as a data collection strategy (Radcliffe, 2013) – despite the fact that diaries are increasingly recognised as a valuable method in organisational and management research (van Eerde et al., 2005). They have the ability to capture the particulars of experience in a way that is not possible using traditional designs, and they permit the examination of reported events and experiences in their natural, spontaneous context (Reis, 1994). Diaries offer the advantage of immediacy (Symon, 2004), offsetting the problems of retrospective accounts and enabling recent events to be recalled in sufficient detail to afford new insights into complex phenomena (Poppleton et al., 2008; Radcliffe and Cassell, 2014).

A method with the ability to capture this dynamism is important in HRM research, where the focus is on understanding people, allowing a picture to be built up of the types of issues that are raised on a daily basis. Diaries that have been employed in previous studies in this area (for example, Butler et al., 2005; Doumas et al., 2003; Weiss et al., 1999; Williams and Alliger, 1994) tend to be quantitative, which act more like surveys, filled in by participants on a daily basis. Such quantitative diaries provide a useful way of capturing the dynamic nature of daily experiences as participants are required to think about events at the end of each day. They highlight daily changes, which other more retrospective techniques would be unlikely to recognise. However, because these diaries use self-report scales, each consisting of a small number of predefined items, they may overlook other important factors, neglecting valuable insights participants may have to offer. For example, Plowman (2010) demonstrated the value of qualitative diaries in one of the few HRM studies to utilise this approach. Her aim was to gain a deeper understanding of the meaning of "gendered" organisational culture in order to identify what needs to change and why. To achieve this, the staff and managers at the case study company were given diaries in order to record their individual self-reflection about daily events in the workplace. Her findings from this application of the diary method affirmed the value of qualitative diaries for uncovering the internal workings of organisations by revealing what goes on in the unofficial sphere of the organisation, which would normally remain undiscovered. This study demonstrates the utility of qualitative diaries in uncovering underlying issues from different perspectives.

This raises the question: why is the qualitative diary method of data collection so rarely utilised as part of HRM research designs? Quite simply, employing this approach entails numerous challenges; from acquiring participants who are willing to give up their time on a regular basis, to ensuring that diaries are effectively completed without the presence of the researcher (Radcliffe, 2013). This chapter discusses such challenges whilst arguing for perseverance in order to achieve the data collection benefits that this method affords.

PROJECT CONTEXT: USING QUALITATIVE DIARIES TO EXPLORE WORK–FAMILY DECISION-MAKING

This research project was concerned with exploring how dual-earner couples experienced, and subsequently made decisions to resolve, incidents of work–family conflict. As with any methodological decision, it is of course important to consider whether diaries are the most appropriate method, taking into account what one is aiming to achieve. In terms of my own research, I had noted that whilst there has been extensive research exploring the work–family interface, numerous methodological deficiencies within this area had been raised (for example, Casper et al., 2007). Research in this area has frequently relied upon examining individuals' general levels of conflict at a particular point in time using surveys rather than research conceptualising and measuring conflict as a specific event or episode (Maertz and Boyar, 2011). Work and family conflict has infrequently been explored in relation to actual interaction despite the everyday reality of people trying to manage work and family involving complex processes and dynamics, where reconciling different interpretations of events is a daily occurrence (Radcliffe and Cassell, 2014). I therefore considered diary studies to be particularly suitable to investigate the work–family interface as both the work and family domains are dynamic, changing daily (Butler et al., 2005; Williams and Alliger, 1994). I hoped that by collecting data using diaries I would have the opportunity to gain in-depth insights into the decision-making processes that dual-earner couples engage in when attempting to resolve daily work–family conflict. I wanted to gain a detailed understanding of the mechanisms and processes of decision-making in incidents of work–family conflict as they occur on a daily basis and in participants' own words.

My participants were 24 dual-earner couples (48 participants), all with child dependents, from a variety of organisations and occupations in both the public and the private sector ranging from school teachers to small business owners. In-depth interviews were conducted with participants prior to diary completion, exploring general work–life experiences as well as asking them to recall specific incidents. The diaries explored factors that are considered when couples make difficult work–family decisions. Each diary page consisted of four open-ended questions based on the aims of the research:

1.   Please describe any decisions where you made a choice between work and family today.
2.   What did you decide to do?
3.   How did you arrive at this decision? Please describe in as much detail as you can the decision process that you went through and ALL the factors that had an impact on the decision you made.
4.   What was the outcome of the decision that you made? Please explain how you felt about the decision and anything that occurred as a result of the decision.

Diaries were completed over 28 consecutive days, including weekends, either in hard copy or electronically (via email) according to preference. Participants were asked to report all incidents of work–family conflict experienced over time, as soon as possible after the incident occurred and in their own words. At the end of the diary period, unstructured telephone interviews were conducted with each individual separately, focusing on the content of the diaries, checking understanding and the participant's reactions to the experience.

USING QUALITATIVE RESEARCH DIARIES: CHALLENGES AND PRACTICAL SUGGESTIONS

In this section I briefly outline three key challenges that I faced when employing the qualitative diary method in my own research. After briefly addressing each challenge I offer practical suggestions, based on my own experiences, which can go at least some way to addressing these difficulties.

Challenge 1: Participant Commitment

The biggest challenge that I found when using qualitative diaries was attaining and maintaining the level of participant commitment and dedication required to successfully complete regular diary entries; a level of commitment rarely required in other types of research (Bolger et al., 2003). It is difficult to maintain this level of commitment to the research over time, without the presence of the researcher and especially when participants are, by the very nature of the research topic, people with little spare time. Subsequently, diaries are not always completed on time; slowing down data collection and analysis and causing concern about the information provided (busy participants may resort to completing diaries in retrospect, thus undermining one of the key benefits of using the diary method).

As a means of addressing this problem, it is especially important to maintain contact with participants throughout. Previous research has highlighted that "personal contact retains participants more so than monetary incentives or dependence upon goodwill towards science" (Bolger et al., 2003, p. 595). It is therefore important to contact participants regularly during diary completion to ensure any concerns are raised by providing further opportunity to ask questions. This helps to ensure that any issues are dealt with as they occur and to prevent loss of data due to misunderstandings or disillusionment with the study. During the initial interview I agreed with participants how they would like to be contacted during this period with the hope of avoiding, or at least minimising, the disruption to their daily lives. As a result, I contacted participants via telephone, text or email several times during the four-week period to provide the opportunity for further questions and to make sure they were happy to continue.

Another useful strategy is to agree exactly when and how diary entries should be made. Whilst some modern electronic diaries do have signalling features with the ability to inform participants of when to record an entry, if participants are being asked to report events as they occur these signalling features are unlikely to be useful. In such 'event-based' studies, it needs to be decided whether or not it is reasonable to ask participants to report an incident in their diaries immediately after the event. This can often be unrealistic; therefore, a more realistic approach might be to allow participants to postpone responding at inopportune moments (see Chong et al., 2014 for innovative approaches to allow for this using smart phone technology). A discussion regarding when participants would complete their diaries during the initial interview, along with encouragement to report events as soon as possible, can help to reduce fabrication due to highly retrospective accounts. For instance, Symon (2004) suggests that a participant regularly completing their diary on the train on the way home from work was free from distractions, therefore producing concise diary entries that were consistently recorded at the same time each day. It could also be useful to ask participants to record exactly when they completed their diary entry, or more specifically to note how much time had passed between the event and the recording. This not only gives researchers a clearer picture of the degree of retrospection within the account but may also encourage participants to make greater efforts to record their experiences as close to the event as possible, therefore minimising the introduction of retrospection as far as possible. In my own research I also gave participants the option to complete diaries either electronically via email or using traditional pen and paper. However, a wider variety of options for recording diary data can also be explored including audio diaries (for example, Boyd et al., 2004), video diaries and the more recent development of smart phone diary apps (Chong et al., 2014). In order to further facilitate regular responses, it is useful to provide participants with options so that they can select the approach that is most comfortable and convenient for them.

Challenge 2: Ensuring Effective and Useful Entries

A separate but related issue is ensuring that significant details are recorded, in sufficient depth, by participants. Unlike other qualitative methods, such as interviews, the researcher is not present to prompt participants or request a more detailed response, which can lead to loss of important information.

In order to encourage effective recording it is important to consider diary design carefully. There are three general categories of diary methods in the literature (Eckenrode and Bolger, 1995). These are:

1. interval-contingent, where experiences are recorded at regular, predetermined intervals of time;
2. signal-contingent, where participants report experiences whenever they are contacted by the researcher;
3. event-contingent, where participants report every time a preestablished event takes place.

Such considerations must, as always, be based on the research aims of each particular study. My own research relied upon an event-contingent schedule, as this made most sense given the purpose of the research (exploring work–family incidents). This type of diary is usually required when diaries are employed with the purpose of exploring particular incidents as they occur, since providing reports at fixed times each day would not ensure that a specific incident had occurred and could be reported. This design requires specific instructions, including a clear definition of the triggering event, because any ambiguities as to which events fall within that definition may cause participants to omit relevant events and a decrease in the number of events reported (Bolger et al., 2003).

In my own research, the initial interviews prior to diary completion were used as an opportunity to ensure that participants had a clear and specific understanding regarding what they were expected to report and in how

much detail. These interviews enabled me to build rapport with the participants, and beyond this it permitted me the opportunity to explain the task
of completing the diaries and the aims of the research in detail. Here I also
emphasised the importance of recording minor and routine work–family
conflicts, including the discussion of specific examples, to emphasise the
amount of detail required in their entries. As part of this initial interview I
employed the critical incident technique (Chell, 2004) asking interviewees
to recall a specific work–family conflict incident that they had experienced
recently. I then talked through this incident with the interviewees in order
to identify their decision-making process, and any factors that had an
impact upon this process, before explaining how this would work in relation to recording such an incident in their diary. This approach enabled
participants to understand the type of incidents that should be recorded in
their diary, as well as the importance of including adequate detail in terms
of their decision-making process and all the factors involved.

A related issue specifically relevant to designing qualitative diaries is
how much structure, if any, to incorporate in the diary. One of the challenges is to focus the research, drawing a line around what can be investigated in a particular study and what is out of the scope of that research,
whilst also avoiding imposing a structure onto participants that is not
their own. There are clear benefits of keeping diaries as unstructured as
possible; namely, to prevent participant's description of incidents being
confined in any way by the researcher's preconceived ideas. Indeed, this
is an important benefit of utilising qualitative rather than quantitative
diaries. However, a blank page might be daunting for some participants,
particularly those who may not have written for a significant period of
time. It is also important that the diary is designed in a way that encourages the reporting of as much relevant information as possible.

In order to make an informed decision regarding structure, pilot studies
can prove highly useful in trialling different layouts. I trialled various
diary structures before commencing with my own research and as a result
decided upon semi-structured diaries, consisting of four open-ended questions for each day. During the pilot studies, unstructured diaries consisting
of a blank page for each day led to daily reports that were not entirely relevant and lacking sufficient detail. Participants explained that without the
prompts of the semi-structured diary, they "would just have written what
happened, and not any feelings or why" and that they "did think about
it more" when completing the semi-structured diary. Overall, the semi-
structured diaries tended to produce more detail regarding the decision-
making process. However, there was still concern regarding restriction of
participant expression resulting in information loss since the aim of this
study was to capture participants' experiences from their point of view

and therefore a compromise was reached by including an extra space for further comments each day.

Challenge 3: Ethical Issues

From a researcher's perspective, when qualitative diaries fulfil their potential in terms of leading to the exposing and reflection of in-depth personal issues and insights, this is extremely beneficial in terms of the rich data that can be attained. However, this can also raise ethical issues around the impact that such in-depth reflection could have on participants – especially if the topic under discussion is particularly personal and of a sensitive nature. Such issues are further enhanced when the researcher considers conducting follow-up interviews with participants after reading personal disclosures within their diaries. In my own experience, follow-up interviews were an important element of this research approach, as they provided vital opportunities to clarify and discuss in more detail the issues raised in the diaries, in order to gain a more complete and in-depth understanding. However, bringing up emotive issues can be difficult and potentially have a negative impact on participants' emotional state (Corbin and Morse, 2003). In some cases, where sensitive issues and conflicts arise, it may not be ethical to raise the topic in the follow-up interview. Other authors have chosen not to conduct follow-up interviews because of such difficulties, and have instead chosen only to undertake single interviews (for example, Gatrell, 2009). As qualitative researchers, we must prioritise the interests of participants above our own desire to collect data and ethical guidelines iterate the need for researchers to protect participants from potentially harmful effects of qualitative research interviews (for example, British Psychological Society, 2010).

Subsequently any follow-up interviews should be conducted with careful consideration of whether it is appropriate to raise any issues that could cause harm to participants. Whilst these interviews provide an important opportunity to question the meaning and significance of events to the participant with the potential of producing a valuable depth of information (Zimmerman and Wieder, 1977), judgement calls are extremely important. One consequence of such considerations in designing my own research was that I made the decision to conduct follow-up interviews via telephone in an attempt to make participants more comfortable talking about any sensitive issues by permitting some degree of personal distancing (Gatrell, 2009).

It is also good practice to discuss impact with participants. Follow-up interviews provide an opportunity to discuss what impact, if any, keeping the diaries had on participants. Diaries can be used not only as a research tool but also as an intervention having the capacity to enable reflection and raise consciousness about the reported topic, allowing for a deeper understanding and space for thinking and acting on change (Alford et al., 2005; Plowman, 2010). It is useful, interesting and good practice to ascertain how taking part in the research affected the participants. For instance, in my own research, participants expressed how this process "made me think more about what I actually do" with some suggesting that it led to greater self-awareness such as enabling them to "analyse my motives" and others expressing greater awareness of their partner's roles and responsibilities, "realising more what the demands are on each other". For some participants this led to decisions to change behaviour and often participants reflected positively upon the experience in terms of enabling positive change.

SO WHY USE QUALITATIVE DIARIES?

There are clearly numerous challenges, which are not always straightforward to address, when it comes to using qualitative diaries for the purpose of HRM research. This is undoubtedly why this method is underutilised. So why should HRM researchers consider using qualitative diaries despite these challenges?

Qualitative diaries have the potential to offer several key benefits for HRM research; the ability to capture the specifics of events, including thoughts, feelings, considerations and reactions; the ability to capture these events as they happen to avoid the problems associated with retrospect; and their capacity to do this over numerous days, therefore enabling a longitudinal research design. Such an approach can lead to the revelation of new and interesting insights and details that remain unnoticed when employing other methods of data collection. Indeed, in my own research, the use of qualitative diaries led to a greater understanding of the actual conflicts experienced by employees on a daily basis, as well as how they were experienced and resolved, which is vital in the creation of successful policies or supportive strategies. This section explores each of these key benefits in a little more depth.

Qualitative Diaries Focus on the Detailed Exploration of Discrete Episodes

Qualitative diaries allow researchers to explore events and processes within the context of daily life in a way that is not possible with more traditional methods. This approach, in conjunction with the qualitative nature of the research, allows participants to express their own perception of their experiences of a specific event without restriction, therefore providing the opportunity to uncover thoughts and feelings that have not previously been exposed. In my own research on managing daily work–life conflict, taking an episodic approach enabled the discovery of thought processes and concurrent feelings leading to, and predicting, the selection of particular strategies for dealing with these conflicts. One example of this was the negotiation of reciprocal arrangements with others, which involved building, and maintaining, agreements of mutual reciprocation both within couples and externally with other parents. This was predicted by the estimated ability to reciprocate and maintain such relationships equitably and was also stimulated by various emotions including stress and guilt. It is argued that such depth of understanding regarding the complexity of how these strategies were (de)selected by participants would not have been possible using other, more traditional approaches to data collection.

Qualitative Diaries Take a Non-retrospective Approach

The lesser time lapse between the event occurrence and recording of the event also offers the opportunity for as much detail as possible to be recalled and reported. This enhances the benefits of the episodic approach by not only capturing the specifics but as many of the specifics as possible due to better participant recall. A better recollection of thought processes and emotions attached to events, experiences and decisions is much more likely if these events are recorded as soon after they happen as possible (Bolger et al., 2003). For example, by allowing participants to express their own perception of their experiences of a specific event freely, and with a lesser time lapse between the event occurrence and recording, the qualitative diaries used in my research permitted the revelation of previously undiscovered factors considered by participants when making decisions in incidents of work–family conflict (for example, Powell and Greenhaus, 2006). For example, participants frequently recalled making fairly intricate fairness judgements regarding others when deciding how best to manage specific conflicts. This might include decisions to seek support from an available party being influenced by the amount of support they had already provided over a particular time period, their reaction to support-giving in the past and their own personal circumstances at that particular time. Such considerations had not previously been explored in relation to work–family conflict (Radcliffe and Cassell, 2014). These factors may not have been recalled in an interview, at a time far removed from the actual event, as it is less likely that a person will be able to remember exactly what they were thinking at that time, as well as recalling all the influencing factors that led to a specific outcome (Radcliffe, 2013).

Qualitative Diaries Permit a Longitudinal Element

Rather than examining a specific topic at one specific point in time, the qualitative diary has the ability to capture context by demonstrating the impact of past events on subsequent events. Taking events, feelings or decisions in isolation often gives an incomplete picture of events. This method also enables the researcher to capture immediate, and not so immediate, outcomes. A within person analysis over time, exploring both practical and emotional outcomes over numerous days, permitted by the qualitative diary method, can lead to deeper insights – particularly in terms of emotions and the impact that these emotions have on a person over time. The more in-depth recall of specific events and related feelings permits the mapping of the impact of such emotions on emotions and events on subsequent days. For example, with regards to my own research I had noted that previous literature had highlighted mixed results regarding the benefits of flexible working. Some studies have reported that 'family-friendly' policies, such as flexible working arrangements, actually demonstrate positive relationships with family to work conflict (Hammer et al., 2005; Lapierre and Allen, 2006). Whilst the possibility of an increase in such conflict incidents for those with flexible working was found in my research, previous studies have not shown the longer-term daily impact on the employees themselves, and subsequently the organisation. My findings demonstrated how, despite some problems with flexible work arrangements, a lack of flexibility can continue to be damaging after the event due to the constraints this puts on daily decision-making (Radcliffe and Cassell, 2015). For example, one participant reported experiencing constraints placed upon her decision-making by an unsupportive and inflexible supervisor who refused to allow her to start work at 10 am rather than 9 am on an occasion where she was required to work away from home. Her concern about this decision continued to have a knock-on effect on both her work and personal life over the following days. The longitudinal nature of the research enabled the observation of the impact that imposing such constraints on decision-making can have over time. Beyond this, the necessity to continuously make decisions under such constraints was shown to lead to individuals leaving their organisation or intending to do so. Specific events and experiences are inextricably linked to previous and subsequent events, and how these are experienced. Qualitative diaries provide an opportunity to capture and explore these links in a way that other methods cannot.

IN CONCLUSION

This chapter highlights the numerous benefits of using qualitative diaries as well as addressing some of the challenges of employing this method and provides suggestions and design considerations for those considering collecting data in this way. Although the use of the qualitative diary method can entail numerous challenges, it is argued here that the benefits outweigh the problems.

Using qualitative diaries enables the exploration of everyday situations and aids in understanding events from the perspectives of individuals by gaining detailed descriptions of their experiences rather than trying to find explanations. In my own research, new findings were enabled by the substantial amount of detail attained using a non-retrospective, episodic and longitudinal approach that also allowed participants free expression to report their own perception of experiences. Beyond this, the use of qualitative diaries enabled emotional experiences to be captured at the time of event occurrence, which could otherwise have been lost or diluted using retrospective techniques (Symon, 2004). There was a focus on both practical and emotional outcomes providing greater insight into the actual daily experiences of participants as well as the impact that such emotional outcomes had on subsequent work–family scenarios. Such findings can throw new light on important HR issues. By using a new approach that has the ability to look at issues in a new light, important new insights have the opportunity to be uncovered, and the daily dynamics of complex issues and experiences can begin to be understood. In this way, qualitative diaries are extremely useful tools that should be considered by researchers looking to add new and valuable contributions to the existing HRM literature.

FURTHER READING

Radcliffe, L.S. (2013), "Qualitative diaries: uncovering the complexities of work–life decision-making", *Qualitative Research in Organizations and Management: An International Journal*, **8** (2), 163–80.

Symon, G. (2004), "Qualitative research diaries", in C.M. Cassell and G. Symon (eds), *Essential Guide to Qualitative Methods in Organizational Research*, London: Sage, pp. 98–114.

REFERENCES

Alford, W.K., Malouff, J.M. and Osland, K.S. (2005), "Written emotional expression as a coping method in child protective services officers", *International Journal of Stress Management*, **12** (2), 177–87.

Bolger, N., Davis, A. and Rafaeli, E. (2003), "Diary methods: capturing life as it is lived", *Annual Review of Psychology*, **54**, 579–616.

Boyd, D., Egbu, C., Chinyio, E., Xiao, H. and Lee, C.C.T. (2004), "Audio diary and debriefing for knowledge management in SMEs", in F. Khosrowshahi (ed.), *Proceedings 20th Annual ARCOM Conference*, Vol. 2, Heriot Watt University, Association of Researchers in Construction Management, 1–3 September, pp. 741–7.

British Psychological Society (2010), *Code of Human Research Ethics*, available at http://www.bps.org.uk (accessed 1 April 2016).

Butler, A.B., Grzywacz, J.G., Bass, B.L. and Linney, K.D. (2005), "Extending the demands-control model: a daily diary study of job characteristics, work–family conflict and work–family facilitation", *Journal of Occupational and Organizational Psychology*, **78** (2), 155–70.

Casper, W.J., Eby, L.T., Bordeaux, C., Lockwood, A. and Lambert, D. (2007), "A review of research methods in IO/OB work–family research", *Journal of Applied Psychology*, **92** (1), 28–43.

Chell, E. (2004), "Critical incident technique", cited in C.M. Cassell and G. Symon (eds), *Essential Guide to Qualitative Methods in Organizational Research*, London: Sage, pp. 98–114.

Chong, M.K., Whittle, J., Rashid, U. et al. (2014), "Methods for monitoring work–life balance in a digital world", Paper presented at the Socio-Technical Practices and Work–Home Boundaries Workshop at MobileHCI 2014, Toronto, Canada, 23 September.

Corbin, J. and Morse, J.M. (2003), "The unstructured interactive interview: issues of reciprocity and risks when dealing with sensitive topics", *Qualitative Inquiry*, **9** (3), 335–54.

Doumas, D.M., Margolin, G. and John, R.S. (2003), "The relationship between daily marital interaction, work, and health-promoting behaviors in dual-earner couples: an extension of the work–family spillover model" *Journal of Family Issues*, **24**, 3–20.

Eckenrode, J. and Bolger, N. (1995), "Daily and within-day event measurement", in S. Cohen, R.C. Kessler and L.U. Gordon (eds), *Measuring Stress: A Guide for Health and Social Scientists*, New York: Oxford University Press, pp. 80–101.

Gatrell, C. (2009), "Safeguarding subjects? A reflexive appraisal of researcher accountability in qualitative interviews", *Qualitative Research in Organizations and Management: An International Journal*, **4** (2), 110–22.

Guest, D.E. (2011), "Human resource management and performance: still searching for some answers", *Human Resource Management Journal*, **21** (1), 3–13.

Hammer, L.B., Neal, M.B., Newsom, J., Brockwood, K.J. and Colton, C. (2005), "A longitudinal study of the effects of dual-earner couples' utilization of family-friendly workplace supports on work and family outcomes", *Journal of Applied Psychology*, **90**, 799–810.

Kiessling, T. and Harvey, M. (2005), "Strategic global human resource management research in the twenty-first century: an endorsement of the mixed-method research methodology", *International Journal of Human Resource Management*, **16** (1), 22–45.

Lapierre, L.M. and Allen, T.D. (2006), "Work-supportive family, family-supportive supervision, use of organizational benefits, and problem-focused coping: implications for work–family conflict and employee well-being", *Journal of Occupational Health Psychology*, **11**, 169–81.

Maertz, C.P. Jr and Boyar, S.L. (2011), "Work–family conflict, enrichment, and balance under 'levels' and 'episodes' approaches", *Journal of Management*, **37**, 68–98.

Ohly, S., Sonnentag, S., Niessen, C. and Zapf, D. (2010), "Diary studies in organizational research: an introduction and some practical recommendations", *Journal of Personnel Psychology*, **9** (2), 79–93.

Plowman, P.J. (2010), "The diary project: revealing the gendered organisation", *Qualitative Research in Organisations and Management: An International Journal*, **5** (1), 28–46.

Poppleton, S., Briner, R.B. and Kiefer, T. (2008), "The roles of context and everyday experience in understanding work–non-work relationships: a qualitative diary study of white- and blue-collar workers", *Journal of Occupational and Organizational Psychology*, **81**, 481–502.

Powell, G.N. and Greenhaus, J.H. (2006), "Managing incidents of work–family conflict: a decision-making perspective", *Human Relations*, **59**, 1179–212.

Radcliffe, L.S. (2013), "Qualitative diaries: uncovering the complexities of work–life decision-making", *Qualitative Research in Organizations and Management: An International Journal*, **8** (2), 163–80.

Radcliffe, L.S. and Cassell, C. (2014), "Resolving couples' work family conflicts: the complexity of decision making and the introduction of a new framework", *Human Relations*, **67** (7), 793–819.

Radcliffe, L.S. and Cassell, C. (2015), "Flexible working, work–family conflict, and maternal gatekeeping: the daily experiences of dual-earner couples", *Journal of Occupational and Organizational Psychology*, **88** (40), 835–55.

Reis, H.T. (1994), "Domains of experience: investigating relationship processes from three perspectives", in R. Erber and R. Gilmore (eds), *Theoretical Frameworks in Personal Relationships*, Hillsdale, NJ: Erlbaum, pp. 87–110.

Symon, G. (2004), "Qualitative research diaries", cited in C.M Cassell and G. Symon (eds), *Essential Guide to Qualitative Methods in Organizational Research*, London: Sage, pp. 98–114.

Travers, C. (2011), "Unveiling a reflective diary methodology for exploring the lived experiences of stress and coping", *Journal of Vocational Behavior*, **79** (1), 204–16.

van Eerde, W., Holman, D. and Totterdell, P. (2005), "Editorial: special section on diary studies in work psychology", *Journal of Occupational and Organizational Psychology*, **78**, 151–4.

Weiss, H.M., Nicholas, J.P. and Daus, C.S. (1999), "An examination of the joint effects of affective experiences and job beliefs on job satisfaction and variations in affective experiences over time", *Organizational Behavior and Human Decision Processes*, **78** (1), 1–24.

Williams, K.J. and Alliger, G.M. (1994), "Role stressors, mood spillover, and perceptions of work–family conflict in employed parents", *Academy of Management Journal*, **37** (4), 837–68.

Zimmerman, D.H. and Wieder, D.L. (1977), "The diary: diary-interview method", *Urban Life*, **5** (4), 479–98.

15 Autoethnographic vignettes in HRM
Mark Learmonth and Michael Humphreys

INTRODUCTION

Many members of faculty in business schools have had relatively lengthy industrial experience prior to joining academia. Mark, for instance, the first author of this chapter, worked for 17 years in the UK National Health Service (NHS) before his PhD. Similarly, Mike worked in technical and further education colleges for 25 years before his PhD. Indeed, according to Higher Education Statistics Agency (HESA) data (employee statistics for UK universities), the average business PhD student graduates at 31 years of age – implying that many business PhDs have had careers prior to academia – while there is also a large cohort of DBA and executive MBA students who continue working as managers in the course of pursuing practice-orientated degrees. What this chapter will do, therefore, is to discuss the idea of "autoethnographic vignettes" – theoretically informed stories (vignettes) drawn from our own lives (auto) about our observations of working life (ethnography).

Indeed, a potentially rich well of data exists among business academics and students concerning their own personal, insider accounts – vignettes of working life. However, this well of experience remains relatively untapped, in part because there are few outlets to publish work based on one's own personal accounts. The aim of this chapter is to explore the value and potential impact of practitioner knowledge within academic writing, especially writing concerned with the lived experience of working lives. The intent is to develop methods in which:

1. Practitioners (or former practitioners) can provide personal, autobiographic vignettes about aspects of their own working lives that are of interest to non-academic audiences.
2. These same people can also critically analyse their own accounts within the conventions of academic writing.

One particular contribution of scholars' own personal vignettes is potentially to create new windows on "difficult-to-research" areas. Indeed, there are signs of an emergent interest within social sciences to make such writing more acceptable (see, for example, Doloriert and Sambrook,

2012). However, for us, the value of using vignettes is not just to analyse – it is also to evoke as powerfully as possible some of the personal consequences of being at work. We see potential for this sort of research within a range of current human resource management (HRM) issues including, for example, workplace bullying, work/life balance, home working and coping with the challenges of redundancy or unemployment. Vignettes about such issues, written by people who have directly experienced such things themselves, should appeal to non-academic audiences – particularly if the evocative element is done well. For academics too, these evocative autobiographical stories can provide a fine grain of detail, enabling analyses to reveal in new ways some of the contradictions inherent in working life, as well as the connections between one's personal dilemmas and wider social structures. In sum, they have potential to inform policy debates and management action.

In this chapter, therefore, we start by discussing a potential theoretical framework for presenting personal vignettes within academic writing – autoethnography. Then we look at the ways in which this kind of writing has already been attempted in management and organisation studies, finishing with some pitfalls to avoid as well as some ideas for those who are interested in constructing their own vignettes.

INTRODUCING AUTOETHNOGRAPHY

In recent years, certain leading ethnographic researchers have begun to place an increasingly strong emphasis on highly personal, experiential and emotionally evocative narratives. Often using drama, poetry and other experimental modes of literary and artistic expression in their quest for evocation (Denzin, 2003; Humphreys, 2005; Learmonth and Humphreys, 2012; Spry, 2009), the narratives produced seek to encourage empathy and identification in readers, along with a wide variety of other personal responses, which might range, for example, from therapeutic catharsis to political action. Furthermore, in seeking to "change the world by writing from the heart" (Denzin, 2006, p. 422), this mode of enquiry typically sets aside conventional social scientific preoccupations (with method, validity, reliability, generalizability and so on) in favour of factors like personal meaning, empathetic connection and identification. Indeed, in conducting such experimental ethnography, as Denzin explains, the "focus [is] on epiphanies, on the intersection of biography, history, culture and politics, turning point moments in people's lives" (2009, p. 335).

What is perhaps especially distinctive about this new genre, however, is its autobiographical nature. Researchers typically make their own life and experience the "focus of the [ethnographic] story, [it is, therefore, the author who is both] the one who tells and the one who experiences, the observer and the observed" (Ellis, 2009, p. 13). For its proponents, then, the principal contribution of such writing is that it offers:

> methodological alternatives to what one typically finds in academic scholarship . . . to put on display a researcher who, instead of hiding behind the illusion of objectivity, brings himself forward in the belief that an emotionally vulnerable, linguistically evocative, and sensuously poetic voice can place us closer to the subjects we wish to study . . . [an important consideration because] too often . . . claims of truth try to triumph over compassion, try to crush alternative possibilities, and try to silence minority voices. (Pelias, 2004, p. 1)

We think that the following narrative, drawn from a widely cited journal article, gives a flavour both of the literary style and the evocative, highly personal accounts that many in this new mode of experimental ethnography are attempting. The paper's narrator, Jim, "presents a story about the embodied struggles" (Sparkes, 2007, p. 521) he believes his job as a university academic involves. And in this excerpt, we join him by the copying machine in the midst of a chance encounter with Louise, a PhD student:

> Look Jim, I *know* you are busy. I *know* how stressed you are. You're *always* busy and stressed. But I'm also busy and stressed. *And* you *are* my supervisor and I have *got* to get my PhD on time. That's not going to happen if I can't get to you when I need to. And I need to right now. Not yesterday, not tomorrow, but today! I shouldn't have to feel guilty about asking for your time should I?
>
> Jim simply nodded in agreement. She was right on all counts. Bright, intelligent, dynamic and passionate about her research, she also worked four nights a week and some weekends in a restaurant to help fund her studies. Louise had every right to expect Jim to be readily available as her supervisor and guide her along the way. She should not have to feel guilty about asking for his time. But guilt was the feeling that washed over Jim as the photocopier continued to churn out the multiple copies of student notes for his lecture in 10 minutes' time. He felt guilty about the lack of concentrated time he could give any of his PhD students. He felt guilty about hastily skim reading their drafts of chapters and embryonic analyses. He felt guilty that he could not keep up with the reading he needed to do to push their ideas forward and support their thinking. He felt guilty because he was selling them short. He *hated* this feeling being associated with an aspect of the job he loved. But, even in this domain, the manic pressures of saturated time, the sheer busy-ness at UWA thwarted his desire to be the kind of supervisor he wanted to be and the kind of supervisor his doctoral students had the right to expect him to be.
>
> Standing there, Jim felt slightly disorientated. His emotions had swung from intense hostility to intense guilt in the space of a few moments. And now raw anger was seeping into the corporeal mix. Anger with a system that made him feel these emotions so often in his daily life. Each in their own way drained

> him, diminished him, eroded him, dehumanized him. (Sparkes, 2007, p. 533, emphasis in original)

This is a highly evocative vignette of academic life. Perhaps unsurprisingly though, critics of this kind of writing have been far from slow to point to its apparent avant-garde distance from – perhaps even outright diametric opposition to – the received aims and norms of social science. After all, as Behar puts it:

> No-one objects to autobiography, as such, as a genre in its own right. What bothers critics is the insertion of personal stories into what we have been taught to think of as the analysis of impersonal social facts. Throughout most of the twentieth century, in scholarly fields ranging from literary criticism to anthropology to law, the reigning paradigms have traditionally called for distance, objectivity and abstraction. The worst sin was to be too personal. (1996, pp. 12–13)

But one measure of how influential this intellectual current is becoming, nevertheless, is that it has acquired an increasingly widely recognised label: autoethnography. The term was appropriated from a somewhat older anthropological tradition with which it shares little, at least in terms of method; even so, in the early years of the twenty-first century, the popularity and influence of this newer version of autoethnography has started to take off. Indeed, according to the Proquest PhD dissertation index, over the ten years to 2009, there were 206 PhDs completed that focused centrally on autoethnography or similar personalised accounts.

THE RISE (AND RISE) OF AUTOETHNOGRAPHY

> The more one looks for the origins of autoethnography, the more they recede into the misty beginnings of the discipline now routinely censured for denying the possibility of autoethnography by silencing the native voice. One may even find oneself slipping far back beyond that, all the way back to the Socratic injunction "know thyself" which Malinowski was fond of quoting in his seminars. (Buzard, 2003, p. 66)

The classic fieldwork studies of twentieth-century anthropologists, sociologists (and, of course, organisational ethnographers) typically construct narratives in which the participant-observer enters into an alien culture, gets a view of that culture from within and then, as it were, escapes from that culture to present a vision of it unavailable to those inside. Early versions of autoethnography seem almost exactly to reverse this process: they concern looking at one's own culture from without, writing about it, then returning to that culture. Indeed, the earliest published work to use the term "auto-ethnography" for an approach to qualitative research discusses it as the anthropological analysis of one's "own people" (Hayano, 1979, p. 99). Instead of studying "a distinctly different group than their own" (1979, p. 100) – the standard practice in anthropology – Hayano's version of auto-ethnography envisages ethnographers who "possess the qualities of often permanent self-identification with a group and full internal membership, as recognized both by themselves and the people of whom they are a part" (1979, p. 100). In a subsequently published monograph, Hayano provides an extended example of this version of auto-ethnography, analysing a group to which he himself had long belonged: Poker's (that is, the card game) loose network of nocturnal devotees (Hayano, 1982; see Van Maanen, 1988, pp. 106–7 for a contemporaneous commentary).

It is clear, therefore, that the way Hayano originally envisaged auto-ethnography differs significantly from today's dominant "experimental" version. The latter after all seeks to fuse intimate and embodied autobiography with ethnography. Indeed, Hayano proposes what now seem fairly conventional methods and foci. In particular, Hayano's version of auto-ethnography remains intent upon the observation and analysis of others (albeit others who share membership of the same group as the ethnographer). Unlike experimental autoethnography, Hayano is relatively uninterested in the details of the researcher's own autobiography, and does not trouble the conventional ethnographic distinction between the observer and the observed – a distinction that experimental autoethnography seeks at least to deconstruct; perhaps to dissolve entirely.

Nevertheless, there are still elements of Hayano's work that are shared with today's experimental autoethnography. Hayano questions the taken for granted benefits of an ethnographer's status as an objective outsider; he also makes pertinent his own biography, at least in the sense that explicit analytical use is made of his (previous and ongoing) personal relations with the group studied. So, while injecting into his own definition a stress on autobiographical detail not found in Hayano's work, Norman Denzin, a leading proponent of today's experimental autoethnography, seems to have been influenced by Hayano's arguments in this, his own early formulation of auto-ethnography (note, for instance, their shared hyphen that Denzin is soon to drop):

> An *auto-ethnography* is an ethnographic statement which writes the ethnographer into the text in an autobiographical manner . . . This is an important variant in the traditional ethnographic account which positions the writer as an objective outsider in the texts that are written about the culture, group or person in question . . . A fully grounded biographical study would be

auto-ethnographic and contain elements of the writer's own biography and personal history. (1989, p. 34, emphasis in original)

Another early definition of autoethnography as "insider account", which, like Hayano's comes from a cultural anthropological tradition, is rather more self-conscious than Hayano about the power relations inherent in representing "the other":

> "autoethnography" or "autoethnographic expression" . . . refers to instances in which colonized subjects undertake to represent themselves in ways that *engage with* the colonizer's terms. If ethnographic texts are a means by which Europeans represent to themselves their (usually subjugated) others, autoethnographic texts are texts the others construct in response to or in dialogue with those metropolitan representations. . . . Autoethnographic texts differ [therefore] from what are thought of as "authentic" or autochthonous forms of self-representation . . . [because autoethnography] involves partly collaborating with and appropriating the idioms of the conqueror . . . [and] are usually addressed both to metropolitan readers and to literate sectors of the speaker's own social group. (Pratt, 1992, p. 9, emphasis in original)

Pratt's version of autoethnography shares Hayano's focus on insiders' accounts of themselves (rather than outsider-ethnographers' accounts of the other), but it is much more explicit about the power asymmetries involved in rendering to the other an account of one's own self or group. For Pratt, autoethnography always emerges from the receiving (or resisting) end of ethnographic work. She argues that subjugated groups, should they wish to speak of themselves in ways intelligible to their oppressors (and thereby producing her version of an autoethnographic account), are obliged to appropriate certain of their oppressor's intellectual resources. Indeed, her main example is a 1200-page account of the history and culture of the Inca. Dated 1613, and addressed to King Philip III of Spain, the account was written in a mixture of Spanish and Quechua by Felipe Guaman Poma de Ayala as a response to Spanish misrepresentations of the conquered people's way of life.

Thus, while Pratt's version of autoethnography is again rather different from experimental autoethnography, it seems to us that Pratt shares with experimental autoethnographers important debts to similar intellectual traditions. For instance both versions were borne, at least in part, out of a concern to be responsive to the problematic nature of ethnographic authority. Both are sensitive, in other words, to the question: How can one speak about or on behalf of the other? Indeed, Ellis and Bochner (2000, p. 735) chart the development "of reflexive, experimental, autobiographical and vulnerable texts" within an intellectual framework indebted to major poststructuralist and feminist thinkers, one that encourages the uncovering of:

multiple perspectives, unsettled meanings, plural voices, and local and ille-
gitimate meanings that transgress against the claims of a unitary body of
theory . . . [as well as] exposing how the complex contingencies of race, class,
sexuality, disability, and ethnicity are woven into the fabric of concrete personal lived experiences. (2000, p. 735, emphasis omitted)

There is a sense then in which today's experimental autoethnography can
be seen as one of a number of the more radical ethnographic responses to
emerge from the crisis of representation in the 1980s and 1990s.

ORGANISING AND MANAGING AUTOETHNOGRAPHY

In a brief review, Doloriert and Sambrook (2012) classify current organisational and management autoethnographic research into three "streams",
namely: studies within higher education (HE) organisations; accounts of
"previous/other life" organisations; and complete member research in
other organisations. Unsurprisingly perhaps, given the relative convenience of writing about self within one's own organisation, there is an ever-
growing list of autoethnographies of academic life covering the areas of
teaching, research and administration particularly in the perceived mana-
gerialist context of recent research assessment exercises.

The second and third streams of management literature identified
by Doloriert and Sambrook (2012) are broadly speaking the kinds of
approaches we are advocating in this chapter. The second of their streams
consists of autoethnographic accounts written by academics about their
"experiences elsewhere, particularly their work experiences prior to enter-
ing HE, although this could include work experiences simultaneously with
HE" (p. 86). The third category identified by Doloriert and Sambrook
(2012) encompasses autoethnographies written by "complete" members
of non-academic organisations. Doloriert and Sambrook (2012) seem to
be particularly advocating the notion of the "co-produced autoethnography where at least one author is researcher and the other a practitioner
working in a non-academic organisation" (p. 87). We ourselves feel that
a very useful way of getting practitioners (and/or academics who were
practitioners) to provide autoethnographic accounts of their working lives
is through the explicit use of vignettes. After all, we all have these kinds of
experiences to draw upon; the key issue is to make use of these experiences
in a scholarly way, while still making them fully accessible to a practitioner
audience. How to do it – not just in published work but also in student
theses and dissertations – is the question to which we now turn.

AUTOETHNOGRAPHIC VIGNETTES

Vignettes have been variously defined as: "short scenarios in written or pictorial form, intended to elicit responses" (Hill, 1997, p. 177); "concrete examples of people and their behaviours on which participants can offer comment or opinion (Hazel, 1995, p. 2); "stories about individuals, situations and structures which can make reference to important points in the study of perceptions, beliefs and attitudes (Hughes, 1998, p. 381). Such vignettes have been used in the study of attitudes, perceptions, beliefs and norms across a wide and diverse range of social research topics including, for example, violence between children in residential care homes (Barter and Renold, 2000), drug injectors' perceptions of HIV risk and safer behaviour (Hughes, 1998) and social work ethics (Wilks, 2004). These vignettes, often generated from ethnographic research, are constructed as plausible, vivid examples of situations with which the different groups can identify and are intended to be effective in generating conversations, ideas, group discussion. Thus, as a qualitative research tool vignettes appear accepted, quite commonly used and effective not only as a vehicle for empirical social science research but also a training resource.

However, we would like to examine and, indeed advocate, a more controversial use of vignettes in research, specifically their use in autoethnographic texts where they may be used as an evocative "representational strategy of authorial voice and narrative form" (Jeffcutt, 1994, p. 242). Sparkes's tale of academic life previously cited is a good example of such a vignette, which in Spry's terms "reveal[s] the fractures, sutures and seams of self-interacting with others in the context of researching lived experience" (2001, p. 712). We suggest that the combination of vignettes and autoethnography presents an opportunity for synergy between academics and management practitioners by giving voice to both the researcher and the researched. As Jarzabkowski et al. (2014, p. 280) put it, "The evidentiary power of such vignettes lies in their plausible, vivid, and authentic insights into the life-world of the participants, which enables readers to experience the field, at least partially." Here are two examples from our own previously published work:

Mike in a Turkish Technical College

The taxi turns right out of the honking traffic through the main gate set within a forbidding, three metre high, spiked wrought iron fence. The taxi driver asks us, in English, whether the fence is there to keep students in, or others out. Students mill about in the yard, between the fence and the dull grey concrete buildings. They are nearly all female, and there seem to be two styles of dress. Some wear short skirts or jeans, sweaters, shirts, boots and long hair. In contrast to this there are some in Islamic dress, their hair and head fully covered by the hijab or scarf and only the skin of the face and hands visible. We enter the main door, and are greeted by the caretakers, all brown-suited middle aged men with moustaches, leaning against, grey unadorned walls. We pass the student common room and tobacco smoke billows from the door. We walk along a tile-floored corridor past a large black bust of Atatürk, a Turkish National flag, tall glass cabinets with examples of costume and embroidery, and continue onto a grimy stone floor, passing hundreds of students along the way. (Humphreys and Watson, 2009, p. 43)

Mark Working in Health Care
As a health care manager I had been tasked with implementing a new ward-based MIS [management information] system. What I had assumed would be minor changes in nurses' work in exchange for substantial gains in terms of the management systems was seen very differently by the nurses themselves. They argued that looking after patients would be seriously compromised, to an extent that far outweighed what they thought were the cosmetic gains in having a slicker administrative system. Whatever the rights and wrongs, it was clear that the political benefits to the top managers in being seen as leaders in MIS meant that there was no question of not implementing the new system. During the implementation, I happened to overhear two nurses expressing to one another their strong personal animosity against me because of my involvement. The realization of their hostility left me quite shocked and hurt. I had not anticipated it, and at the time, could not work out why it should have been so vociferous. (Griffin et al., 2015, p. 29)

Mike's vignette is a contextual scene-setting story in the style of Van Maanen (1988, p. 136) who described such vignettes as "personalised accounts of fleeting moments of fieldwork in dramatic form", adding flavour to an account of a difficult consultancy visit and subsequent discussion of culture difference. Mark's vignette is more organisationally focused and formed the basis of an exploration of alternative approaches to HRM. We consider that using vignettes of work experience in this way can enhance the theory and practices of both academics and practitioners. This has particular application in published research papers by addressing things like intimacy, insider knowledge and difficult research subjects where ethics might make access difficult. Thus, "vignettes can illustrate the nexus of concepts and relationships, often within a richly conveyed context, which the surrounding text can then tease out" (Jarzabkowski et al., 2014, p. 281). However, while authors' personal involvement in both telling stories and analysing them arguably means that they may be able to bring a greater understanding of the personal issues at stake, there is also a range of problems inherent in providing one's own personal accounts.

PITFALLS AND IDEAS FOR CONSTRUCTING AUTOETHNOGRAPHIC VIGNETTES

Problems with the use of autoethnographic vignettes include, for example: (1) memory and forgetting (that is, as opposed to standard ethnography, most autobiographical accounts are necessarily written without diaries or other records); (2) narcissism and methods for the re-presentation of self (that is, self-stories attract the criticism that they are really just about satisfying researchers' self-regard); (3) the creation of critical distance (that is, the extent to which it is possible, or desirable, to detach oneself from the emotions involved in one's own stories). We have explicitly acknowledged the problems with autoethnographic vignettes in a previously published piece:

> From a methods point of view, it is worth making explicit that these texts of our stories were not derived from any kind of ethnographic field notes – none were taken because the significance of the events only became evident to us later. Thus the tales were constructed, initially from memory, and subsequently evolved through discussions with one another, and also from presentations of proto-versions at various conferences. (Learmonth and Humphreys, 2012, p. 115)

Crucially, autoethnographic scholarship requires a literary kind of writing skill, in order to avoid being boring, unimaginative and unreadable. But, practically speaking, how do you start? As autoethnography is about your own lived experience, you do need to have lived and had some experiences and, of course, you also have to recall your lived experiences. In this regard, diaries and other forms of records (email threads, files on previous papers, old CVs, as well as more personal stuff – letters, photographs, scrapbooks and so on) are all invaluable sources for your stories – as is your own imagination and your ability to make sense through theoretical lenses. There is no "blueprint" for autoethnography (fortunately). But it does mean that to write a tale that other people will find interesting you need to have a wide awareness of the almost infinite variety of ways in which stories can be told successfully. And that reminds us of another point – we don't think autoethnographies are something that can be knocked off over night. In other words, autoethnography is not an easy option – just writing down your thoughts may be the start but to be most likely to interest anyone, the story needs to be told well, has to have a (theoretical/analytical) point and you need to persist.

THE POTENTIAL OF AUTOETHNOGRAPHIC VIGNETTES FOR MANAGEMENT RESEARCH AND PRACTICE

In organisation and management studies autoethnography remains on the margins of scholarly endeavour; a marginality that in our view represents a loss, overall, to the discipline. Indeed, while we would hardly wish it to displace the primacy of more conventional forms of organisational ethnography (Watson, 2011) we nevertheless find much to commend in the best autoethnographies. The emphasis on the personal and evocative, along with autoethnography's often literary and storied nature, seems to us to open up new opportunities for a range of novel contributions to be made – including, importantly, contributions by practitioners. These characteristics of autoethnography can, we believe, also provide illuminating parallels with more established modes of representation within management studies and management practices. Autoethnographic accounts are also enhanced and made more vivid by "vignettes [which] are a particularly useful way to illustrate the messy and entangled interrelationships between concepts as they actually occur within the field" (Jarzabkowski et al., 2014, p. 280). Management practitioners can use their experiences to construct such evocative vignettes that in turn can form the basis for analytical autoethnographic research papers. This could not only improve working relationships between practising managers and academics (thereby enhancing MBA Executive education!) but also, potentially, provide synergistic insights into topical and perhaps difficult organisational issues.

FINAL THOUGHTS ON PUBLICATION

We conclude with a note of academic caution. Publishing autoethnographic work can sometimes be problematic because of the restricted range of publication possibilities in management and organisation studies. Currently, it is rare for the "big" US management journals to publish anything calling itself autoethnography (though see Pilegaard et al., 2010 in *Academy of Management Perspectives* and Karra and Phillips, 2008 in *Organizational Research Methods* for exceptions). At the moment, however, sympathetic homes for management autoethnography include *Qualitative Research in Organization and Management: An International Journal* (for example, Doloriet and Sambrook, 2009) and *Culture and Organization* (which recently published a special edition on autoethnography, Boyle and Parry, 2007). Others that we know have published autoethnography include *Organization* (for example, Keenoy and Seijo, 2010); *Management Learning* (for example, Bell and King, 2010); *Critical Perspectives on Accounting* (for example, Haynes, 2006); *Human Relations* (for example, King and Learmonth, 2015) and *Journal of Business Ethics* (for example, Boje and Tyler, 2009). We recommend trying!

REFERENCES

Barter, C. and Renold, E. (2000), "I wanna tell you a story: the use of vignettes in qualitative research", *International Journal of Social Research Methodology*, **3** (4), 307–23.

Behar, R. (1996), *The Vulnerable Observer: Anthropology that Breaks Your Heart*, Boston, MA: Beacon.

Bell, E. and King, D. (2010), "The elephant in the room: critical management studies conferences as a site of body pedagogics", *Management Learning*, **41** (4), 429–42.

Boje, D. and Tyler, J.A. (2009), "Story and narrative noticing: workaholism autoethnographies", *Journal of Business Ethics*, **84**, 173–94.

Boyle, M. and Parry, K. (2007), "Telling the whole story: the case for organizational autoethnography", *Culture and Organization*, **13** (3), 185–90.

Buzard, J. (2003), "On auto-ethnographic authority", *The Yale Journal of Criticism*, **16**, 61–91.

Denzin, N.K. (1989), *Interpretive Biography*, Newbury Park, CA: Sage.

Denzin, N.K. (2003), *Performance Ethnography: Critical Pedagogy and the Politics of Culture*, Thousand Oaks, CA: Sage.

Denzin, N.K. (2006), "Analytic autoethnography, or deja vu all over again", *Journal of Contemporary Ethnography*, **35**, 419–28.

Denzin, N.K. (2009), *Qualitative Inquiry Under Fire*, Walnut Creek, CA: Left Coast Press.

Doloriert, C. and Sambrook, S. (2009), "Ethical confessions of the 'I' of autoethnography: a student's dilemma", *Qualitative Research in Organization and Management: An International Journal*, **1** (1), 27–45.

Doloriert, C. and Sambrook, S. (2012), "Organisational autoethnography", *Journal of Organizational Ethnography*, **1** (1), 83–95.

Ellis, C. (2009), *Revision: Autoethnographic Reflections on Life and Work*, Walnut Creek, CA: Left Coast Press.

Ellis, C. and Bochner, A.P. (2000), "Autoethnography, personal narrative, reflexivity: researcher as subject", in N.K. Denzin and Y.S. Lincoln (eds), *Handbook of Qualitative Research*, 2nd edn, Thousand Oaks, CA: Sage, pp. 733–68.

Griffin, M., Humphreys, M. and Learmonth, M. (2015), "Doing free jazz and free organizations, 'a certain experience of the impossible'? Ornette Coleman encounters Jacques Derrida", *Journal of Management Inquiry*, **24** (1), 25–35.

Hayano, D.M. (1979), "Auto-ethnography", *Human Organization*, **38**, 99–104.

Hayano, D.M. (1982), *Poker Faces*, Berkeley, CA: University of California Press.

Haynes, K. (2006), "A therapeutic journey? Reflections on the impact of research on researcher and participant", *Qualitative Research in Organizations and Management: An International Journal*, **1** (3), 204–21.

Hazel, N. (1995), "Elicitation techniques with young people", *Social Research Update*, No. 12, Department of Sociology, University of Surrey, available at http://www.soc.surrey.ac.uk/sru/SRU12.html (accessed 24 October 2011).

Hill, M. (1997), "Research review: participatory research with children", *Child and Family Social Work*, **2**, 171–83.

Hughes, R. (1998), "Considering the vignette techniques and its application to a study of drug injecting and HIV risk and safer behaviour", *Sociology of Health & Illness*, **20** (3), 381–400.

Humphreys, M. (2005), "Getting personal: reflexivity in autoethographic vignettes", *Qualitative Inquiry*, **11** (6), 840–60.

Humphreys, M. and Watson, T.J. (2009), "Ethnographic practices: from 'writing-up ethnographic research' to 'writing ethnography'", in S. Ybema, D. Yanow, H. Wels and F. Kamsteeg (eds), *Organizational Ethnography: Studying the Complexities of Everyday Organizational Life*, London: Sage, pp. 40–55.

Jarzabkowski, P., Bednarek, R. and Le, J.K. (2014), "Producing persuasive findings: demystifying ethnographic textwork in strategy and organization research", *Strategic Organization*, **12** (4), 274–87.

Jeffcut, P. (1994), "From interpretation to representation in organizational analysis: postmodernism, ethnography and organisational symbolism", *Organization Studies*, **15** (2), 241–74.

Karra, N. and Phillips, N. (2008), "Researching 'back home' international management research as autoethnography", *Organizational Research Methods*, **11** (3), 541–61.

Keenoy, T. and Seijo, G. (2010), "Re-imagining email: academics in the Castle", *Organization*, **17** (2), 177–98.

King, D. and Learmonth, M. (2015), "Can critical management studies ever be 'practical'? A case study in engaged scholarship", *Human Relations*, **68**, 353–75.

Learmonth, M. and Humphreys, M. (2012), "Autoethnography and academic identity: glimpsing business school doppelgängers", *Organization*, **19**, 99–117.

Pelias, R.J. (2004), *A Methodology of the Heart: Evoking Academic and Daily Life*, Walnut Creek, CA: AltaMira Press.

Pilegaard, M., Moroz, P.W. and Neergaard, H. (2010), "An autoethnographic perspective on academic entrepreneurship: implications for research in the social sciences and humanities", *Academy of Management Perspectives*, **24** (1), 46–61.

Pratt, M.L. (1992), *Imperial Eyes: Travel Writing and Transculturation*, 2nd edn, London: Routledge.

Sparkes, A.C. (2007), "Embodiment, academics, and the audit culture: a story seeking consideration", *Qualitative Research*, **7**, 521–50.

Spry, T. (2001), "Performing autoethnography: an embodied methodological praxis", *Qualitative Inquiry*, **7** (6), 706–32.

Spry, T. (2009), "Bodies of/as evidence in autoethnography", *International Review of Qualitative Research*, **1**, 603–10.

Van Maanen, J. (1988), *Tales of the Field*, Chicago, IL: University of Chicago Press.

Watson, T.J. (2011), "Ethnography, reality and truth: the vital need for studies of 'how things work' in organisations and management", *Journal of Management Studies*, **48** (1), 202–17.

Wilks, T. (2004), "The use of vignettes in qualitative research into social work values", *Qualitative Social Work*, **3**, 78–87.

PART IV

INNOVATIVE DATA ANALYSIS

16 Computer-supported qualitative research
Julie Cogin and Ju Li Ng

INTRODUCTION

For many years, qualitative analysis has largely been undertaken using manual techniques. Since the late 1980s, dedicated software has been developed to aid qualitative analysis. The first generation of computer programs was largely designed to assist researchers in managing data by enabling the structuring of information from focus groups, field notes and interviews. One of the first computer-assisted qualitative data analysis software (CAQDAS) packages (developed by Australian academic Tom Richards) was called NUD*IST, which stands for Non-numerical Unstructured Data Indexing, Searching and Theorising. It was designed to provide a program like SPSS but as a non-Statistical Package for Social Scientists.

Second generation CAQDAS packages introduced functions for coding text and manipulating, searching and reporting on the coded text. This assisted researchers in the retrieval of text from data, enabled scholars to code that data and develop a system of relating codes to each other using tree-like structures.

Recent third generation CAQDAS packages have become more advanced and go beyond manipulating, searching and reporting on coded text to assist in analysis by providing tools to help researchers examine relationships in the data, support in the development of theories and in testing hypotheses. Some programs (for example, QSR NVivo) support the analysis of rich text, websites, social media, diagrams and the incorporation of images, movies and other multimedia data.

In the following section we outline some of the benefits of CAQDAS so that its potential can be more fully realised in the human resource management (HRM) field.

BENEFITS OF CAQDAS

Robust analysis of qualitative data is demanding, repetitive and laborious. Primarily a manual exercise, it requires a researcher to be intuitive, to reason and theorise and most of all to be patient. Essentially, analysis is a process of reduction and accumulation to manage and classify data. Richards calls this process "decontextualizing and recontextualizing" (2002, p. 200). The process enables the development of concepts and theories to help understand the phenomena under study. As such, qualitative research is an inductive (or abductive) approach to the development of theory, rather than a deductive approach that tests theories that have already been proposed as quantitative research follows.

In order to pursue a qualitative approach a scholar must immerse him or herself into a context, spend time becoming familiar with data and subjects and, through subjective interpretation, build knowledge. It is a continuous process that dominates the research activity, beginning with data collection through to conceptualisation and beyond.

In an attempt to better manage time throughout this process, some scholars have turned towards CAQDAS. Reducing the time needed in decontextualising and recontextualising as well as minimising repetition is one of the central benefits of CAQDAS. One example of how time can be saved using CAQDAS can be seen in the calculation of intercoder reliability scores. Instead of manual handling and sorting of data using the various formulas, CAQDAS can calculate scores with ease (see Lombard et al., 2002 for a full description).

Another benefit is that CAQDAS effectively supports an abductive approach that begins with an unexpected observation before working backward to understand this anomaly (Saunders et al., 2012). In this way, CAQDAS is extremely helpful in moving back and forth between ideas, data and theories to produce new knowledge, providing opportunities for reflection during the data collection process, with consequent redirection if necessary. Monks et al.'s (2013) study seeking to understand how HR systems work, the role of HR philosophy and HR processes, is a good example of this. In the study, 56 semi-structured interviews with employees in seven information and communications technology (ICT) firms were undertaken. The authors used three stages of NVivo data analysis. In phase one, coding focused on identifying the broad HR configurations identifiable within the data. The results of phase one led to phase two coding, seeking to identify hierarchical structures and breaking down the categories into subcategories to better understand the meanings embedded therein (the HR philosophies, HR policies and HR processes). This led to phase three that consisted of analysing employees' experiences of each system. In this project, coding using CAQDAS would have made continuous data analysis a much easier process, as well as enabled the evolution of inquiry throughout the study. This approach was also utilised by Kellner et al. (2014) in a study on the degree of HRM corporate control and autonomy in franchised coffee chains. The authors used a two-step coding procedure via NVivo of reading and rereading data, assigning keywords (second-order categories) to passages of text, and sorting and identifying emerging themes (first-order categories).

Another benefit of CAQDAS is that it can assist researchers by providing improved data management by compiling all of the documents, coding information and associated files needed for analysis. The HRM field is becoming more sophisticated using multi-source and multi-level data with larger sample sizes (Sanders et al., 2013) and subsequently projects are becoming more complex. CAQDAS provides a versatile and efficient system of collecting, storing and reporting, becoming an important project management resource. In our own research we used QSR Nvivo 10 as a central management tool while employing a grounded theory approach. Specifically, we used the memo function in NVivo to document the research log and chronologically outline the entire research process, including the logic surrounding a three-phase participant recruitment process and two-phase theoretical sampling method as well as our reasoning behind all coding and abstraction. This provided us with a faster method of inquiring into the data and enhanced our ability to sort, sift, search and think through the identifiable patterns and idiosyncrasies in the large dataset that was constructed. Given the project was fully funded by an external government body, using CAQDAS as a project management resource greatly assisted in regular reporting of research progress.

In the past, qualitative research has been criticised because of lack of transparency with some suggesting qualitative research has a reputation for untrustworthy results supported by cherry-picked anecdotes. The use of CADQAS, when grounded in good theory and appropriate research design, is often more readily accepted as "legitimate" research (Richards and Richards, 1991, p. 308). Sinkovics and Alfoldi (2012, p. 5) note that CAQDAS can create an "auditable footprint of the progressive dialogue between the researcher and their data". Tansley et al.'s (2014, p. 403) study on the efficiency and effectiveness of electronic HRM systems used NVivo as a tool to provide a more transparent and rigorous research approach and avoid perceptions of stumbling "through a mass of data". As such, one of the benefits is that CAQDAS provides an accurate and transparent representation of data as well as an audit of the entire research process.

MISCONCEPTIONS AND PITFALLS

Despite the benefits, the use of CAQDAS has not been without controversy. In this section we review some of the "myths" and "truths" of CAQDAS.

Myth: CAQDAS is the answer and end to all laborious coding and data analysis.
Truth: CAQDAS does not replace competence in qualitative research techniques.

It is often misconstrued that software does the analysis for the researcher – this is not the case. The researcher must still collect the data, decide what to code and how to conceptualise. As noted above, software can increase the ease at which analysis is undertaken by minimising repetitive and mechanical tasks. Computer assistance is merely a tool that facilitates more effective and efficient analysis.

Before employing CAQDAS, a researcher must first be competent in qualitative research. Fundamental principles such as philosophical stands, ontology, epistemology or positivism, post-positivism, critical theory and constructivism are all important. One must also be able to: (1) ask the right research questions; (2) design qualitative research; and (3) select which data analytical method to use (see Denzin and Lincoln, 2000). It is only after obtaining this crucial knowledge that a researcher should begin to explore and choose an appropriate CAQDAS. Table 16.1 provides suggestions for further reading.

Myth: CAQDAS converts qualitative data into quantitative data.
Truth: CAQDAS facilitates a more efficient and sophisticated exploration and analysis of data.

Contrary to the goals of qualitative inquiry, quantitative research does

Table 16.1   Suggestions for further reading

Subject area	Recommended authors/sources
Qualitative research design	Darlington and Scott (2002); Marshall and Rossman (1999); Onwuegbuzie and Leech (2007); Patton (2002)
Qualitative methods (major examples)	*Spectrum of qualitative research*: Leech and Onwuegbuzie (2007); Taylor and Bodgan (1984) *Grounded theory*: Glaser (1965); Strauss and Corbin (1990) *Content analysis*: Berelson (1952) *Thematic analysis*: Boyatzis (1998)
Data coding and data analysis	Glaser (1965); Miles and Huberman (1994); Taylor and Bodgan (1984)
Rigour and quality of qualitative research	Creswell and Miller (2000); Golafshani (2003); Morse et al. (2002); Riegen (2003)

not attempt to first understand the context being studied. While quantitative data describes data numerically, it cannot and does not go one step further, as qualitative inquiry does, to first make sense of what is being observed before attempting to discover meaning through detailed explanations (Filstead, 1979). With this in mind, there has been active debate with regard to digital intervention in what is fundamentally a human endeavour.

Opponents argue that methodological impurities may result as data are transferred into a digital – ones and zeros – environment. The abstraction that results from this transfer may misrepresent or simplify the multi-dimensional qualities of the original data. Another argument emphasises the utility of computers for counting and producing numbers. It is seen by some that this may force researchers into the trap of turning qualitative accounts into semi-quantitative arrays of analysis by enumerating the facts rather than interpreting them.

CAQDAS helps in organising and structuring volumes of qualitative data. This feature is important and useful when researchers have multiple sources of data such as archival data, webpages, observation videos of HRM practices, focus groups and different types of interviews. Most CAQDAS have a query function that allows scholars to search for specific keywords to explore the breadth and depth of data. For instance, in our own research (Cogin et al., under review), NVivo helped to facilitate a systematic and efficient approach to explore and analyse multi-site, multi-actor and multi-level data sources. Specifically, we organised our data using folders that mapped the research design and data source. As we progressed with our coding and data analysis, NVivo helped us to have an in-depth understanding of how various sources of data were linked and more importantly NVivo's "coding comparison query" allowed us to explore the depth of a specific theme compared to other theme or across groups of participants or organisations. A more detailed explanation of how this was carried out is illustrated later in the chapter.

Myth: CAQDAS is easy and merely "a push of a button".
Truth: CAQDAS is a tool to facilitate qualitative data analysis.

This myth could potentially be due to the misinterpretation or lack of understanding of the functions of some software packages (for example, NVivo's visualisation function and Leximancer's concept maps). Leximancer promotes its features as "useful results fast, minimal set-up, no training sets or key terms, no human bias in analysis" (http://info.lexi mancer.com/), which implies that data analysis comes with a "press of a button". We encourage scholars to be fully aware of the prerequisites of such features. The way data are collected, prepared and formatted and aligned with research goals is vitally important before any meaningful concept maps can be produced by Leximancer.

Cretchley et al.'s (2010) work illustrates how Leximancer can be used as a text-mining tool by tracking the history of the *Journal of Cross-Cultural Psychology* research articles. This article highlights how CAQDAS can be effectively employed at the initial stage of data exploration when there is little understanding of the field or where overwhelmingly diverse data are collected (that is, 40 years of research articles). Specifically, Leximancer helped to produce a set of concept maps and reports that provided an overview of the data. Even with these helpful features, it is important to note that the authors had to analyse the relationships between the concepts to make sense of the data and that Leximancer (like other packages) does not provide an automated feature that generates immediate findings.

In another example, Verreynne et al. (2011) reveal how their data had to be organised and coded using specific criteria in chronological order before Leximancer was employed to explore the connection between employment practices and performance in small firms. The paper further reinforces the notion that while Leximancer helped to provide an initial understanding and patterns in the data, the authors had to recode iteratively and redevelop the concepts in Leximancer several times before concept maps were acceptable and trustworthy.

In a similar way, NVivo promotes a feature known as "Auto Coding", which technically allows data to be automatically coded. We again emphasise that the preparation of qualitative data, an understanding of context and the research design are absolutely essential first steps. Hence, while CAQDAS often promote automated features, it is not a "press of a button" result because CAQDAS do not replace the critical thinking and analysis skills required for qualitative data analysis. Hence, CAQDAS should not be a short cut to skip the quest for knowledge when carrying out qualitative research.

Myth: CAQDAS is a platform for analysing all forms of data (for example, interview transcripts, survey, video, social media and so on) in one go.

Truth: CAQDAS can be used to triangulate data from different sources *or* functionality may be limited to data storage. Before deciding on the role of CAQDAS you first need to have a clear understanding of the research question, the data collected and its purpose.

Most CAQDAS packages promise to be able to analyse different types of data ranging from interview transcripts/audio, websites, videos and survey data at one time. Technically, this is correct; however, such a promise oversimplifies the complexity of qualitative analysis. An important pre-requisite to employing CAQDAS is that the researcher is grounded in the knowledge of and use of different data analytical methods that are appropriate for the research question and data source.

For example, before analysing data derived from interviews, videos and open-ended surveys it is essential to understand the purpose of the data collection method and how the data relate to the research question(s). A helpful question to ask is: Does each of the data sources help to answer a central research question or three different research questions? If all three data sources help to answer one research question, then CAQDAS can be used to triangulate data via comparison and contrasts of the findings obtained from these different data sources and converge and corroborate results (Leech and Onwuegbuzie, 2007). On the other hand, if the three sources of data help to answer three different research questions, then CAQDAS' functionality is limited to a storage hub for different sources of data.

Another important requirement when dealing with different sources or types of data is knowledge of the most appropriate data analytical method. For example, most CAQDAS packages claim that researchers can analyse observational video. This is somewhat deceiving because what is actually provided is software that can import and "play back", produce transcripts or notes for specific segments of a video and facilitate collaboration across a research team. While extremely useful, this does not negate the need to understand different data analytical methods to produce findings from video content. In this example, an understanding of Bales's (1951) content analysis method may be particularly useful. Hence, it is the knowledge about content analysis methodology that lays the foundation for data analysis of video content, not the CADQAS package.

CASE STUDY

In this section, we illustrate how CAQDAS has been used as a central research management tool to systematically and chronologically design and manage an externally funded research project.

Research Context and Brief Background

Using a grounded theory approach, our research aimed to explore how HRM systems influence hospital outcomes with a specific focus on the HRM practices of recruitment, reward and recognition and appraisal. Given the complexities of HRM systems in hospitals, we employed a multi-level, multi-site and multi-actor research design. NVivo 10 was utilised to manage and analyse the data as well as act as a central project management resource. A three-phase research design emerged as detailed below.

Phase One

We began data collection via interviews using maximum variation sampling because it was important to recruit participants who were diverse in age and gender from metropolitan, outer-metropolitan and rural hospitals. Following a grounded theory approach, we began to analyse the data at the same time as it was collected. We employed a systematic analytical process of open coding and axial coding. The NVivo inquiry tool "Coding Comparison Query" permitted a constant comparison method (an important element of grounded theory). After analysing seven interviews, we discovered that HR practices were implemented differently across different organisational levels (that is, directors, unit managers and staff) and professional groups (that is, doctors, nurses and allied health workers).

Phase Two

Given the preliminary findings, we proceeded with our first theoretical sampling at the second stage of data collection to include specific numbers of doctors, nurses and allied health professionals to better probe and understand these variations. Interview guides were further developed with additional questions to probe into this phenomenon and loaded into the data management filing system of NVivo so different members of the research team could retrieve and update documents at any time. Once again, data collection and data analyses (open coding and axial coding) were carried out simultaneously. Following 19 interviews, and using the coding comparison tool, we were able to sort and compare our findings across themes, organisational levels and professional groups as well as across HR practices. Through this analysis we learned that apart from the variations across professional groups, there were: (1) variations across HRM practices; (2) negative perceptions of HRM; and (3) inconsistences in HRM practices within professional groups.

Phase Three

Given these findings, we proceeded with an additional theoretical sampling and new questions were included in the interview guide to better understand our discoveries. We proceeded to recruit HR executives and more directors, unit managers and staff from different professional groups. Data collection and data analyses (open coding and axial coding) were carried out simultaneously. Data analyses continued to follow a chronological approach of open coding, axial coding and theoretical coding. The functionality of "query" in NVivo allowed us to compare our themes and nodes across organisational levels, professional groups and HRM practices. This query function also permitted us to compare the coding agreement and calculate intercoder reliability scores. The themes were linked to various sources, which enabled the query function to compare how the findings were similar (and different) across locations and groups using themes, keywords or other defined criteria.

NVivo, like many CADQAS, comes with a server version that allowed our team to work simultaneously on the project from different locations and make updates virtually. This also provided the potential for the lead chief investigator to manage access based on each team member's role and monitor progress of team members. This not only facilitated an efficient approach but captured the various contribution weightings across a large team. We used memos to document the entire data collection process to ensure that decisions were made in a systematic and unbiased manner. The full process is illustrated in Figure 16.1.

Phases one, two and three in Figure 16.1 show that the research design included multi-site (metro, outer-metro and rural hospitals), multi-actor (doctors, nurses, allied health specialists) and multi-level data (employees, unit managers and hospital directors) as well as highlight that emerging themes across these multiple categories were diverse and complex in the first few codings and iterations. CAQDAS helped us to organise, code and recode the categories while constantly comparing the emerging themes to make sense of and meanings for each of the themes. For instance, one of the initial themes obtained in our open coding and axial coding was that there were different forms of control used in hospitals. However, NVivo was beneficial in helping us to organise our codes or nodes, while constantly comparing the emerging themes (that is, through matrix comparison). Through the analysis and sensemaking it became more and more apparent that different forms of controls were employed in different HR practices (for example, hiring, performance appraisal, training, rewards and so on) across different levels and professional groups. This finding would not have been made if CAQDAS was not used throughout each stage of the project.

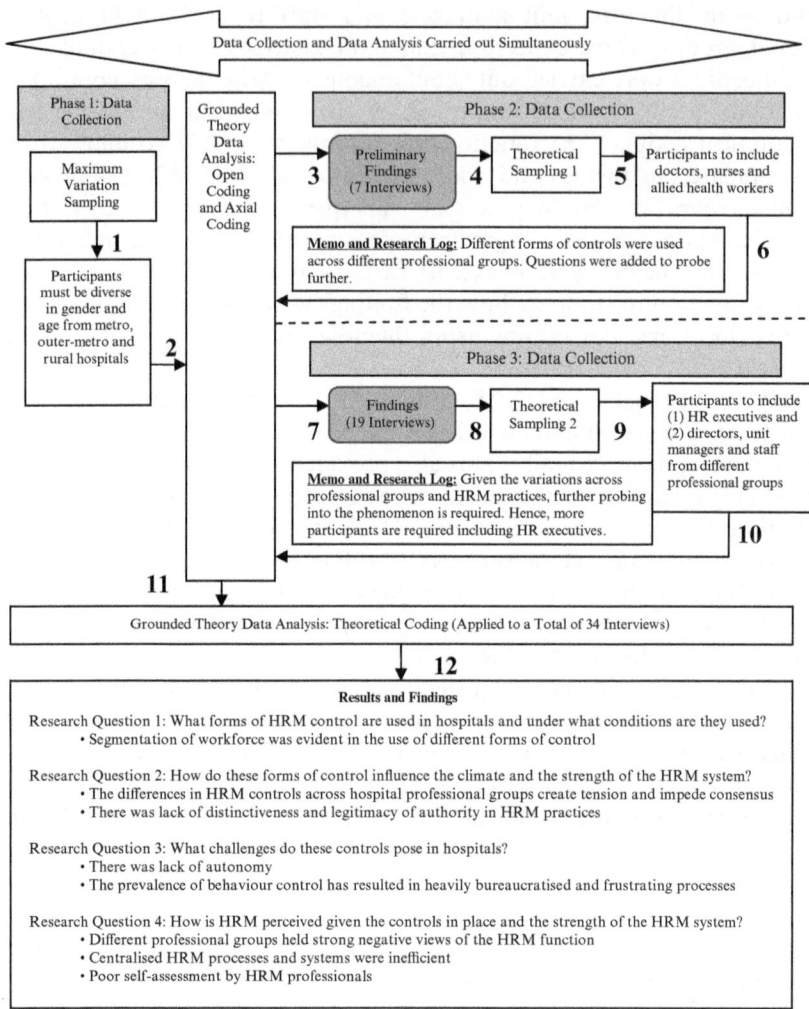

Figure 16.1   Grounded theory data collection and data analysis strategies

THE CURRENT STATUS AND FUTURE OF CAQDAS IN HRM RESEARCH

QRS NVivo has been the most heavily utilised CAQDAS in the HRM literature. In the majority of studies, NVivo has been employed to analyse interview transcripts using a multi-stage inductive process. One exception is Rees and Johari (2010), who investigated the role played by the HRM function in strategic organisational change initiatives. Interview transcripts were examined with the aid of ATLAS.ti, a visual qualitative data analysis computer software.

There are a number of opportunities for HRM researchers to employ CADQAS in novel ways. In the past, most HRM research has been either organisation or individual focused, however more recent research is attempting to bridge the macro-micro divide (Sanders et al., 2013). As a result, there is enormous potential for qualitative research to assess gaps between organisational "intended" HR practices with "actual" or "perceived" practices (Nishii and Lepak, 2008).

Further, with an evolving interest in social embeddedness in the HRM literature (Kaše et al., 2013) and the fast growing development of voluntary speech and expression on social media, CADQAS could be used to import social media sites as another source of analysis. This may be particularly relevant for the study of hiring practices and talent attraction strategies. Not only does this facilitate more efficient data collection but also highlights the need to acknowledge the force and dominance of social media.

CADQAS can be used to analyse videos of top management teams in action to better understand the breakdown in intended HR messages (for example, the valuing of employees) and perceived HR experiences of employees (for example, inconsistent messaging or unfair practices). Hence, through a comparison of interview data, an analysis of written HR policy and a review of videos taken of top management team meetings, and then utilising NVivo's constant comparison and query function in the comparison process, researchers can assess the strength of the HRM system (Bowen and Ostroff, 2004). There are also possibilities for using data found on websites, blogs, media releases and archival data that remain relatively underutilised.

The new generations of CADQAS now come with functionalities that allow researchers to ask more complex research questions. These functionalities are primarily underexplored in the HRM literature. CAQDAS is most beneficial when there are different sources of data or the qualitative research design is complex because CAQDAS serves as the central data management and analytical tool. As the findings are stored in the same software, scholars are able to use the different in-built tools and features such as maps, graphical mapping and comparison to enhance sensemaking processing. For instance, CADQAS is now built with a higher capacity to deal with diverse types of data such as website, social media, video and audio. Further, the functionality of display and visualisation helps with report or manuscript writing as the findings are centrally stored and analysed in one central hub. Leximancer and NVivo have functions such as concept maps, charts and graphs that allow research-ers to create charts and models to better present their findings using the results obtained from the data analysis. This helps to reduce duplication when trying to recreate tables or charts using other software. Likewise, NVivo has a "Reports and Extracts" function that allows researchers to print customised reports and extracts using the "report wizard" that can be exported to another format such as Microsoft Word, Excel and Portable Document Format.

We anticipate that these functionalities will not only bring efficiencies to the qualitative research process but allow HRM researchers to be innova-tive and bold in asking more complex questions. Practically, CAQDAS has been extremely useful when dealing with reviewers' comments when revising manuscripts as researchers are able to easily examine the audit trail and coding process to provide a trustworthy and dependable justifica-tion and explanation of the findings.

DISCUSSION

Despite misconceptions and debates, a number of notable qualitative theorists have encouraged the use of CADQAS (Denzin and Lincoln, 1998; Miles and Huberman, 1994). We support this view and suggest that CADQAS can facilitate more innovative designs and rigorous processes in qualitative research. Even though there is increased usage of CADQAS in qualitative research, the full functionality and capabilities of CADQAS have not been fully explored in the HRM field.

Specific to HR research, we recommend that researchers extend their exploration to more complex and integrative phenomena because CADQAS can facilitate this type of research efficiently. However, it is important that researchers understand how the features of the CADQAS chosen can help to answer research questions. Researchers should read with caution claims made by CADQAS packages and avoid the situation where data are forced into a specific software. We recommend that in the exploration and evaluation of software, scholars first have a deep under-standing of the research objective, questions and the methodology. For instance, both NVivo and Leximancer can facilitate content analysis and grounded theory methodology. However, the two softwares are built very differently and are based on different foundations. Hence, the analytical process and the representation of data and findings will be different. While features such as graphical representation are a matter of preference on the surface, it is crucial for researchers not to be distracted by cosmetic fea-tures and later settle for a less effective CADQAS.

In concluding this chapter, it is important to note that CADQAS is not a short cut to qualitative research analysis. We emphasise the need to first understand and master the key pillars of research outlined in Table 16.1 before employing CADQAS. Through our experience, we know that an eagerness to jump into CADQAS can derail focus from fundamental research knowledge.

REFERENCES

Bales, R.F. (1951), *Interaction Process Analysis: A Method for the Study of Small Groups*, Cambridge: Addison-Wesley Press.

Berelson, B. (1952), *Content Analysis in Communication Research*, Glencoe, IL: The Free Press.

Boyatzis, R.E. (1998), *Transforming Qualitative Information: Thematic Analysis and Code Development*, Thousand Oaks, CA: Sage.

Bowen, D.E. and Ostroff, C. (2004), "Understanding HRM-firm performance linkages: the role of 'strength' of the HRM system", *Academy of Management Review*, **29**, 203–21.

Cogin, J.A., Ng, J. and Lee, I. (under review), "Controlling healthcare professionals: job attitudes and operational efficiency".

Creswell, J.W. and Miller, D.L. (2000), "Determining validity in qualitative inquiry", *Theory into Practice*, **39** (3), 124–30.

Cretchley, J., Rooney, D. and Gallois, C. (2010), "Mapping a 40-year history with Leximancer: themes and concepts", *Journal of Cross-Cultural Psychology*, **41** (3), 318–28.

Darlington, Y. and Scott, D. (2002), *Qualitative Research in Practice*. Crows Nest, NSW: Allen and Unwin.

Denzin, N. and Lincoln, Y. (1998), *The Landscape of Qualitative Research: Theories and Issues*, Thousand Oaks, CA: Sage.

Denzin, N.K. and Lincoln, Y.S. (2000), *The Handbook of Qualitative Research*, 2nd edn, Thousand Oaks, CA: Sage.

Filstead, W.J. (1979), "Qualitative methods – a needed perspective in evaluation research", in T.D. Cook and C.S. Reichardt (eds), *Qualitative and Quantitative Methods in Evaluation Research*, London: Sage, pp. 33–48.

Glaser, B.G. (1965), "The constant comparative method of qualitative analysis", *Social Problems*, **12** (4), 436–45.

Golafshani, N. (2003), "Understanding reliability and validity in qualitative research", *The Qualitative Report*, **8** (4), 597–607.

Kaše, R., King, Z. and Minbaeva, D. (2013), "Editors' note: using social network research in HRM: scratching the surface of a fundamental basis of HRM", *Human Resource Management*, **52** (4), 473–83.

Kellner, A., Townsend, K., Wilkinson, A. and Peetz, D. (2014), "Decaf or double shot? The strength of franchisor control over HRM in coffee franchises", *Human Resource Management Journal*, **24**, 323–38.

Leech, N.L. and Onwuegbuzie, A.J. (2007), "An array of qualitative data analysis tools: a call for data analysis triangulation", *School Psychology Quarterly*, **22** (4), 557–84.

Lombard, M., Snyder-Duch, J. and Bracken, C.C. (2002), "Content analysis in mass communication research: an assessment and reporting of intercoder reliability", *Human Communication Research*, **28**, 587–604.

Marshall, C. and Rossman, G.B. (1999), *Designing Qualitative Research*, Thousand Oaks, CA: Sage.

Miles, M.B. and Huberman, A.M. (1994), *Qualitative Data Analysis: An Expanded Sourcebook*, 2nd edn, Thousand Oaks, CA: Sage.

Monks, K., Kelly, G., Conway, E., Flood, P., Truss, K. and Hannon, E. (2013), "Understanding how HR systems work: the role of HR philosophy and HR processes", *Human Resource Management Journal*, **23** (4), 379–95.

Morse, J.M., Barrett, M., Mayan, M., Olson, K. and Spiers, J. (2002), "Verification strategies for establishing reliability and validity in qualitative research", *International Journal of Qualitative Methods*, **1** (2), 13–22.

Nishii, L. and Lepak, D. (2008), "Employee attributions of HR practices: their effect on employee attitudes and behaviors, and customer satisfaction", *Personnel Psychology*, **61**, 503–45.

Onwuegbuzie, A. and Leech, N. (2007), "Sampling designs in qualitative research: making sampling process more public", *The Qualitative Report*, **12** (2), 238–54.

Patton, M.Q. (2002), *Qualitative Research and Evaluation Methods*, 3rd edn, Thousand Oaks, CA: Sage.

Rees, C. and Johari, H. (2010), "Senior managers' perceptions of the HRM function during times of strategic organizational change: case study evidence from a public sector banking institution in Malaysia", *Journal of Organizational Change Management*, **23** (5), 517–36.

Richards, T. (2002), "An intellectual history of NUD*IST and NVivo", *International Journal of Social Research Methodology*, **5** (3), 199–214.

Richards, T. and Richards, L. (1991), "The NUD*IST qualitative data analysis system", *Qualitative Sociology*, **14** (4), 307–24.

Riegen, A.M. (2003), "Validity and reliability tests in case study research: a literature review with 'hands-on' application for each research phase", *Qualitative Market Research*, **6** (2), 77–86.

Sanders, K., Cogin, J.A. and Bainbridge, H.T.J. (2013), *Research Methods for Human Resource Management*, London: Routledge.

Saunders, M., Lewis, P. and Thornhill, A. (2012), *Research Methods for Business Students*, 6th edn, London: Pearson.

Sinkovics, R. and Alfoldi, E. (2012), "Facilitating the interaction between theory and data in qualitative research using CAQDAS", in G. Symon and C. Cassel (eds), *Qualitative Organizational Research: Core Methods and Current Challenges*, London: Sage, pp. 1–24, available at http://www.manchester.ac.uk/escholar/uk-ac-man-scw:159596/ (accessed 20 February 2015).

Strauss, A.L. and Corbin, J. (1990), *Basics of Qualitative Research: Grounded Theory Procedures and Techniques*, Newbury Park, CA: Sage.

Tansley, C., Kirk, S., Williams, H. and Barton, H. (2014), "Tipping the scales: ambidexterity practices on e-HRM projects", *Employee Relations*, **36** (4), 398–414.

Taylor, S.R. and Bodgan, R. (1984), *Introduction to Qualitative Research Methods: The Search for Meanings*, New York: Wiley.

Verreynne, M., Parker, P. and Wilson, M. (2011), "Employment systems in small firms: a multilevel analysis", *International Small Business Journal*, **31**, 405–30.

17 Cross-cultural HRM research: the potential of causal cognitive mapping
Gail Clarkson

INTRODUCTION

Historically, the important insights of cross-cultural research have come from the discipline of anthropology, with researchers conducting ethnographic studies across a range of geographical and social settings. Tales of bizarre or barbaric cultural rituals, such as Takuna girls having their hair plucked out or Luiseno initiates having to lie motionless while being bitten by angry ants (Sosis, 2004), are fascinating but, of course, it is likely that in the context of contemporary human resource management (HRM) the questions being posed will be rather less colourful. However, across all contexts it is notoriously difficult to bring about any forms of change that pose a challenge to the shared beliefs and values, rituals and cultural "norms" of a community. Problems are magnified in the context of large change initiatives such as those of organisational merger and/or acquisition, but even in small organisations and, seemingly, simple contexts, change is rarely devoid of complication. It is becoming increasingly clear that HRM researchers need to take additional account of worker perceptions of such change initiatives. For example, longitudinal research has provided evidence that merely the anticipation of job loss has a negative influence on health even before employment status has changed (Ferrie et al., 1995). Moreover, even when the objective data reveals that there is nothing of concern, heightened employee perceptions of job insecurity may cause organisations to suffer financially due to the associated costs of increased absenteeism and sickness resulting from lowered employee wellbeing.

Many of the basic assumptions about how people think and of their self-perceptions and perceptions of others have been shown to be culturally bounded. Cognitive insight into cultural variation is viewed as being crucial to understanding (Fiske and Taylor, 2010). As revealed in the managerial and organisational cognition (MOC) literature, cognitive mapping has been used as a potentially powerful means of representing actors' belief systems for many years (see, for example, Bougon et al., 1977; Fiol, 2001; Ford and Hegarty, 1984; Gioa and Thomas, 1996). Cognitive mapping procedures provide a way to structure and simplify thoughts and beliefs, to make sense of and communicate information about them. Cognitive mapping methods have been employed to advantage in the discipline of HRM (see Budhwar, 2000; Budhwar and Sparrow, 2002), and further application could hold considerable potential in the cross-cultural context. This includes the international operation of companies, where strategies may be to manage the human resource in a similar manner across all locations (as dictated by central headquarters), and alternative attempts to develop multi-national markets by the exploitation of the peculiarities of local or destination countries and to manage the human resource in a rather more localised context. In either strategy mistaken assumptions regarding cultural context can have negative and potentially dramatic consequences.

To facilitate reader considerations as to if, and how best, cognitive mapping might usefully be employed in the context of their own studies of cross-cultural HRM research, the use of mapping methods is considered in the context of one research study. However, before this, a broad introduction is provided for the cognitive mapping novice.

CAUSAL COGNITIVE MAPPING

There are two distinct branches of MOC research: the computational approach, which examines how actors process information, and the interpretive approach, which investigates how meaning is created around information in a social context (Lant and Shapira, 2001, p. 2). The latter "interpretive" approach, which has a sociological background (see Berger and Luckmann, 1967 on the social construction of reality), and is also embedded in the inter-related fields of social psychology, appears to hold particular potential for the cross-cultural researcher. Not least as from this viewpoint cultural processes play a constitutive rather than solely a causal role in map development (see recent work by Heft, 2013).

The choice of mapping method depends largely upon whether the model of cognition is seen to be relatively simple, where, for example, simple counting and weighting of words in a text would be acceptable (making the assumption that concepts used often are more significant), or rather more complex and involving a considerable amount of researcher interpretation to get from the raw data to the finished map. Researchers have employed a variety of methods in an attempt to gain insights into actors' fundamental belief systems, from the simple process of having participants list basic concepts (de Chernatony et al., 1993) to more sophisticated procedures such as the development and multivariate analysis of questionnaire items (Fombrun and Zajac, 1987).

Axelrod (1976) developed a causal cognitive mapping method that was used in political science. A causal cognitive map is a graphical representation where constructs (or nodes) represent concepts, and links (arcs or lines) represent the perceived causal relationships between concepts, the rationale being that when a map is pictured in graph form it is relatively easy to see how each of the concepts and causal relationships relate to each other and to see the overall structure of the whole set of portrayed assertions concerning a particular domain (Figure 17.1).

Here, Construct A is perceived to have a positive influence on Construct B, no influence on Constructs C and E, and a negative influence on Construct D. The only construct influencing Construct A is Construct B.

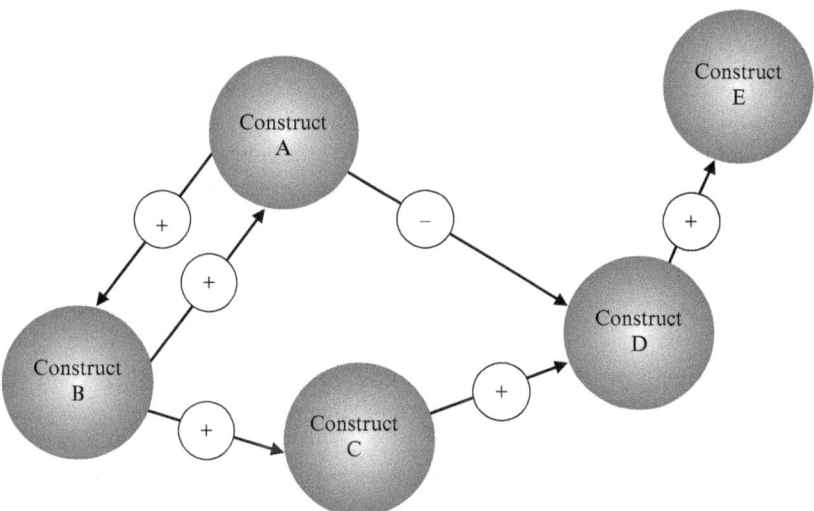

Note: For any given pair of constructs, there may be a circular link, a "loop" whereby a construct ends up affecting itself. Loops can be either positive (deviation amplifying) or negative (deviation counteracting). For example, examining AB and BA, if the link A,B is negative and the B,A link is positive, then we have a deviation counteracting loop because an increase in A lowers B, but this decrease in B, in turn, lowers A. If, on the other hand, both constructs are signed the same, then the loop is deviation amplifying (Axelrod, 1976; Voyer and Faulkner, 1989; Weick, 1979). The indegrees (number of links into a construct from other constructs) reveal the extent to which a construct is directly or indirectly influenced by another construct. The outdegrees (number of links out of a construct to other constructs) are indicators of the extent to which a construct exerts a direct or indirect (reachability) causal influence on another construct (Axelrod, 1976; Ford and Hegarty, 1984; Harary et al., 1965). Generally, the greater the number of indegrees into/outdegrees from a construct, the more important that construct (or salient) is considered to be (Markóczy and Goldberg, 1995; Salancik and Porac, 1986; Swan and Newell, 1998; Weick and Bougon, 1986).

Figure 17.1   An illustrative causal cognitive map

The indegrees (number of links into a construct from other constructs) reveal the extent to which a construct is directly or indirectly influenced by another construct. The outdegrees (number of links out of a construct to other constructs) are indicators of the extent to which a construct exerts a direct or indirect (reachability) causal influence on another construct. Generally, the greater the number of indegrees into/outdegrees from a construct, the more important (or salient) that construct is considered to be.

In the words of Huff (1990, p. 16):

> Causal maps allow the map maker to focus on action – for example, how the respondent explains the current situation in terms of previous events, and what changes he or she expects in the future.

The direct links to action implicit within this approach that make it a method worthy of consideration in a wide range of contexts. However, there are many methodological choices facing the causal cognitive mapping researcher and in this chapter this is considered in the context of a study of the UK call centre industry.

ILLUSTRATIVE STUDY: KEY DECISIONS

Direct mapping procedures can be sub-divided in terms of the extent to which the elicitation process permits participants to use their everyday language. Undoubtedly, ideographic techniques (whereby maps are captured in their natural language form) are inherently more meaningful to the individual participants and, of course, more appealing to the qualitative researcher. As with indirect methods (where a cognitive map is derived from, for example, documentary source material), the major disadvantage with this technique relates to the laborious coding methods required for comparative analyses. Nomothetic elicitation, which entails the use of standardised lists of concepts, for example, in the form of highly structured questionnaires, obviates the need for such procedures and facilitates systematic comparisons. They do, however, run the risk that the basic map construction task might prove meaningless for participants and, again, are likely to hold little appeal for the qualitative researcher. Where more interactive methods are used, for example, interviewing procedures, there is no agreement as to the best way of transforming this material into a cause map. In some cases, individuals are involved in validating their own maps; while in others the link between data collection and map is managed solely by the researcher or interventionist (Eden, 1992).

In the illustrative study, in order to determine if there was evidence of institutional effects across call centre organisations, and to ensure that the study was not simply detecting an organisational effect in relation to culture and process, a relatively large-scale investigation was required. Essentially, the main concerns were to collect data in a manner that did not unduly restrict participant response yet which was also amenable to systematic comparison. In the pilot phase of the illustrative study, maps were first drawn freehand and then using commercially available computer software, that is, Decision Explorer® that Eden and colleagues have successfully developed in order to capitalise on the utility gained from reflective mapping (see, for example, Eden et al., 1992). This software has proved to be of immense benefit in areas where interactively generated maps have helped to build up a comprehensive qualitative map or model, which is then explored and analysed to help develop strategy, decision making and business problems. Use of this package confirmed the author claims that Decision Explorer® engages participants who can not only view and validate their maps but also, with researcher support, carry out their original construction.

However, as the first maps were developed for the call centre study, it was possible to see that while the cognitive mapping procedure enabled a deep understanding of a variety of issues, it was clear that acquiring a mass of potentially non-comparable data would not be helpful. In addition, as building up the necessary bank of maps would be carried out over a period of several months, there was a need to ensure that as understanding evolved over the course of the project this did not result in a lack of consistency in approaching participants. Clearly, the skills of the facilitator are key in helping manage the demand characteristics of the social situation, which could lead to overly simplistic or complex and "messy" maps at the original stage of data collection. Eden and Ackermann (1998) acknowledge that comparison of maps is methodologically problematic but their epistemological stance leads them to oppose any form of nomothetic method to simplify or standardise the procedures. However, the perceived issues of reliability and limits on any subsequent analysis, beyond ideographic methods, were determined to prohibit this methodology in the context of this study.

Markóczy and Goldberg (1995) developed a "hybrid" form of causal cognitive mapping with considerable potential for the systematic collection and analysis of large-scale data, made technically feasible using computer software (Clarkson and Hodgkinson, 2005). Development of the pool of constructs is done prior to the data collection so that each participant selects constructs from the same pool, obviating the need for subjective researcher judgement in making such comparisons. The pool can be developed in a variety of ways, for example, initial interviews or extensive

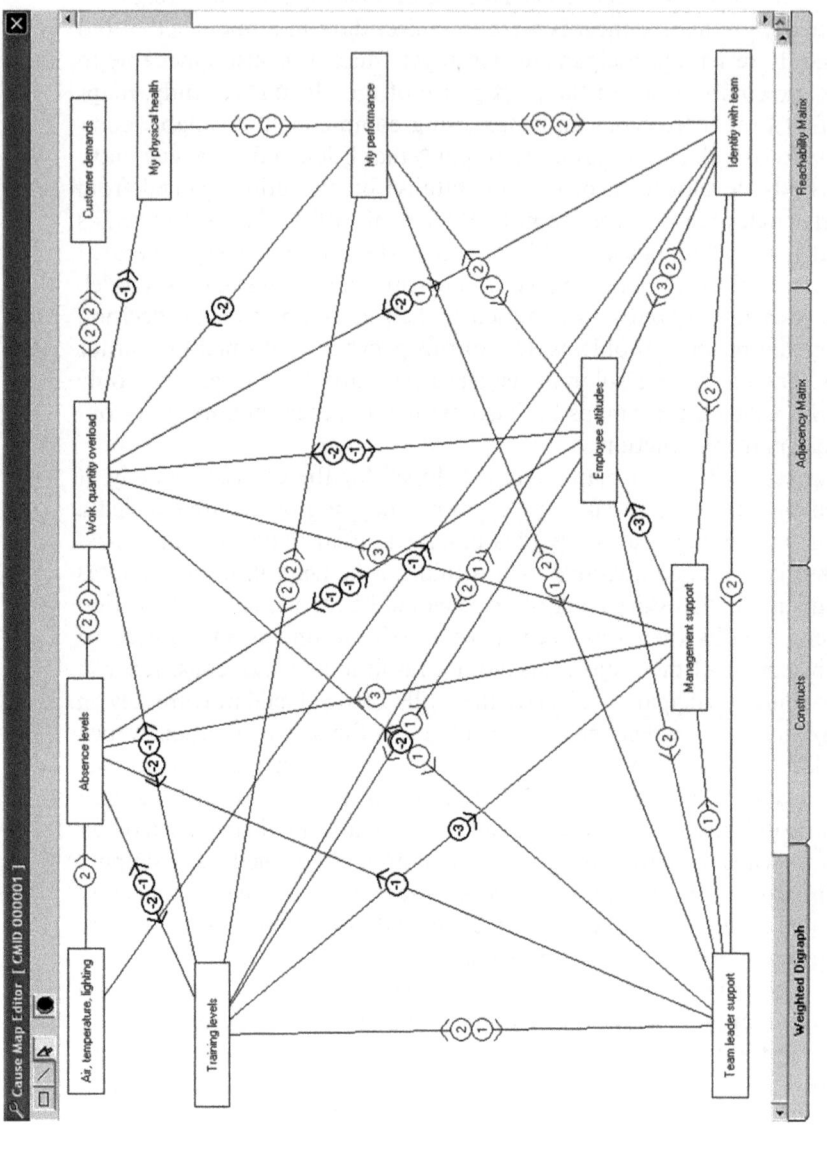

Note: Magnitude of effect is defined as 1 = increase slight; 2 = increase moderate; 3 = increase strong; −1 = decrease slight; −2 = decrease moderate; −3 = decrease strong.

Figure 17.2   Causal cognitive map in weighted digraph format

literature review. However, the main point is that participants choose only constructs that are personally salient (meaningful), and selection from a pool of constructs is said to allow participants additional freedom of choice, while the systematic elicitation of constructs lays the ground for systematic comparison and analysis.

Using this procedure, a common pool of constructs (developed via interview analysis or literature review) is presented to all participants, who select a fixed number to form the basic content of their map. Each participant then assesses the influence of each of her or his chosen constructs in a pair-wise manner. A complex map with many links between constructs will produce a dense network compared to another where the constructs do not have many connections. In the latter case, the resulting map may look like a configuration of isolated constructs.

As in the illustrative study, some researchers then give participants the option to modify the resulting diagram (as shown in Figure 17.2) on an iterative basis – until they are fully satisfied that it constitutes an adequate representation of their causal beliefs (Hodgkinson and Clarkson, 2005).

RECOMMENDATIONS

The major strength of qualitative data collection is, of course, the benefits it brings in relation to deep exploration and rich insights that are usually obtained in the context of a small sample of participants. Yet, cross-cultural research presents particular challenges to the qualitative researcher in that many theoretical notions can only be subjected to adequate empirical scrutiny by the collection of relatively large-scale data, for example, to ascertain if we are *really* capturing cultural differences and influences – be that in national, organisational or geographical context – and not just those of individual representatives. Clearly, when investing intellectual effort, and valuable time and money in a study, it is important to have a real chance of finding any "real" difference in, for example, attitudes to work or any form of HRM practice in relation to cultural type/dimension.

It is clearly inappropriate to capture data that is, in reality, not actually meaningful to participants but it is also clearly less than helpful to acquire a mass of potentially non-comparable material and this chapter has a particular focus upon causal cognitive mapping elicitation procedures that ultimately hold maximum potential in the context of large-scale studies. While it is accepted that the use of any construct list will focus thinking in particular directions (though, of course, and as pointed out by Eden and Ackermann, 1998, even open-ended interviews will have some focus), the method used in the illustrative study is recommended for researchers looking to elicit and compare anything other than a small number of cause maps on a longitudinal or cross-sectional basis.

CONCLUSIONS

The basis of much HRM research relates in some manner to social inter-action, in many forms such as employees and managers, peers with peers, managers and union representatives. The causes of such interactions often lie in the perceived world while the consequences of such perceptions are profound, in relation to feelings, motivations and behaviour. We have some understanding that reveals fundamental cultural differences in cognition (many of which are examined by Fiske and Taylor, 2010). For example, configurations of belief have been shown to differ across cultures (Leung and Bond, 2004), with implications for influence strategies (Fu et al., 2004) and many other issues relevant to HRM, such as expected reward for effort, and so – at least – (some form of) cognitive mapping method may be worthy of your consideration.

Clearly, even after extensive piloting to produce a representative range of potentially salient constructs (as in the illustrative study presented in this chapter), this may be seen as too confining for some researchers because of fundamental philosophical considerations or specific meth-odological concerns in the context of the study in question. For some researchers, the degree of standardisation employed would simply not be acceptable. For example, Eden and Ackermann (1998, p. 198) clearly acknowledge that comparison of maps is methodologically problematic but their epistemological stance leads them to being opposed to any form of method to simplify or standardise the procedures. Instead, they place additional emphasis on the skills of the facilitator in helping to manage the demand characteristics of the social situation, which could lead to overly simplistic or complex and "messy" maps at the original stage of data input: "it becomes important to see the researcher as the research instrument, rather than the data collection and analysis techniques or tools as the research instrument". Moreover, alternative forms of mapping may be more compatible with smaller-scale inductive research (see, for example, Eden and Ackermann, 1998). It has been difficult to do justice to the range of possibilities in one chapter but the interested reader is likely to find the annotated references a good start-ing point.

ANNOTATED FURTHER READING

Clarkson, G.P. and Hodgkinson, G.P. (2005), "Introducing Cognizer™: a comprehensive computer package for the elicitation and analysis of cause maps", *Organizational Research Methods*, **8**, 317–41.
This paper provides details of the mapping procedure used in this chapter and technical aspects that will be helpful to the interested reader.
Fiske, S.T. and Taylor, S.E. (2010), *Social Cognition: From Brains to Culture*, Boston, MA: McGraw-Hill.
This book provides not only a good introduction to social cognition but a considerable range of examples and references that will be particularly pertinent to the cross-cultural researcher.
Hodgkinson, G.P. and Clarkson, G.P. (2005), "What have we learned from almost thirty years of research on causal mapping? Methodological lessons and choices for the information systems and information technology communities", in V.K. Narayanan and D.J. Armstrong (eds), *Causal Mapping for Research in Information Technology*, Hershey, PA: Idea Group Inc., pp. 46–79.
This is a comprehensive chapter that guides the reader through philosophical considerations, and the strengths and weaknesses of different mapping methods.
Lant, T.K. and Shapira, Z. (eds) (2001), *Organizational Cognition: Computation and Interpretation*, Mahwah, NJ: Lawrence Erlbaum Associates, pp. 1–12.
This book provides a review of the many diverse methods for accessing thinking in organisational settings, and a collection of work that clarifies the contribution and limitations of each.

REFERENCES

Axelrod, R. (1976), *Structure of Decision: The Cognitive Maps of Political Elites*, Princeton, NJ: Princeton University Press.
Berger, P. and Luckmann, T. (1967), *The Social Construction of Reality: A Treatise in the Sociology of Knowledge*, London: Penguin.
Bougon, M., Weick, K. and Binkhorst, D. (1977), "Cognition in organizations: an analysis of the Utrecht Jazz Orchestra", *Administrative Science Quarterly*, **22** (3/4), 606–39.
Budhwar, P.S. (2000), "Strategic integration and devolvement of human resource management in the UK manufacturing sector", *British Journal of Management*, **11**, 285–302.
Budhwar, P.S. and Sparrow, P.R. (2002), "Strategic HRM through the cultural looking glass: mapping the cognition of British and Indian managers", *Organization Studies*, **23**, 599–638.
Clarkson, G.P. and Hodgkinson, G.P. (2005), "What can diaries tell us that questionnaires can't?", *Personnel Review*, **36**, 684–700.
de Chernatony, L., Daniels, K. and Johnson, G. (1993), "A cognitive perspective on managers' perceptions of competition", *Journal of Marketing Management*, **9**, 373–81.
Eden, C. (ed.) (1992), "On the nature of cognitive maps (Editorial)", *Journal of Management Studies*, **29** (Special Issue), 261–5.
Eden, C. and Ackermann, F. (1998), "Analysing and comparing idiographic cause maps", in C. Eden and J.-C. Spender (eds), *Managerial and Organizational Cognition: Theory, Methods and Research*, London: Sage, pp. 192–209.
Eden, C., Ackermann, F. and Cropper, S. (1992), "The analysis of cause maps", *Journal of Management Studies*, **29**, 309–24.
Ferrie, J.E., Shipley, M.J., Marmot, M.G., Stansfeld, S. and Smith, G.D. (1995), "Health effects of anticipation of job change and non-employment. Longitudinal data from the Whitehall II Study", *British Medical Journal*, **311** (7015), 1264–9.

Fiol, C.M. (2001), "All for one and one for all? The development and transfer of power across organization levels", *Academy of Management Review*, **26** (2), 224–42.

Fiske, S.T. and Taylor, S.E. (2010), *Social Cognition: From Brains to Culture*, Boston, MA: McGraw-Hill.

Fombrun, C.J. and Zajac, E.J. (1987), "Structural and perceptual influences on intra-industry stratification", *Academy of Management Journal*, **30**, 33–50.

Ford, J.D. and Hegarty, W.H. (1984), "Decision makers' beliefs about the causes and effects of structure: an exploratory study", *Academy of Management Journal*, **27** (2), 271–91.

Fu, P.O., Kennedy, J., Tata, J. et al. (2004), "The impact of societal cultural values and individual social beliefs on the perceived effectiveness of managerial influence strategies: a meso approach", *Journal of International Business Studies*, **35**, 284–305.

Gioia, D.A. and Thomas, J.B. (1996), "Identity, image, and issue interpretation: sensemaking during strategic change in academia", *Administrative Science Quarterly*, **41** (3), 370–403.

Harary, F., Norman, R.Z. and Cartwright, D. (1965), *Structural Models: An Introduction to the Theory of Directed Graphs*, New York: Wiley.

Heft, H. (2013), "Environment, cognition, and culture: reconsidering the cognitive map", *Journal of Environmental Psychology*, **33**, 14–25.

Hodgkinson, G.P. and Clarkson, G.P. (2005), "What have we learned from almost thirty years of research on causal mapping? Methodological lessons and choices for the information systems and information technology communities", in V.K. Narayanan and D.J. Armstrong (eds), *Causal Mapping for Research in Information Technology*, Hershey, PA: Idea Group Inc., pp. 46–79.

Huff, A.S. (ed.) (1990), *Mapping Strategic Thought*, Chichester: Wiley.

Lant, T.K. and Shapira, Z. (eds) (2001), *Organizational Cognition: Computation and Interpretation*, Mahwah, NJ: Lawrence Erlbaum Associates, pp. 1–12.

Leung, K. and Bond, M.H. (2004), "Social axioms: a model for social beliefs in multicultural perspective", in M.P. Zanna (ed.), *Advances in Social Experimental Social Psychology*, Vol. 35, San Diego, CA: Academic Press, pp. 119–97.

Markóczy, L. and Goldberg, J. (1995), "A method for eliciting and comparing causal maps", *Journal of Management*, **21**, 305–33.

Salancik, G.R. and Porac, J.F. (1986), "Distilled ideologies: values derived from causal reasoning in complex environments", in H.P. Sims, Jr, D.A. Gioia and associates (eds), *The Thinking Organization: Dynamics of Organizational Social Cognition*, San Francisco, CA: Jossey-Bass, pp. 75–101.

Sosis, R. (2004), "The adaptive value of religious rituals: rituals promote group cohesion by requiring members to engage in behaviour that is too costly to fake", *American Scientist*, **92** (2), 166–72.

Swan, J. and Newell, S. (1998), "Making sense of technological innovations: the political and social dynamics of cognition", in C. Eden and J.-C. Spender (eds), *Managerial and Organizational Cognition: Theory, Methods and Research*, London: Sage, pp. 108–29.

Voyer, J. and Faulkner, R. (1989), "Organizational cognition in a jazz ensemble", *Empirical Studies of the Arts*, **7** (1), 57–77.

Weick, K.E. (1979), *The Social Psychology of Organizing*, 2nd edn, New York: McGraw-Hill.

Weick, K.E. and Bougon, M.G. (1986), "Organizations as cognitive maps: charting ways to success and failure", in H.P. Sims, Jr, D.A. Gioia and associates (eds), *The Thinking Organization: Dynamics of Organizational Social Cognition*, San Francisco, CA: Jossey-Bass, pp. 102–35.

18 Deriving behavioural role descriptions from the perspectives of job-holders: an illustrative example
Richard Winter

INTRODUCTION

Understanding the individual knowledge, skills and abilities (KSA) and key demands of a job has traditionally been seen as the cornerstone of the human resource (HR) function (Brannick et al., 2007). Implicit in job analysis and associated employee selection activities is the notion recruiters must gain accurate and realistic job information to assess the degree of congruence between an applicant's KSA and the job requirements (Breaugh and Starke, 2000; Meglino et al., 2000). Armed with realistic job previews, recruiters are thought to be better equipped to hire applicants who match job classifications (person-job fit) and who are "just right" (person-organisation fit) for their organisations (Kristof-Brown, 2000; Sekiguchi, 2007). Achieving person-job (PJ) and person-organisation (PO) fit by way of realistic job previews has been associated with a range of positive HR outcomes, including intentions to accept a job offer, low attrition from the recruitment process and high job satisfaction (Carless, 2005; Meglino et al., 2000).

To achieve PJ and PO fit, recruiters have traditionally taken the attribute approach of considering jobs in terms of which KSA of individuals, or attributes of the job itself, fit recruiters' PJ and PO fit perceptions (Kristof-Brown, 2000). By classifying jobs in terms of the qualifications an individual needs to possess in order to fulfil a particular open position (Huffcutt and Youngcourt, 2007), or by specifying the personality characteristics and social skills associated with selecting individuals in team-based settings (Morgeson et al., 2005), the attribute approach provides a solid foundation by which recruiters can justify PJ and PO hiring decisions. However, in the process of standardising jobs across HR levels for employee classification and selection purposes (Campion et al., 1997), an attribute approach may disregard the important performance role that "employees play in actively shaping both the tasks and social relationships that compose a job" (Wrzesniewski and Dutton, 2001, p. 179). In essence, an attribute approach to job analysis may decouple the job from the broader social context that shapes relationships between individuals or jobs.

One possible solution to the decoupling problem of traditional job analysis is to focus on work analysis from the perspectives of job-holders (Morrison, 1994; Parker, 2007). Work role analysis conducted this way can expand the study of jobs by capturing sets of behaviours a job-holder considers important to fulfil the performance demands of their role position (Morgeson and Dierdorff, 2011; Welbourne et al., 1998). Including a job-holder's "role orientation" in the work analysis means taking account of how narrowly or broadly the job-holder defines their job, including which responsibilities are seen as integral or external to their work role (Parker, 2007). For example, in knowledge-based work contexts role orientations may broaden beyond the traditional focus on core task performance to include proactive and adaptive behaviours that demonstrate a job-holder's capacity to "anticipate and prevent problems, rather than to only react to problems" (Parker, 2007, p. 407).

By making job-holders themselves an integral part of the work analysis process, it is possible to collect a broader array of cognitive-social information relating to the interpersonal, interdependent and contextual nature of work (Sanchez and Levine, 2001). This information includes beliefs about how best to approach complex project tasks and work collaboratively in uncertain contexts (Griffin et al., 2007), be proactive in response to changes in the internal-external environment (Plouffe and Grégoire, 2011) and create networks of interpersonal relationships with others inside and outside the organisation (Gibson et al., 2014). Hence, by including more description of the social context in which jobs are embedded, it is possible to understand *what* job-holders believe they do in their roles to be successful, and *why* certain relational behaviours between individuals and jobs may be critical to individual, team and organisational performance (Plouffe and Grégoire, 2011).

This chapter presents an inductive process for deriving behavioural role descriptions from the perspectives of job-holders. Adopting an interpretive viewpoint, project managers are portrayed in the following data descriptions as sensemakers (Weick, 2008), not merely recipients of attributes compiled by others, but active thinking, feeling and intentional social actors constructing their jobs to fit their perceived project manager role demands (Cheng et al., 2005). Casting project managers as active "job crafters", as having the latitude to define and enact their jobs, places importance on the meanings individual managers "make in the task or relational boundaries of their work" (Wrzesniewski and Dutton, 2001, p. 179). These relational boundaries are considered important in understanding the social and knowledge-based demands of project-based work. For instance, emergent projects and prosocial activities have been associated with beneficial organisation outcomes, such as the "garnering of tangible or intangible resources" (Plouffe and Grégoire, 2011, p. 694), and the development of human capital (Hollenbeck and Jamieson, 2015). Hence, behavioural role descriptions can be evaluated as important strategic tools in helping HR recruiters understand "what kinds of employees maximise team potential and the flow of knowledge through the organisation" (Hollenbeck and Jamieson, 2015, p. 378).

In the following sections, the process of using inductive methods (semi-structured interviews, grounded theory) to derive a behavioural role description from the perspective of one project manager is described. Stages of inductive analysis are described using code mapping techniques, tables and a role map. The chapter concludes with a discussion of how behavioural role descriptions may make distinct contributions to future work in HR research and practice.

WORK ROLE ANALYSIS

Work analysis can be defined as "the systematic investigation of (a) work role requirements and (b) the broader context within which work roles are enacted" (Morgeson and Dierdorff, 2011, p. 4). Work role requirements encompass the KSA needed to fulfil the behavioural demands of others inside and outside the organisation. Hence, a role subsumes traditional task responsibilities by placing importance on the behaviours role incumbents need to demonstrate to fulfil the demands being voiced by other significant role holders, such as customers, suppliers and other team members (Welbourne et al., 1998). Understanding how the role incumbent construes and crafts their work roles (role conception), in terms of deciding how best to satisfy the demands of other role holders (role demands), draws attention to the social and discretionary nature of effective work (role performance) in professional service organisations (Griffin et al., 2007; Rodham, 2000).

Work role analysis, when part of a high-involvement HR process and knowledge-based employment mode, can connect jobs to an environment of HR practices that creates value for customers, contributes to the organisation's strategic goals and responds to changes in business conditions (Boxall and Macky, 2009; Monks et al., 2013). Crucially, work role analysis can make these multilevel connections when it reflects an HR philosophy whereby role and team behaviours are part of a larger statement of human capital recruitment, knowledge management, teamwork and communication, and employee satisfaction values (Hollenbeck and

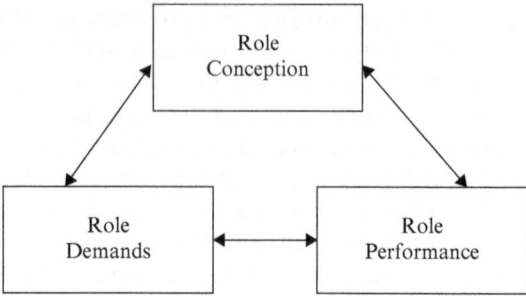

Figure 18.1   Work role analysis

Jamieson, 2015). As part of this HR philosophy, strategic HR performance assumptions apply to ensure individual role behaviours and HR
systems align with the organisation's business strategy, culture and goals
(Schuler, 1992). The most important of these states role performance will
meet the collaborative goals of the organisation when job-holders' flexible
role orientations meet the knowledge demands of other team members and
the changing work context (Parker, 2007; Plouffe and Grégoire, 2011).

To help capture the expanded scope of work requirements in managerial positions, Figure 18.1 illustrates a work role analysis framework for
deriving behavioural role descriptions. Using the framework to derive
work roles inductively means placing importance on: (1) the intentions,
expectations and meanings individual job-holders attribute to their role
requirements (role conception); (2) rich descriptions of task behaviours
and pressures associated with the role (role demands); and (3) key activities and interactions the job-holder engages in to perform the role successfully (role performance).

INDUCTIVE METHODS

Using inductive methods to derive behavioural role descriptions places
primary importance on studying social action from the perspective of
the job-holder (manager) rather than the HR consultant (researcher).
Grounded theory is an inductive research methodology that allows
researchers to systematically develop theory (in this case behavioural role
descriptions) from the accounts of people who are enacting action in its
natural social setting (Lincoln and Guba, 1985). Currently, grounded
theory is the "most widely used and popular qualitative research method
across a wide range of disciplines and subject areas" for discovering theory
from data rather than testing or verifying existing theories (Bryant and

Charmaz, 2010, p. 1). Inductive analysis, an essential component of the methodology, allows researchers to discern how employees and managers construe their world of work from the way they talk about it (Phillips and Hardy, 2002).

Interviews as Conversations

Treating interviews as conversations offers scope for managers to describe the "milieu of managerial work" (Dierdorff et al., 2009) and focus on aspects of work context that give rise to key social-political pressures and performance demands (Rodham, 2000). Managers are more likely to "open up" about aspects of their role if the style and pace of questioning is flexible, non-leading, enjoyable and focused on the manager's actual experiences at work (King and Horrocks, 2010). If the conversation proceeds well, then the manager is more likely to share important information about how they craft their role descriptions (Wrzesniewski and Dutton, 2001), including the breadth of tasks, goals and problems they see as within their in-role responsibilities (Morrison, 1994). Adopting good conversational techniques (for example, making eye contact, active listening, use of humour) translates into helping managers relax and talk about important social interactions, particularly social-political aspects of networking where they may encourage, cajole, praise, reward, manipulate and influence others in informal teams and face-to-face situations (Gibson et al., 2014).

HR researchers use semi-structured qualitative interviews to capture the reasoning and evaluative beliefs managers and employees describe with respect to their work roles and work practices (Townsend et al., 2012; Winter and Jackson, 2014). As a data collection technique, semi-structured interviews allow for new insights into employees' job contexts, social interactions and job performance by anchoring questions in relevant theory whilst allowing employees the freedom to construct their job requirements in their own language and terms. HR researchers and practitioners may find the following open-ended questions useful in deriving behavioural work role descriptions:

1. What does your job/work entail? (*Role conception*: Probe for key job responsibilities; types/breadth of tasks and goals; role ethos and principles.)
2. What things do you feel must be done in your job? Why? (*Role demands*: Probe for activities that must be done; key people inside/outside the organisation; pressures/dilemmas of role.)
3. Who do you interact/engage with in your job? Why these people? (*Role demands/role performance*: Probe for social interactions with respect

to key tasks/projects and problems; nature/purpose of interactions; networking behaviour.)

4. What do you see as effective job/role performance? Is it realisable? How? (*Role performance*: Probe for activities that constitute "effective" and/or "successful" performance; links to organisation's strategic purpose/goals.)

Stages of Inductive Analysis

Doing inductive analysis centres on comparing and contrasting data items into meaningful categories. Such categories draw the researcher's attention to the many similarities and differences between data items whilst remaining coherent and meaningful to employees themselves (Charmaz, 2006). Categorical development begins by identifying (coding) the content of an employee's responses to interview questions. In this stage, code labels assign words to the meanings an employee infers to their role (role conception); the activities that must be done in their work role (role demands); and the types of interactions the employee engages in to perform the role successfully (role performance). In the following example, the code labelling process is illustrated with respect to the role descriptions of a project manager in an Australian mining company (Winter, 1998).

ILLUSTRATIVE EXAMPLE

Once an employee's interview data has been recorded and transcribed, it can be "marked-up" (Turner, 1981) using a coloured marker pen and/or using computer-assisted tools such as the comments reference boxes in Word or Adobe Acrobat software. The Word program can assist with the inductive process of "initial coding" (Charmaz, 2006, pp. 54–5) by assigning line numbers to the text, a feature that allows text location points to be added for coding segments of the interview data.

Coding Role Data

In Figure 18.2, code labels have been attached relating to Manager A's Job Conception (job conc: 1–23). Within this data segment, different facets of the role have been labelled such as the Coordinator Role (7–15); the Technical Role (15–17); and the Administrative Function (17–23). Within these role labels, smaller codes have been added such as the role is a "focal point" (*InVivo* code) for clients to bring jobs and queries to (focpoint 8–9). Manager A makes reference to his coordination role in terms of

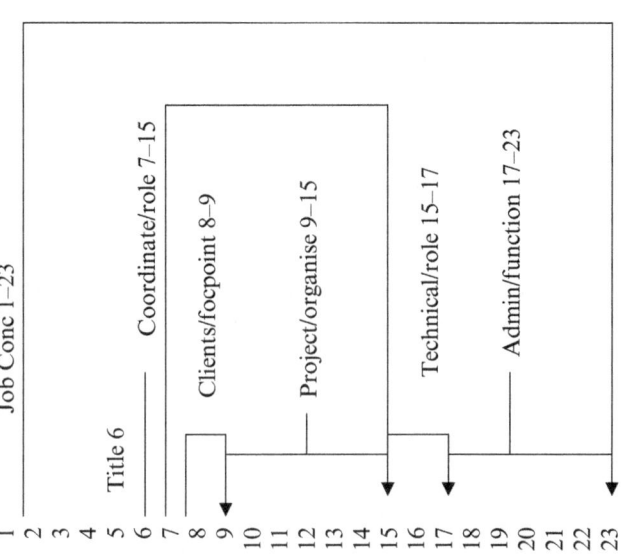

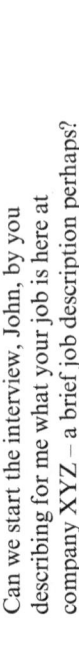

R1: Can we start the interview, John, by you describing for me what your job is here at company XYZ – a brief job description perhaps?

A1: The job is physical geologist, resources, which involves the coordination of all work in the geology sphere, providing a focal point for clients to bring jobs to and bring queries to. It is my task to decide who works on which project, who leads which project, to be involved in the vetting of quotes, proposals, reports, going out: to ensure the overall – that all jobs are progressed in a timely fashion and that resources are allocated adequately to all the jobs in the geology sphere. It's primarily a coordination role. It is not a full-time administrative role in that I work on projects as well. I'm a technical person as well. The administrative function also covers reporting to management, monthly reports, quarterly, six-monthly reports; also things like performance appraisals of the staff in line geology area, career planning for the staff in the geology area, training coordination – all those aspects as well as mundane stuff like leave.

Figure 18.2   Manager A's code mapping extract

deciding "who works on which project" and "who leads which project" (10). Further searches of the transcript found additional descriptions of this coordination role. Inspection of the language used to describe this role revealed different but related role properties whereby the manager has "to know where everyone is on all projects and where they're going to be at any point in time" (246–286, not shown). An important part of this coordination role is "making sure all projects go along on track and that all the client's demands are met" (298–300). Further comparison of these related role definitions revealed Manager A construed his role in terms of two related functions: the "Coordination of Project Work" (Coordination Role) and "Taking on the Client's Perspective" (Supervisory Role).

Creating Tables

Creating tables of related role properties provides valuable insights into the perceived breadth of an employee's construed work role (Morrison, 1994; Parker, 2007). Perceived breadth directs attention to the types of activities the role incumbent considers as "in-role" and necessary to justify their role performance. Table 18.1 illustrates some of the social activities (properties) Manager A considers to be essential components of his "coordination role" (that is, "informal face-to-face interactions with project

Table 18.1   Manager A – coordination role and supervisory role conceptions and properties

Role conceptions	Properties
Coordination of project work	Major job responsibility is getting projects out on time and within cost
	Focal point for clients to bring jobs and queries to
	Assembles project teams
(Coordination Role)	Informal face-to-face interactions with project managers to get updates, progress reports
	Circulation/vetting of reports
	Help/advice given to project managers (firefighting)
Taking on the client's perspective	Client's expect 100% attention
	Major job responsibility is meeting client's expectations
	Practical solutions to client's problems encouraged
(Supervisory Role)	Project managers motivated to conceptualise project's requirements and to succeed
	Mediates between clients and project team members

managers to get updates, progress reports") and "supervisory role" (that is, "mediates between clients and project team members").

Continued inspection of Manager A's role conception revealed a preference for informal networks both inside and outside the organisation. Effective networking behaviour was construed in terms of "catching up with people on an informal basis . . . to solve project problems, like plotting, drafting and computing bottlenecks" (1863–1864; 1849–1850). Informal social networks were seen as vital to "co-opting whatever resources [are needed] to get the job done" (257–259), a role performance behaviour described as proactive and contextually relevant in uncertain and interdependent work contexts (Griffin et al., 2007). Additional properties of why Manager A considers informal networks to be important components of his social role (that is, need for "friendly and close team relationships" and the "cross-fertilisation of ideas between team members") are shown in Table 18.2.

Role Maps

Role maps represent excellent tools for illustrating the social-relational aspects of managerial work in professional occupations (Fiol and Huff, 1992; Stetz et al., 2011). Instead of dividing a job into smaller units as traditional job analysis techniques demand (Brannick et al., 2007), role

Table 18.2   Manager A – main network role conceptions and properties

Role conceptions	Properties
Friendly and close team relationships	Informal social contacts with free and regular face-to-face communication
	Close-knit social groups
	Social contacts reduce work pressures and motivates team members
	Social banter intermixed with work-related exchanges
	Firefighting between projects makes gaining team's consent easier
Cross-fertilisation of ideas between team members	Sharing of ideas and information to solve complex project problems
	Project managers encouraged to inform manager of project developments, ideas, techniques
	Word of mouth information disseminated to team members
	Project tasks set up where team members work together, learn from and assist each other

maps focus on the activities employees state they must perform to satisfy their role demands and be effective at work. An essential quality of role maps is that they contain sufficient amounts of cognitive reasoning to link work context to emerging managerial role requirements (Dierdorff et al., 2009). That is, just how the manager construes their work role highlights the agency inherent in managerial work and helps to understand why managers may prioritise certain activities and not others (Parker, 2007). Including scope for employees to voice their rationales for certain behaviours at work is a proactive HR strategy as it can account for emergent job behaviours and human capital networks that lead to beneficial teamwork and knowledge sharing outcomes in organisations (Parker and Collins, 2010; Plouffe and Grégoire, 2011).

In Figure 18.3, two interrelated supervisory ("taking on the client's perspective") and coordination ("coordination of project work") roles are shown at the centre of Manager A's role map. Both roles are considered by Manager A to be of central importance to fulfilling his key role demands: meeting the demands and expectations of individual clients. To meet these role demands, Manager A stated he relied on a network of "friendly and close team relationships" to encourage the "cross-fertilisation of

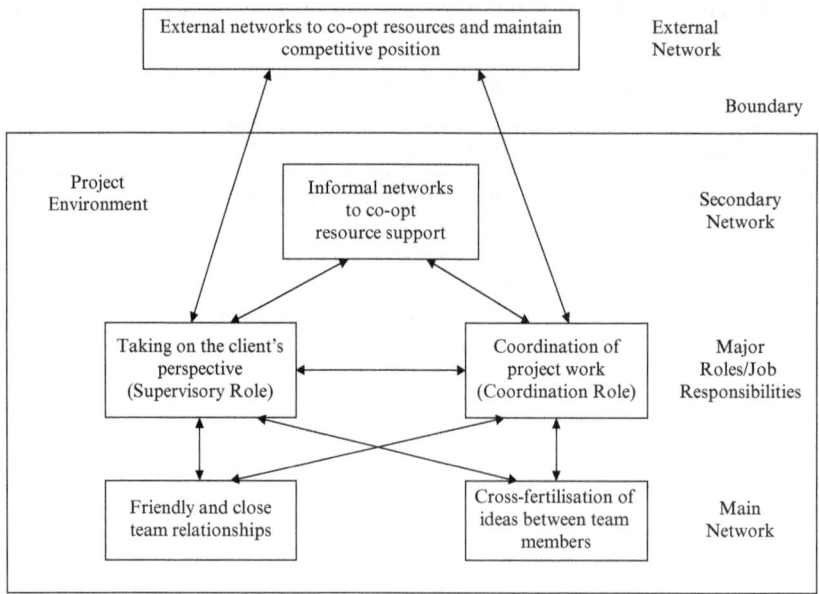

Figure 18.3   Manager A's role map

ideas between team members" (Main Network). A secondary network of informal, cooperative relationships also helped Manager A keep projects on track (coordination role) and ensure projects did not get stalled (supervisory role). Finally, an external network of contacts helped the manager support his major role responsibilities (double-headed arrows in Figure 18.3 show these interdependent role relationships).

Behavioural Role Descriptions

Based on these role conception descriptions, together with Manager A's role map, a behavioural role description for Manager A (Box 18.1) was written and fed back to the manager for his comments. He and other managers commented on the benefits of seeing their own job profiles linking critical aspects of role performance (for example, effective relationships with clients and other project teams) with their rationales for specific role behaviours (for example, the need for informal networks and face-to-face interactions). Engaging managers in the process of checking and where necessary amending their own role descriptions meant some "member validation" criteria could be assigned to the final stage of data collection – a useful process in strengthening the overall quality of the inductive analysis (Oxtoby et al., 2002). Giving managers a voice in how their role descriptions were portrayed was seen as enhancing the credibility of the interview analysis as it paid detailed attention to the work context as interpreted by job-holders (Patton, 1990).

DISCUSSION

As an employee's work environment becomes more complex and interdependent (Griffin et al., 2007; Plouffe and Grégoire, 2011), job and organisational performance are increasingly dependent on proactive workplace behaviours whereby employees actively exchange information support and resources with others in teams across the organisation (Parker and Collins, 2010). Creating role descriptions using inductive qualitative techniques makes it possible to understand how some employees manage to skilfully navigate their organisations and work collaboratively with others (Morgeson et al., 2005; Plouffe and Grégoire, 2011). For example, Manager A's role description gives insights into the kinds of informal networks a project manager needs to establish inside and outside the organisation to meet clients' demands and expectations. These social interactions not only highlight the social skills a project manager needs to work effectively in a dynamic project-based environment (Cheng et al., 2005), they

BOX 18.1   MANAGER A'S BEHAVIOURAL ROLE DESCRIPTION

Major Role Responsibilities

Supervising and coordinating project work to meet client's expectations of individual attention is a major role responsibility. To meet these expectations, the manager spends time making sure project managers and team members are focused on finding practical solutions to each client's problems. This means ensuring adequate resource support is available to prevent projects getting stalled and delayed. A "main" and "secondary" network of informal and friendly relationships is utilised to co-opt resource support and meet each client's specific needs.

Networking Requirements

- By interacting informally with project managers, and motivating them to succeed, the manager is made aware of each project's status and possible problems that could cause project delays. This information is vital if the manager is to know where individual projects are going to be at some point in time. In these informal interactions, the manager encourages the team to "cross-fertilise ideas" with each other so new techniques are learnt to solve client's complex problems.
- Free and regular communication builds friendly and cooperative team relationships vital to the exchange of ideas and information to solve client's problems. In this team climate, the manager gathers work-related ideas and gains the consent of the team with respect to the client's requirements. The close-knit nature of team relationships allows the manager to "firefight" between projects whenever his technical input is needed.
- In meeting client's deadlines, resource support is critical. The manager is aware of the importance of priorities to the extent and timing of resource support. By working informally across work structures, the manager co-opts support by determining and resolving priorities in close, interactive discussions with drafting, plotting and computing resource staff. During this process, new ways around bottlenecks are found.
- External networks are also vital to accomplishing major role responsibilities. Networks outside the organisation allow the manager to tap into specific skills, advice, expertise and information not accessible internally. In the process of networking with professional colleagues, the manager gains access to highly specialised, up-to-date information to enrich his own knowledge base.
- External networks also help maintain the organisation's competitive position by increasing the manager's awareness of "who is doing what projects" in the mining community. Networks also provide the manager with information on competitor's services that the company may need to incorporate in the future. Finally, networks provide a means for head hunting key personnel.

also suggest that effective role performance amongst project managers is as much about "socialising and networking" with internal and external organisational members as it is about "planning and decision making" (Gibson et al., 2014).

Deriving role descriptions from the perspectives of job-holders does not imply this approach should replace the KSA attribute approach to job analysis. KSA are still important in describing the tasks specific to a particular work role, as well as representing generic behaviours applicable across a wide variety of work roles (Morgeson and Dierdorff, 2011). However, behavioural role descriptions may make a significant contribution to understanding the "larger team and organisational context" within which jobs are embedded (Morgeson and Dierdorff, 2011, p. 4). As useful supplements to existing KSA fit methods, they can help to identify the kinds of social skills and interpersonal interactions that maximise teamwork and flows of knowledge through an organisation (Plouffe and Grégoire, 2011). As such, behavioural role descriptions are ideally suited to self-managing, enriched job roles characterised by high degrees of task complexity, autonomy and organisational responsibility (Parker and Collins, 2010). With a richer and more accurate description of an enriched role like project leadership (Briner et al., 1990), recruiters are better equipped to search for people who match a team-based skills profile or have the potential to do so after training (Morgeson et al., 2005).

Behavioural role descriptions offer distinct advantages to recruiters interested in assessing complex workplace behaviours such as project leadership. When grounded in a role analysis framework, tasks can be assessed in terms of the demands of other role holders (for example, the need to take on the client's perspective) and the behaviours critical to task performance (for example, using informal and external networks to co-opt resource support and gain project advice). A key virtue of experience-based role descriptions is that they increase the amount and accuracy of job information, an attribute found to lessen employees' anxiety in the stages of recruitment, selection and induction (Wanous, 1992). More accurate descriptions of how existing job-holders respond effectively to the problems of clients should have positive effects on the job performance of new recruits when integrated into selection, induction and training activity (Meglino et al., 2000). For instance, in this chapter's project management example an HR recruiter may treat industry knowledge as a given in their recruitment activity and use a behavioural role description to identify the crucial "networking skills" needed to boundary span and work effectively with other individuals, work groups, functional areas and other business units (Gibson et al., 2014).

Finally, behavioural role descriptions direct attention to the self-management of job-holders – agency that can be captured in HR training and development programmes to help new and existing job-holders construe their jobs differently and achieve higher levels of job performance (Fondas and Stewart, 1994; Parker, 2007). A different understanding of roles may emerge when job-holders reflect on their own role maps with respect to colleagues in similar positions. Reframing how other job-holders enact different social interactions and networking behaviours to achieve their role responsibilities may provoke a "qualitatively new framework or template" for seeing and doing project work (Bartunek, 1988, p. 138). Shifting understanding of project work to include more scope for networking behaviours could send an important signal to future job applicants that project work is a valuable form of social capital (Hollenbeck and Jamieson, 2015). Not only does project work reframed in stronger social terms build stronger trust ties in HRM. It also provides an important collegiate foundation for the free exchange of ideas conducive to knowledge sharing in professional service organisations (Monks et al., 2013).

Future Challenges and Shortcomings

Using role descriptions and role maps grounded in the language of job-holders, recruiters can create more accurate classifications of manager occupations providing improvements to both concurrent and predictive validation of job analysis and selection processes (Stetz et al., 2011). A real challenge for HR recruiters is to use the firsthand knowledge gained from interviewing critical employees for the purpose of augmenting existing HR selection practices and processes. Semi-structured interviews featured in this chapter provide a method of sourcing "thick description" (Geertz, 1973) of an employee's work context – context to help understand why certain social role behaviours are considered beneficial to the employee and may result in effective job performance (Parker et al., 2010).

However, a word of caution is necessary with respect to relying on an employee's description of their work roles. The manager depicted above may have over-reported their "good networking" behaviour and under-reported their "bad politicking" behaviour out of a concern their role description may be seen by senior managers, or used to evaluate their job performance. To minimise such "social desirability bias" (Nederhof, 1985), recruiters are advised to corroborate the role description by gaining feedback from others in the employee's social network and/or by observing the employee over a particular timespan. Using multiple methods to construct a behavioural role description is likely to give more confidence in the internal validity of the data by controlling for employee biases and distortions (Patton, 1990). But of course recruiters will need to consider the increased time and costs involved.

In conclusion, an inductive approach to work role analysis seems most effective in the context of understanding complex managerial roles and situations where employees craft proactive role orientations to define the relational boundaries of their work (Parker et al., 2010). Although constructing behavioural role descriptions is a time-consuming and relatively expensive (for example, interview transcription costs) process, they can with faithful practice produce more accurate and reliable performance-based descriptions for key managerial positions in an organisation (Griffin et al., 2007; Welbourne et al., 1998). Importantly, behavioural role descriptions can identify a range of social skills and actual workplace behaviours to complement competency job attribute frameworks. As HR recruiters well know, job previews are more accurate and useful when they are informed by the work experiences of actual job-holders.

ANNOTATED FURTHER READING

Charmaz, K. (2006), *Constructing Grounded Theory: A Practical Guide through Qualitative Analysis*, London: Sage.
Excellent introductory text to coding data in grounded theory practice.
King, N. and Horrocks, C. (2010), *Interviews in Qualitative Research*, London: Sage.
Text draws attention to the flexible, open-ended nature of the qualitative interview intent on capturing the interviewee's personal experience.
Parker, S.K. (2007), "'That is my job': how employees' role orientation affects their job performance", *Human Relations*, **60**, 403–34.
Two UK quantitative studies illustrating how a flexible role orientation predicted job performance in self-managing contexts.

REFERENCES

Bartunek, J.M. (1988), "The dynamics of personal and organisational reframing", in R.E. Quinn and K.S. Cameron (eds), *Paradox and Transformation: Toward a Theory of Change in Organisation and Management*, Cambridge, MA: Ballinger, pp. 137–68.
Boxall, P. and Macky, K. (2009), "Research and theory on high-performance work systems: progressing the high involvement stream", *Human Resource Management Journal*, **19** (1), 3–23.
Brannick, M.T., Levine, E.L. and Morgeson, F.P. (2007), *Job and Work Analysis: Methods, Research, and Applications for Human Resource Management*, 2nd edn, Thousand Oaks, CA: Sage.
Breaugh, J.A. and Starke, M. (2000), "Research on employee recruitment: so many studies, so many remaining questions", *Journal of Management*, **26**, 405–34.
Briner, W., Geddes, M. and Hastings, C. (1990), *Project Leadership*, Aldershot: Gower.

Bryant, A. and Charmaz, K. (2010), "Introduction, grounded theory research: methods and practices", in A. Bryant and K. Charmaz (eds), *The Sage Handbook of Grounded Theory*, Los Angeles, CA: Sage, pp. 1–28.

Campion, M.A., Palmer, D.K. and Campion, J.E. (1997), "A review of structure in the selection interview", *Personnel Psychology*, **50**, 655–702.

Carless, S.A. (2005), "Person-job fit versus person-organisation fit as predictors of organisation attraction and job acceptance intentions: a longitudinal study", *Journal of Occupational and Organisational Psychology*, **78**, 411–29.

Charmaz, K. (2006), *Constructing Grounded Theory: A Practical Guide through Qualitative Analysis*, Thousand Oaks, CA: Sage.

Cheng, M.I., Dainty, A.R.J. and Moore, D.R. (2005), "What makes a good project manager?", *Human Resource Management Journal*, **15** (1), 25–37.

Dierdorff, E.C., Rubin, R.S. and Morgeson, F.P. (2009), "The milieu of managerial work: an integrative framework linking work context to role requirements", *Journal of Applied Psychology*, **94** (4), 972–88.

Fiol, C.M. and Huff, A.S. (1992), "Maps for managers: where are we? Where do we go from here?", *Journal of Management Studies*, **29** (3), 267–85.

Fondas, N.J. and Stewart, R. (1994), "Enactment in managerial jobs: a role analysis", *Journal of Management Studies*, **31** (1), 86–103.

Geertz, C. (1973), *The Interpretation of Cultures*, New York: Basic Books.

Gibson, C., Hardy III, J.H. and Buckley, R.M. (2014), "Understanding the role of networking in organisations", *Career Development International*, **19** (2), 146–61.

Griffin, M.A., Neal, A. and Parker, S.K. (2007), "A new model of work role performance: positive behaviour in uncertain and interdependent contexts", *Academy of Management Journal*, **50** (2), 327–47.

Hollenbeck, J.R. and Jamieson, B.B. (2015), "Human capital, social capital, and social network analysis: implications for strategic human resource management", *Academy of Management Perspectives*, **29** (3), 370–85.

Huffcutt, A.I. and Youngcourt, S.S. (2007), "Employment interviews", in D.L. Whetzel and G.R. Wheaton (eds), *Applied Measurement: Industrial Psychology in Human Resource Management*, London: Psychology Press, pp. 181–99.

King, N. and Horrocks, C. (2010), *Interviews in Qualitative Research*, London: Sage.

Kristof-Brown, A.L. (2000), "Perceived applicant fit: distinguishing between recruiters' perceptions of person-job and person-organisation fit", *Personnel Psychology*, **53**, 643–71.

Lincoln, Y.S. and Guba, E.G. (1985), *Naturalistic Inquiry*, Newbury Park, CA: Sage.

Meglino, B.M., Ravlin, E.C. and DeNisi, A.S. (2000), "A meta-analytic examination of realistic job preview effectiveness: a test of three counterintuitive propositions", *Human Resource Management Review*, **10**, 407–34.

Monks, K., Kelly, G., Conway, E., Flood, P., Truss, K. and Hannon, E. (2013), "Understanding how HR systems work: the role of HR philosophy and HR processes", *Human Resource Management Journal*, **23** (4), 379–95.

Morgeson, F.P. and Dierdorff, E.C. (2011), "Work analysis: from technique to theory", in S. Zedeck (ed.), *APA Handbook of Industrial and Organisational Psychology*, Vol. 2, Washington, DC: American Psychological Society, pp. 3–41.

Morgeson, F.P., Reider, M.H. and Campion, M.A. (2005), "Selecting individuals in team settings: the importance of social skills, personality characteristics, and teamwork knowledge", *Personnel Psychology*, **58**, 583–611.

Morrison, E.W. (1994), "Role definitions and organisational citizenship behaviour: the importance of the employee's perspective", *Academy of Management Journal*, **37**, 1543–67.

Nederhof, A.J. (1985), "Methods of coping with social desirability bias: a review", *European Journal of Social Psychology*, **15**, 263–80.

Oxtoby, B., McGuiness, T. and Morgan, R. (2002), "Developing organisational change capability", *European Management Journal*, **20** (3), 310–20.

Parker, S.K. (2007), "'That is my job': how employees' role orientation affects their job performance", *Human Relations*, **60**, 403–34.

Parker, S.K. and Collins, C.G. (2010), "Taking stock: integrating and differentiating multiple proactive behaviours", *Journal of Management*, **36**, 633–62.

Parker, S.K., Bindl, U.K. and Strauss, K. (2010), "Making things happen: a model of proactive motivation", *Journal of Management*, **36**, 827–56.

Patton, M.Q. (1990), *Qualitative Evaluation and Research Methods*, 2nd edn, Newbury Park, CA: Sage.

Phillips, N. and Hardy, C. (2002), *Discourse Analysis: Investigating Processes of Social Construction*, Thousand Oaks, CA: Sage.

Plouffe, C.R. and Grégoire, Y. (2011), "Intraorganisational employee navigation and socially derived outcomes: conceptualisation, validation, and effects on overall performance", *Personnel Psychology*, **64**, 693–738.

Rodham, K. (2000), "Role theory and the analysis of managerial work: the case of occupational health professionals", *Journal of Applied Management Studies*, **9** (1), 71–81.

Sanchez, J.I. and Levine, E.L. (2001), "The analysis of work in the 20th and 21st centuries", in N. Anderson, D.S. Ones, H.K. Sinangil and C. Viswesvaran (eds), *Handbook of Industrial Work and Organisational Psychology*, Vol. 1, Thousand Oaks, CA: Sage, pp. 71–89.

Schuler, R.S. (1992), "Strategic human resources management: linking the people with the strategic needs of the business", *Organisational Dynamics*, **21** (1), 18–32.

Sekiguchi, T. (2007), "A contingency perspective of the importance of PJ fit and PO fit in employee selection", *Journal of Managerial Psychology*, **22** (2), 118–31.

Stetz, T.A., Button, S.B. and Scott, D.W. (2011), "Creating occupational groups using visual job classification", *Management Research Review*, **34** (3), 294–310.

Townsend, K., Wilkinson, A., Allan, C. and Bamber, G. (2012), "Mixed signals in HRM: the HRM role of hospital line managers", *Human Resource Management Journal*, **22** (3), 267–82.

Turner, B.A. (1981), "Some practical aspects of qualitative data analysis: one way of organising the cognitive processes associated with the generation of grounded theory", *Quality and Quantity*, **15**, 225–47.

Wanous, J.P. (1992), *Organisational Entry: Recruitment, Selection, Orientation and Socialisation of Newcomers*, 2nd edn, Reading, MA: Addison-Wesley.

Weick, K.W. (2008), "Sensemaking", in S.R. Clegg and J.R. Bailey (eds), *The Sage International Encyclopedia of Organisation Studies*, Thousand Oaks, CA: Sage, pp. 1403–6.

Welbourne, T.M., Johnson, D.E. and Erez, A. (1998), "The role-based performance scale: validity analysis of a theory-based measure", *Academy of Management Journal*, **41** (5), 540–55.

Winter, R.P. (1998), "Focus on work roles: a value-added approach to work redesign", in D. Mortimer, P. Leece and R. Morris (eds), *Readings in Contemporary Employment Relations*, Sydney: Harcourt Brace, pp. 455–74.

Winter, R.P. and Jackson, B.A. (2014), "Expanding the younger worker employment relationship: insights from values-based organisations", *Human Resource Management*, **53** (2), 311–28.

Wrzesniewski, A. and Dutton, J.E. (2001), "Crafting a job: revisioning employees as active crafters of their work", *Academy of Management Review*, **26** (2), 179–201.

Index